S0-DQW-467

GERALD M. PHILLIPS, Ph.D. is a certified marriage and family counselor and professor of speech communication at Pennsylvania State University. A prolific author, Dr. Phillips has written fifteen books on business, education, and communication, including *Help for Shy People* (Prentice-Hall/Spectrum Books).

H. LLOYD GOODALL, Ph.D., is assistant professor in organizational communication at University of Alabama in Huntsville. He has written numerous professional books and articles on topics including interpersonal communication and relationship skills.

GERALD M. PHILLIPS
H. LLOYD GOODALL, JR.
Illustrated by Esther Szegedy

Loving &
Living

Improve Your Friendships
and Marriage

A SPECTRUM BOOK

Prentice-Hall, Inc. Englewood Cliffs, New Jersey 07632

Library of Congress Cataloging in Publication Data

Phillips, Gerald M.
  Loving and living.

  "A Spectrum Book."
  Includes bibliographical references and index.
  1. Friendship.   2. Marriage.   3. Interpersonal communication.   I. Goodall, H.
Lloyd.   II. Title.
  BF575.F66P46   1983   158'.2   82-18617
  ISBN 0-13-541136-X
  ISBN 0-13-541128-9 (pbk.)

This book is available at a special discount when ordered in bulk quantities.
Contact Prentice-Hall, Inc., General Publishing Division,
Special Sales, Englewood Cliffs, N.J. 07632.

© 1983 by Prentice-Hall, Inc., Englewood Cliffs, New Jersey 07632

A SPECTRUM BOOK

ISBN 0-13-541128-9 {PBK.}

ISBN 0-13-541136-X

10   9   8   7   6   5   4   3   2   1
Printed in the United States of America

Manufacturing buyer Christine Johnston
Cover design © 1982 by Jeannette Jacobs

Prentice-Hall International, Inc., *London*
Prentice-Hall of Australia Pty. Limited, *Sydney*
Prentice-Hall of Canada, Inc., *Toronto*
Prentice-Hall of India Private Limited, *New Delhi*
Prentice-Hall of Japan, Inc., *Tokyo*
Prentice-Hall of Southeast Asia Pte. Ltd., *Singapore*
Whitehall Books Limited, *Wellington, New Zealand*
Editora Prentice-Hall do Brasil Ltda., *Rio de Janeiro*

Contents

Preface

Our thanks to the many respondents who contributed bits of their life to this study. Thanks also to the colleagues at various locations around the country who made the effort to solicit respondents for us. A special thanks to our wives, Nancy and Donna, who read the manuscript at various stages and commented extensively and who helped us define ourselves as a result of this work.

The study of human behavior is a very personal kind of study. The act of writing is a solitary act. Our study made us "experts" on being with others; our writing made us "experts" on solitude. We learned something important from our work: that the company of others is valuable so long as the others are valuable and that being alone is not necessarily lonely. By doing this study and writing this book, we became better able to be friends with ourselves.

G.M.P.
H.L.G.

ACKNOWLEDGMENTS

First excerpt p. 11 from Leon Cooper, "Source and Limits of Human Intellect." Reprinted by permission of *Daedalus*, Journal of the American Academy of Arts and Sciences, Spring 1978, p. 16.

Second excerpt p. 11 from E.O. Wilson, *On Human Nature* (Cambridge: Harvard University Press, 1979), p. 75.

Excerpt pp. 89–90 from Lane Jennings, "Brave New Words," *The Futurist*, June 1981. *The Futurist* is published by the World Future Society, 4916 St. Elmo Avenue, Washington, D.C. 20014.

Excerpt pp. 104–105 from Christine Rigby Arrington, "The Paupered Princesses," *Savvy*, July 1981, pp. 32–37.

Excerpts pp. 155–156 from *The Synonym Finder*, ed. J.I. Rodale (Emmaus, PA: Rodale Books, Inc., 1961 edition, p. 439.

Introduction

HERE'S HOW WE GATHERED THE INFORMATION ABOUT THE PEOPLE WE DESCRIBE IN THIS BOOK

This book started as a textbook that got good reviews but that no one read (Gerald M. Phillips and Nancy J. Metzger, *The Study of Intimate Communication* [Boston: Allyn and Bacon, 1976]). The book was based on a long questionnaire originally given in 1973–1974 to 446 people. Their replies ran from four to ninety-one pages. In addition about 50 were interviewed extensively. During 1979–1981 three thousand more replies were obtained to an expanded questionnaire. The populations surveyed looked like this:

THE 1973–1974 SAMPLE	Male	Female	THE 1979–1981 SAMPLE	Male	Female
Schoolteachers	70	141	Professional managers	345	111
Employed adults	65	36	Blue collar	141	48
College students	45	59	Clerical	58	118
Secondary/elementary	12	18	Housepersons	0	310
Total	192	254	Teachers	24	35
			Professors	33	8
			College students[a]	1243	1331
			Total	1844	1961

[a] Includes the entire student body of a small state college.

1

The questionnaire was open-ended. Respondents were told to use the questions as guidelines for their comments rather than attempt to respond to each item. Not every item would apply in each case anyway. Thus, we will not report item by item. What we got were essays on love, marriage, and friendship from a great number of people with varying degrees of literacy.

Respondents were told to provide name and phone number if they were willing to be interviewed. Approximately 85 percent were willing. We selected interview subjects on the basis of availability and typicality of responses.

Here is the questionnaire form we used:

Think of a person (not a relative) of the same sex whom you regard as your closest friend. Describe your relationship with this person. Use the following questions as a guide to your answer. You need not answer all items.

1. Describe the person. Describe physical appearance. Identify occupation, values, interests. Discuss similarities and differences between you.
2. How often are you together? What do you do and talk about when together?
3. When and how did you make the decision that this person was your friend? How did you know it was mutual?
4. Compare the way your friend sees you with how you wish to be seen?*
5. Do you loan and borrow? What are your rules?
6. Do you ever talk about the nature of your friendship? Describe the talk. How do you resolve disputes between you? How do you make rules for your friendship? Describe them. What happens when one of you breaks a rule?
7. What goals do you have for your friendship? How do you expect it to change over the next five to ten years?*
8. What personal information do you disclose to and conceal from your friend? What does she or he disclose to you? What do you think he or she conceals? Why do you think she or he keeps information from you?
9. How does this person get along with your family and other friends? How do you get along with his or her friends and family. Does this relationship impede making new relationships? What would you do if it ended?*
10. What do you get out of the friendship: goods? services? sentiments? time? What do you give your friend? Do you think your exchange is even?
11. How do you use other friends when your friend is not available?*
12. Do you have fantasies about your friend? Describe.

Discuss the topic of friendship with the following questions as a guide:

1. Define each of the following words: *friend, friendly, enemy.* How do you fit people into your categories.† What is the opposite of friend?*
2. How do you make friends? How do you tell someone you want to be friends? What response do you look for? What do you do if your overtures are rejected? How do you reject unwanted overtures?
3. What is the nature of your dependency on others?*
4. Do you have empathy with your friend? What does "empathy" mean?*
5. What does "trust" mean? How do you show you trust someone? What must another person do before you trust them? Have you ever had a trust betrayed? How did you feel? Did you ever knowingly betray a trust? How did you feel? How did you think the other person felt? What did you do to make up for it? What do you do to get even when you are betrayed?*
6. What kinds of people do you select for friends? Are you friends with older people? Younger? Different races, religions, economic levels?
7. How can your friends hurt you? What was the nature of the hurt? Did you ever hurt someone? What do you feel like when you are hurt?*
8. What risks are taken in friendship? What can you gain or lose?*
9. What does being a friend obligate you to?*
10. Do you fantasize about your friends? How does that affect the friendship?
11. How does time spent with your friends affect your private time?
12. Do you ever sacrifice friends to your personal needs? For material goods? Are your commitments to ideas more important than your friends?*
13. Explain each of the following words with examples from your friendships: *intimacy, love, confidence, disclosure, authenticity, spontaneity.*†
14. Describe how you feel and what you do when you are lonely or bored.†

The following questions relate to male/female relationships:

1. Can you be friends with someone of the opposite sex on the same terms as with someone of your own sex? If there are differences, what are they?
2. What role does sex play in male/female friendships? Can you be intimate with a person of the opposite sex without sexual contact? Does the sex act cement a relationship? Is homosexuality a sign of a deep relationship?
3. What meaning does intercourse have for you? If you used the word *love*, what does it mean? Can there be "love" in a male/female relationship without intercourse? How does intercourse obligate you?

* Deleted from 1979–1981 survey. We deleted items that proved nonproductive in the earlier survey.
† Added to 1979–1981 survey. The 1979–81 survey included additional questions on male/female relationships.

4. Are you sexually aggressive? Are others aggressive with you? Have you ever physically hurt someone while having sex? Have you been hurt?
5. How possessive are you about the people with whom you have intercourse? Are others possessive with you? Is intercourse a sign of possession?
6. Would you remain in a relationship with a person of the opposite sex who was using and hurting you if the alternative was no relationship at all?
7. What possible meanings are there for intercourse? Are they different for men and women? What happens in a male/female relationship when intercourse is terminated? Do you think it is possible to be monogamous, or faithful to one sex partner?
8. Do you believe in couples living together without marriage? What do you think is the future of the family? What changes do you see in the future in relationships between men and women?
9. What is your view of homosexuality?
10. Are you engaged, living together, or married? Describe your relationship.[†]
11. What is the nature of the exchange in this intimate relationship?[†]
12. Describe how you quarrel and how you resolve your conflicts?[†]
13. What goals do you have for your relationship?[†] What rituals have you?
14. What changes do you expect in the next few years for the relationship?[†]
15. What is your attitude toward feminism?[†] Divorce?[†] Marriage?[†] Having children?[†] Abortion?[†]
16. When do you think boys and girls should start having intercourse? Under what circumstances?[†]

General questions:

1. What is your attitude toward drugs? Alcohol? Pornography?
2. Are you liberal or conservative politically? Religiously?
3. Are you satisfied with your life so far? What changes would you make in your relationships? Job? Life-style? Intercourse?
4. What do you think of the way the country is being run?
5. What would you like to say to the people who asked these questions?
6. If you are willing to be interviewed, please provide name, address, and phone number. Demographics: Age. Sex. Occupation.

We did not try to develop statistical tables. For one thing, each respondent seemed to emphasize topics of particular importance to himself or herself, so reponses were not comparable. Respondents used the questions as guides, and no one responded to all of them. We make no claim about scholarly rigor. We tried to understand what our respondents meant so that we could capture the emotional content in our report.

This book is about possibilities in relationship, not probabilities. It is not designed to be a textbook. A text has already been written on the basis of the same data (Gerald M. Phillips and Julia Wood, *Communication and Human Relationships* [New York: Macmillan Publishing Co., 1982]). *This book is a source of ideas you can apply to your own relationships.*

For that reason, we do not employ the technique of offering generalizations supported by numbers. It is not possible to generalize about the personal choices individuals make about their own lives. On the other hand, by examining what others do, you can see possibilities for your own choices. To express personal ideas as statistical generalizations or probability estimates would vitiate their power and cancel their uniqueness. Ideas are not important just because they *can* be expressed in formal tables. In facts, tables tend to trivialize, whereas narration makes ideas exciting and personal.

In this book we tried to illustrate typical cases by using the language of ordinary people to illustrate feelings and beliefs. This book is neither a sex manual nor a source of techniques for personal improvement, though it may be useful for both purposes. It is a presentation of the mundane, extraordinary, sacred, and profane aspects of the relationships carried on by ordinary people, presented, where possible, in their own words.

We hope to avoid the wrath of our scientifically oriented colleagues by not addressing this book to them. They may be interested in it as human beings, for in this book we will discuss situations and problems even scientists may encounter. We fervently believe we can learn about our own lives by studying the examples of others. We also believe scientists who study human beings somehow manage to separate themselves from their conclusions. Scientific representations make humans less than human. They become statistics, alike in every respect save in the variable studied. We do not believe humans are independent and dependent variables, but we believe they are both *independent of* and *dependent on* one another.

This book is based on reports by ordinary people. We carefully excluded those who were suffering unusual mental or physical problems or who were under treatment for such disorders. We were interested in what people (including scientists) do or do not do on the job with their mates and friends. The examination of how people live their lives can help people think about how they affect others and how to improve their relationships.

Harry Stack Sullivan believed people needed to check the reality of their own lives with others to confirm that others experienced what they experienced, suffered what they suffered, and found joy in similar ways.

The reports in this book will help ordinary people check their lives against the lives of ordinary people.

We reviewed the responses very carefully and selected those we believed typical. In our reports we combined responses to protect anonymity. Thus, we have fiction/fact statements that express the attitudes and feelings of the greater number of respondents. We *did* use numbers at this point. We grouped and counted similar responses and put together statements representing the largest blocs (usually more than half). We have also taken note of important exceptions and presented them as well.

Humans are experts on their own personal lives, but they are not experts on lives in general. Individuals do not look at their lives similarly. Some people are episodic in orientation, others moralistic, and so on. People defy classification by abstractions. We found immense paradoxes in many responses. People often expressed a belief and reported behavior counter to it. We found, also, most people had an intriguing tendency to change their minds, often for reasons that seemed good enough to them, and accordingly defied classification by feelings, beliefs, or even interpersonal beliefs. Gentleness and hostility, friendliness and distrust, openness and paranoia, humor and solemnity, could be found in some proportion in every response.

We augmented our contact with ordinary people by interviewing a number of experts on human relationships: counselors, psychologists, psychiatrists, social workers, and clergy. We asked their opinions on how to manage problems in relationships. We present their responses as a kind of consumer's report on therapeutic treatment of relationship problems.

Since we could not make our report scientific, we felt free to include some of our own opinions. They are clearly labeled. Our most important conclusion is that, given a basic standard of living, human contentment depends on the skill with which people relate. There do not appear to be common standards of success. People seem to work out unique ways of being happy, though their miseries spring from a common inability to cope with common problems. We share a great deal of the world. We must cope with problems of food, clothing, shelter, earning money, learning, loving, and living. We seem to have consistent ways of hurting one another and making one another happy.

People have devised wonderfully idiosyncratic ways of dealing with their lives. The "secret of success" seems to be in finding a particular solution. Those who rely on the general solutions seem to suffer a good deal. We could not repress the notion that a possible cause for relationship problems is the vast number of words that seek to explain how to solve relationship problems. Hardly anything is written about normal people successfully living normal lives. We think we have done that. We think we have written about people normal enough that you can find yourself in this book. If you can do that, this book will be very useful to you.

chapter one

Why we spend our lives with others

Six Rules for Living to a Happy Old Age.
1) Avoid fried foods which angry up the blood.
2) If your stomach disputes you, pacify it with cool thoughts.
3) Keep the juices flowing by jangling gently as you walk.
4) Go lightly on the vices such as carrying on in society.
5) Avoid running at all times.
6) Don't look back, something might be gaining on you.

SATCHEL PAIGE

Nature ordains friendship with relatives;
but it is never very stable.

CICERO

After your mother dies,
nobody cares all that much.

GEORGE CUKOR

The human is a mysterious talking animal. All we know about the animal is what the animal has told us about itself. We have history, myths, and "official records." For most of what the species refers to as "history," what we have is a record of who did what to whom and with what effect.

We have records about who ruled and whom they executed; when they ruled, what countries they conquered, and how many people died; what plagues hit the country and how many people died; and how much trouble there was collecting taxes. We have some traditional songs about the wildwood, mother, and black hair; there are legends about heroic deaths, loyal friends, royal love affairs, and occasional dragons and other fierce beasties. These records tell us about life on earth from a human perspective, what humans think is important to remember. It reveals humans as purposeful, active, possessive, bellicose, stubborn, and romantic creatures. Our historical records are as confused, contradictory, and contentious as the creature itself.

A more recent human development is systematic examination of almost every human behavior, including why humans examine almost every human behavior. Wilder Penfield, a great neurophysiologist, once commented that the mind could understand the brain, but the mind could never understand the mind because to be understood, a thing must be examined by something greater than itself. Thus, we may conclude, humans will never be able to understand humans, much less the nature of individual human understanding itself.

Certain kinds of examiners look at aspects of human behavior: Anatomists examine how humans are put together, physiologists examine how their parts work, psychologists examine their overt behaviors, sociologists examine how they form groups, philosophers try to explain what it all means, novelists examine human stories, and preachers examine what is good and bad.

Collectively, but each in different ways, we all deal with the same issues: how humans replenish the earth with their own kind, how they behave once they have been replenished, how they meet each other and get together in order to be fruitful and multiply and replenish the earth with their kind. Their studies also include opinions about human biology, food, clothing, shelter, social and political life, recreation and fun, fears and dreams, loves and hates, war and peace, and miscellaneous fooling around. The accounts often make fascinating reading; the ideas they present are fun to discuss; they are excellent sources of questions for both introspection and multiple-choice examinations. However, except for very specific information about body parts and how they work, by and large, explanations of human behavior are inconclusive.

Whatever humans claim to know about themselves at any one time will be revised shortly thereafter. A distinguished scientist once said, "The only claim you will have to fame is as an entry in an encyclopedia, 'Once

Professor X thought such and so, but he was later proven wrong.' " What we have become certain of, in ten millennia of learning, is that there is nothing we can be certain of, for as soon as two humans get together, for a few minutes, a day, or a lifetime, they will invent some new possibility for themselves. This is the strangest fact about humans. As specimens, we can be described and measured, but when we get together with others of our kind, we defy description.

We start with the premise of human uniqueness; that each person is a complete creation unlike anything else that ever was, is, or will be. Says a distinguished Nobel Laureate in physics (Cooper, 1978):

Although we no doubt will find ourselves to be made of ordinary materials, we might still marvel at their incredible organization. Although the entire universe may be determined, there is room for our creativity and for our individuality. What we call "I," the precious individual "I," is a result of genetic direction of the materials of which our bodies are constructed, in particular, the few billion neurons protected by our skull, interacting via the sensory and motor apparatus with all the vagaries of the environment in which we find ourselves. . . . The result is a completely unique object. There is no wiring diagram anywhere in the universe for what is contained in the individual head. Each head, each person, is completely individual in a sense as profound as anyone has imagined. There is no replacement for the individual experience that shapes the person. When an individual dies, he or she is lost irretrievably.

E. O. Wilson (1979), Pulitzer Prize–winning zoologist, claims humans are unique because we all have minds of our own:

Since the mind recreates reality from the abstractions of sense impressions, it can equally well simulate reality by recall and fantasy. The brain invents stories and runs imagined and remembered events back and forth through time: destroying enemies, embracing lovers, carving tools from blocks of steel, travelling easily into the realms of myth and perfection. The self is the leading actor in this neural drama. The emotional centers of the lower brain are programmed to pull the puppeteer's strings more carefully whenever the self steps onto the stage. But granted that our deepest feelings are about ourselves, can this preoccupation account for the innermost self, the soul in mechanistic terms? The cardinal mystery . . . is not self love or dreams of immortality, but intentionality.

The big question is *why do we do what we do?* The best scientists have admitted this question is hard to answer scientifically. We have fragments of information about person*s* but not about *the* person. We have a wealth of generalizations that cannot be applied to individuals. And we know even less about person *plus* person. We know that when we humans get together, we either fight or organize. We form societies, governments, and nations, and we pair off to raise families. We can look at our history, laws, literature, and census reports and piece together something about our common experience, but we know little about the personal and private lives of individuals, about what goes on in those unique creatures' minds.

We believe humans are "creatures," for, as Ernest Becker (1975) tells us, we are "angels with assholes." We seek food, sex, and a "warm place to go to the bathroom." But we are much more. Says Shakespeare in *Hamlet:*

What a piece of work is man! How infinite in faculties! In form and movement how express and admirable! In action how like an angel! In apprehension how like a god! The beauty of the world, the paragon of animals!

What we will do in this book is try to understand some of the ordinary qualities of the human creature as it comes together with others of its own kind to form relationships. We will explore the consequences of two people being together. We will look at couples, friends, lovers, and enemies to find out how they make and destroy their private worlds. We look at their behavior and passions both alone and with one another.

Human history is easy to write because the dead cannot argue with you. Science is relatively easy to do because most of the people who read what you wrote can't understand it, and electrons and ants can't talk back. When you try to comment on people, you risk their wrath. Any of them can say about any conclusion you draw, "That's not like me." For that reason, we will resist drawing conclusions. We will, however, express opinions, about which you can say, "I disagree." However, if you disagree, it is up to you to offer argument and proof to the contrary.

THE PROBLEM WITH ADVICE
ABOUT PROBLEMS

There are serious problems when the human, a curiously rational beast, tries to understand its own nature. Libraries are full of materials about why humans choose to live with other humans, about loving, and about living in general. Some say we are nesting or hunting beasts. Some say we are so frail we cannot solve our problems without collaborating with others of our kind. Some claim our language links us together and the social units we build are so complex we had to learn how to exchange goods and services in order to live.

Much is written about how human relationships ought to be conducted. The books and articles range from simple clichés on the one hand to prurient prying on the other, from obfuscated and unreadable scientific reports to moral and religious directives. Humans are advised how to improve their sex life, the behavior of their kids, and success on the job; how to find inner peace, actualization, fulfillment, and total orgasm. We can learn to accomplish these goals through proper diet, kinky sex, letting it all hang out, meditating, cutting loose, being disciplined, not drinking or smoking, taking pills, running, looking out for Number One, being creative, having a hobby, having kids, going back to work, finding God, taking time off from work, managing money effectively, and many other techniques, any one of which might have worked at one time or another for other individuals. The license to write a self-help book is often the desire to produce an autobiography in order to confirm your private system of success by convincing someone else to do it the same way. Self-help books are essentially evangelistic, although they tend to lack revelation. Some of the advice is expensive and impossible to follow for people who do not have extra cash. Some of the advice calls for physical exertion far beyond the abilities of some. Some calls for belief in systems and causes to which some people cannot commit.

Advice books are useful only when the advice works. You have to try the advice to find out whether it works, and trying it is sometimes dangerous. When it comes to relationships, any experiment is potentially risky. We believe it is important for people to try to understand themselves. Said Socrates, "The unexamined life is not worth living." On the other hand, there is a hazard about giving advice; if someone takes it, the advice giver bears a public, moral responsibility. A truism is that everyone wants to be cared about and everyone wants to believe they care.

"Pray, what are you laughing at?" inquired the Rocket. "I am not laughing."
"I am laughing because I am happy," replied the Cracker.
"That is a very selfish reason," said the Rocket angrily. "What right have you to be happy? You should be thinking about others. In fact, you should be thinking about me. I am always thinking about myself, and I expect everybody else to do the same. That is what I call sympathy."

The foregoing excerpt of *The Remarkable Rocket* by Oscar Wilde was quoted in a remarkable little book by Charles Derber called *The Pursuit of Attention* (1979). Derber believes everyone wants attention, and therefore attention is hard to get. If everyone is concentrating on how much they want attention, they have very little time and energy to devote to giving attention to anyone else. Thus, books that advocate assertiveness, looking out for Number One, or making oneself dominant, aggressive, or powerful simply cultivate the natural tendency of people to demand.

However, relationships cannot be formed on demand. You cannot command people to like you. You may be able to bludgeon them into silence while you are shouting, and you may intimidate them so they nod in agreement. You can force people to conform but not to agree. Learning bullying behavior merely accentuates nihilistic tendencies. You acquire the appearance of authority, but underneath there is the ferment of revolt.

People apparently need to form pairs ("Man is born alone and must acquire twoing," says Dr. Jordan Scher), but it is hard for them to do so because of their tendency to demand center stage. Most of us operate like Robin in Gilbert and Sullivan's *Ruddigore:*

> *My boy, you may take it from me,*
> *That of all the afflictions accurst*
> *   With which a man's saddled*
> *   And hampered and addled,*
> *A diffident nature's the worst.*

> *If you wish in the world to advance,*
> *Your merits you're bound to enhance,*
> *   You must stir it and stump it,*
> *   And blow your own trumpet,*
> *Or trust me, you haven't a chance.*

People care very much about what others think of them. The reason so many of them take assertiveness training, worry about being shy, or look out for Number One is they want to be important, respected, loved. They want their fair share. They want to be looked up to so badly they are prepared to *demand* it of others. Scholars such as George Herbert Mead, Harry Stack Sullivan, and others argue that we form our personality, our identity, from what others think of us, how others react to us. Our lives consist of asserting who we are and trying to motivate others to validate those assertions. Usually, when someone sees us as we wish to be seen, we regard that person as a friend, and when someone pushes us to be something worthwhile in his or her eyes, we may have found an intimate.

The main idea in exploring human relationships is to find out how people get together, stay together, and get satisfaction. The work of systematic social scientists adds little to this study, for they are able only to nitpick about the obvious. For example, some recent findings include the generalizations that people tend to take turns in conversations, speak to each other more when they are seated face-to-face then back-to-back, and to answer questions when they are asked.

Social scientists are not trying to evade the issue. They are careful in what they conclude because they do not know how far they can extend their conclusions. They must carefully confine their generalizations to situations exactly like this experience or their experiment. They are trying to avoid responsibility for people acting on what they have discovered, for they are not yet sure what is effective and ineffective. They take the same attitude as scientists who do research in the so-called hard sciences. The applications must be left to others.

In human relationships, technology has been preempted by amateurs, who make "discoveries" and write books often ignorant of what social scientists have discovered. The study of relationships is a curious blend of abstract and technical findings and folklore. This book is based on three controversial generalizations. If you disagree with any of these generalizations, you will probably disagree with some of our interpretations. On the other hand, you can examine the data from your own point of view and compare your conclusions with our conclusions. Here are our three basic assumptions:

1. People carry on their relationships by talking to one another.
2. We can learn a great deal about people by talking to them and listening to what they say.
3. Humans can choose what they say and to whom they say it.

These three premises separate us from those who believe behavior is determined through conditioning. It also separates us from those who believe in an inner wellspring of personality that works through spontaneous talk.

We are concerned about the fact that much of what has been written about human relationships was drawn from the study of people who have problems. Masters and Johnson did not study people with normal sex lives. A great many treatises on marriage have come from studies of divorces, and much of what is written about friendship is from the viewpoint of friendless and lonely people. Much of what we know comes from psychologists and psychiatrists who work with people who have serious problems. We seem to be lacking information about normal and ordinary people.

No one is really normal and ordinary! Everyone is unique and immensely important to himself or herself. (Way deep down, people still disagree with Copernicus: We really want to believe we are the center of the universe.) We lack information about people who do not seek help, who do not give information to social scientists, who do not participate in experiments and whose lives are coming out satisfactorily, who are not terribly lonely or bored, who have both friends and a close partner of the opposite sex. We need better information about people who have sexual intercourse occasionally and enjoy it some of the time without being self-conscious about it. We must study ordinary folks who can talk with people when they need to and are not self-conscious about it, who do their jobs—although they sometimes don't enjoy them very much—and who pay their bills well enough to stay out of bankruptcy court. When we went out to seek respondents to our questionnaires, we purposely sought people who were not having serious problems. We told people not to respond if they were in treatment or thought they were having major problems with their lives. We have no verification that the people who responded really were exactly what we wanted. A few people handed back our questionnaires because they said they were in therapy or working out a divorce. We counted on the honesty of the rest.

We do not wish to get into a battle like that between Sowell and Greeley reported in the December 1981 issue of *Psychology Today*. These two "distinguished" scholars vituperated at each other about the sample from which they derived their conclusions. Our sample is as fuzzy and amorphous as human life. We do not know whether it is random. We do not know whether it is stratified. We know it is made up of people who were willing to respond, and we know we tried to exclude a particular type of person (those with severe problems) from it. We know we do not have enough minority-group representation to draw conclusions about them. So much for the critique of our sample. We do not think any critic can do any more.

"Moving right along now," said Kermit the Frog. We are off on a journey into relatively uncharted territory, the world of relatively ordinary loving and living relationships. One of the most troubling aspects of this journey is that it is hard to study people when you are a person yourself. It is difficult to get inside other people's relationships when you are locked tightly into your own. It is hard to surrender your biases, and even harder to reveal them so other people can take them into account as they read your work.

It is part of human nature to talk about one's own human nature, and you will find us doing that from time to time. Rather than try to edit out all of our opinions, we will try to label them when we catch them. You will probably find out enough about us to take our ideas with the proverbial "grain of salt" as you examine the information we present.

HUMAN BEINGS
AND HUMAN NEEDINGS

Why do humans need relationships with others? Why do men and women with anything resembling normal intelligence and social skill, with the knowledge that their days on earth are few and that people often get in their way, invariably seek the comfort and kindness of others? What is the purpose of struggling to make and keep relationships?

Human relationship behavior is something like the nuzzling puppies do before they leave their mother. The great psychiatrist, Harry Stack Sullivan, believed that as we grow, we seek the satisfaction of secure support and relationships with others. We also use our relationships to provide the security we need against potential attack. We need satisfying *loving* relationships with the opposite sex, and we need secure *living* relationships with others around us. We live in a public society and a private social world.

One driving force for contact with others is obvious. David Barash (1979) points out our need to sustain the biological imperative to keep the species going. There is an urgency in both men and women to do their part to keep the human species alive. A lot of what men and women do with each other relates to that prime directive. Sometimes, the pressure to be sexual beings prevents us from seeing each other as fellow humans. Because of sexual differences we sometimes build walls between ourselves and thus deny ourselves some exciting relationships. For example, we found ourselves tempted to claim men and women really dislike each other. As we struggled with our data, we got the impression men and women do not understand each other. They tend to respond to each other as stereotypes, and because of that, men and women have unrealistic goals and expectations for each other. People who could regard members of the opposite sex as individuals, not as representatives of their sex, seemed to have the best relationships. Still, we cannot deny our biological imperative.

If the goal of the species is to pass on the strongest genes to the next generation, humans are reproductive machines. Our bodies are programmed for physical joy and emotional immortality, sending these two marvelous messages skipping and bumping along our workway, making us shiver with anticipation, purple with passion, and gratified with completion. Sexual intercourse, for most people, is a supremely desirable event. Seeking to participate in it takes up a lot of our time and energy.

Biology must contend with *both* head and heart. This is where the issue gets complicated. Consider the case of the underbrained and simple-emotioned cottontail rabbit. Nothing pleases this species so much as simply complying with biology's command. Anyone who has owned a pair of rabbits knows they do not wear rings on their paws or hang around singing the blues for the bunny that got away. By comparison, we are, as novelist Barry Hannah puts it, "overbrained and overemotioned." We think about ourselves all the time, about others some of the time, and about "us" occasionally. Sometimes we think so much, it prevents us from complying with biology's command. Sometimes we comply with biology's command so much, we lose our ability to think altogether!

The fundamental difference between rabbits and humans is that when a pair of big rabbits produces a hutch of little rabbits, it is not long before the little ones are off hutching on their own. This is not the case with humans. Small humans need a lot of care. We are helpless as infants, and if we are not given daily attention, we die. We must be protected and that is why Kipling said, "Whoever has children in the cradle had best be at peace with the world." In its simplest form, this is the main reason we need one another. We must organize our society to protect our children, and we must organize secure, small, social units to raise our children. If we cannot advance children to the point where they can make it on their own, we have denied our biological imperative.

The complexities of our own biology have carried us far beyond the needs of rabbiting. We have paid for our complicated bodies and brains by needing one another very, very much. Instead of seeing one another as simple, biological connections or potential helpers in a hunt for food, we "featherless bipeds" search for partnership, compatibility of ideas, shared passion, cooperative action, and a little fun. We pass from person to person, from union to union, trying them out until we find some that meet most of our criteria if we are lucky.

There are limits to the number of people we can manage; about fifteen hundred according to one estimate. After that, other people become strangers, like another tribe. We resist crowding, we crave room. We want order; we fear random events. Studies conducted in the 1950s in crowded urban areas demonstrated that if we are too close to one another for too long, we experience stress and we behave in self-defeating ways. Crowding causes stress, stress breeds hostility, hostility breeds insecurity, and insecure people do not breed well. In Calhoun's famous experiments, rats placed in an environment that gradually grew very crowded became schizophrenic and depressed because of the crowding; they fought, they injured their young, they became homosexual and permanently sterile. Obviously we are not rats. By extending the conclusions to humans, we suggest there is evidence people *must* manage to have at least a few relationships that are permanent and predictable in order to feel secure in a crowded world. People can tolerate being crowded in with strangers only if they have a place to go where they feel secure. It isn't the crowd so much that bothers us; it is, according to David Riesman, "the lonely crowd."

Despite the claims made during the late 1960s and early 1970s that we could all "love one another right now," we have learned that we can't. We all need long-lasting, bonded, permanent relationships, exclusive ones we can count on to maintain pleasure and order in our lives. When we live harmoniously within our own psychological and physiological limits, we can attend to our individual urgencies for security and satisfaction and seek a few people out of the many to share, support, and survive with, even to enjoy. There are only so many hours, only so much energy to expend, and we are aware of the silent ticking of our biological clock reminding us we are not immortal. Thus, in the miraculous flash of a billion electrons that is our mind, we are aware that we need to seek and find others. The hazards of relationship are inexpressible, the possibilities for failure enormous, but the rewards are so gratifying that we cannot give up the search. John Silber reminds us that in our lifetimes we will find only three or four people with whom we will ever become intimate. The search is hard because there are few victories possible but worthwhile because the victories are so satisfying.

One of the main problems we face in our search for others is that our desires often exceed our capabilities. All of us want acceptance, approval, and in Carl Rogers's terms, "unconditional positive regard." This only proves that we can name what we cannot have. People do not parcel emotion equally. They reserve intense emotional energy for people for whom they really care. Society helps focus our efforts by providing traditional relationships we can count on much of the time. The family, for example, is the cornerstone of all societies. Sometimes the family is extended, almost a tribe; sometimes the family is very small: just he and she, and baby makes three. But where there is no family unit, the individual cannot adequately mature.

Families teach compromises needed for social living. George Gilder argues that without families people would revert to forming primitive hunting packs. Compromises must be worked out for the good of the order, so humans organize governments. Government is an abstraction that applies family principles to vast societies. In the final chapter we will show you that every family generates a means of making decisions, carrying them out, and adjudicating disputes, the essential principles upon which societies are built. Thus, our family is a rehearsal for our role in society.

The quest to improve our species compels us to move outside of our families to find mates so the best genetic traits can be spread and the weakest controlled. We are exogamous; we seek our mates away from home to enhance strong traits and dilute weak ones.

Societies run best when everyone lives within the rules. Although we each think ourselves unique, our social behavior must conform to the same rules of conduct. We are narcissistic, although it may well be we have misinterpreted the myth of Narcissus. According to the legend, Narcissus saw his reflection in the water and drowned because he fell in love with it. It may not have been so simple. What Narcissus may have discovered was that he was a *unique* person, and from that moment he began to demand that others treat him as one.

Self-awareness, in part, makes us apprehensive about how we may be treated by others, and this leads us to make laws about how others may treat us. The rules by which we live articulate what we can do and what we must avoid to increase rewards and reduce punishments. We use our language to participate in complex social institutions to avoid the "nature red in fang and claw," characteristic of the life of other animals, yet we sometimes fight in our private worlds and make war in our public ones. We are not peace-loving creatures, and the legislation we impose on ourselves to curb the effects of our aggressive nature is sometimes hard to live by. Occasionally we go berserk in a self-destructive outpouring of egocentrism and we may spend the rest of our lives picking up the pieces. Our mission, however, is somehow to create a world fit for people to live in.

OUR NEED TO NEED OTHERS

We experience people constantly. They happen to us like a long string of accidents. We bump into one another in parking lots, shopping malls, dentist's waiting rooms, and classes. We clash at cocktail parties, restaurants, and on corners when we go this way and they go that. We run into old friends and tell them that they haven't aged a bit and that we ought to get together. We make obligatory visits to the relatives on weekends and holidays. We go to the lodge, the garden club, the political meeting, the lecture, and the movies, and we either go with people, meet people there, or share the experience with people (usually all three). Sometimes, in the crowd, we see a person that looks so appealing we want to reach out and demand that he or she become our friend. But we usually don't.

When we are with people, we furiously bang our vocal cords against our larynxes, contorting our faces into any of roughly 700,000 possible signs. We wave our arms and shout. What we say and do is a matter of choice and opportunity, sometimes a matter of internal urgency, sometimes a cold and calculated declaration made for a purpose. We tend to go with the rules we have memorized about how to deal with one another. Most of us pick our associates from people like ourselves, who we have been taught are reliable. We are aware of society's mandates and evaluations, and if we do something undesirable, we often feel guilty about it.

Homosexuals, for example, are confronted with the problems of believing that their choice of sex practices is perfectly all right even though the bulk of society condemns it. Blacks, Indians, Vietnamese, and Hispanics try to get their share of what society has to offer by conforming as best they can, and at the same time they must maintain their pride in the face of demeaning remarks by the people who have what they want.

Friendships between different types of people are exceedingly rare. (Men and women, we found out, are rarely friends.) Birds of a feather do indeed seem to flock together. Youngsters are kept in school, old people consigned to retirement villages, married people in suburbs, and singles in high-rises. Three decades ago, people of all sorts lived together. Today, we are encouraged to confine our associations to people like ourselves, actually with the people most likely to compete with us and threaten us. We must compete with our peers, the people we work and live with, and it is hard to resist the temptation to try to defeat them.

We are also constrained by the demands others make for their rights and welfare. We are taught to "do unto others as you would have others do unto you," but we find it hard to do that for *all* others, and we often find it easy to make fine distinctions so that some others are less "other" than others. It is really hard to be considerate of people who seem different and peculiar. To be concerned about them might mean denying ourselves something we want and deserve. Nevertheless, the mandate to consider the rights of others has been enacted into law by our legislatures and enforced by our courts, and it is the basis for our social etiquette. Like it or not, we are forced to live and share and exchange with many others whom we do not like, and we are punished for grabbing and keeping. When we choose to violate social rules, we must take the consequences. Sometimes we are regarded as criminals, sometimes as mentally ill. There are a very few extraordinary people who seem to be able to make new rules.

We also seem to need commonplaces, myths to help us make choices. We are taught such "truths" as "men are to be strong and courageous, and woman's place is in the home." We learn our bigotries, whom to hate, and what to believe through bits of "wisdom" passed on to us by the important people in our lives. These myths are capable of blurring our vision and clouding our judgment. They often lead us into destructive choices of whom to trust and whom to avoid. We will discuss them in detail in a later chapter.

PARADOXES OF NEEDS

We face some terrible paradoxes because we are creatures who use our minds. We are primitive despite our civilization, many of our urgencies are primal, and we are capable of harsh, cruel, and deceitful acts. We live in the hope of love, but we act in the fear of hate. We talk about love a lot and about hate a little. We form our relationships and hope that we can love, and that we often find ourselves hating and hurting.

We compete for the limited "goodies" of life using laws to protect ourselves except when we think we can evade laws and get away with it. We are selective in our view of justice. We condemn in others acts we rationalize in ourselves. At one time or another, each of us has been rejected or denied something we wanted very badly. We resent losing, we envy the people who have what we have. The Seven Deadly Sins are still very much with us. We deny our biology but legislate it into our morality.

We know humans are urgent about avoiding pain and obtaining pleasure. We all believe we need to be happy, and in our society we have been guaranteed the right to pursue it. Aristotle told us that happiness is the ultimate goal of life, and we seek "it" often without having a noun to identify the pronoun. Then, when we find "it," we may not know we have "it."

While pleasure may only be the absence of pain, we do seek pleasure and that is one of the reasons we form our private twosomes. The quest for sexual pleasure drives us, shapes literature and art, confuses us, distracts us from our work, and gets us into considerable trouble. When we are not getting enough of what we want, we tend to seek panaceas and sometimes make miserable mistakes in our selection of people to love and trust.

A second paradox we face is the need to be rewarded in relationships by others, despite the fact that our ambitions often exceed our abilities. When we fail, we blame the people closest to us, the very ones we want to shelter us. Because we fear our enemies (to the point where often we will not even admit having them), we respect them, whereas we rail against our friends. We cannot get what we want unless we know what we want, know where it is available, and know how to persuade the person who has it to part with it. Our urgency is to demand, but, for most of us, the only road to success is to trade.

If we do not get what we want, we tend to feel guilty about our lack of ability. Sometimes we blame others for it or hope someone will rescue us and make it possible to win again. Much of what we read about relationships ignores topics such as hate, guilt, anxiety, shame, resentment, and revenge, yet they are very much parts of our lives. In a later chapter we will show you how people refuse to admit that they may have enemies or that they could possibly do anything to justify being hated. We prefer to acknowledge trust, love, and responsibility.

Our paradoxes become even more difficult when we extend them into our public lives. We need to be safe and secure in our homes and neighborhoods despite violence in the streets. If we attempt to curb violence, however, we find that we curb our own rights. We are urged to

value ownership of property despite increasing difficulty in acquiring it, and thus we are constantly forced to reassess our worth. When we cannot have the tangible things we seek, we must compensate by finding intangible rewards. Where we formerly declared success to be synonymous with wealth and power, we must now equate success with interpersonal satisfaction, acquiring love and trust rather than a fine car and an important position.

THE NEED FOR RELATIONSHIPS

Because we are animals, we need other people for simple survival. We need to have them to comfort us and make us secure. When we are separated from other people, we are lonely, afraid, and we feel powerless. When we are angry with other people or hostile to our society, we are alienated; we retreat into sullen distance from others, or we retaliate violently. When we do not have people around, we are bored. We do not know what to do with our time. Virtually everything each of us does is directed at some other person. We seek approval, we seek to please, we seek our rewards, to exchange. Our inventions, our art, our wit, our loyalty, and our love either are directed toward others or are directives about others.

The American philosopher George Herbert Mead argued that our identities are formed by the responses of others. We learn to declare ourselves *to be* something or other, and we are either confirmed or rejected by the people around us. As children, we play roles, and our parents and other important people in our lives make it clear that we are not real pirates, ballet dancers, or cowboys. When we try on roles they believe are reasonable, they encourage us, and so we become what they shape us to be. They help us learn to set goals and ambitions through interaction with others, and from others we learn what is socially acceptable and rewarding. We learn to avoid punishment, to become part of the group, and how to follow our inner urgencies and sense of equity. If we do not, we become criminals, mentally ill, or superstars.

Most of us just want to stand out a little bit from the rest of the bunch. We want approval and acceptance in our public behavior and someone to help us feel important in our private life. Only a few ever win

big public rewards. Thus, everyone needs a way to win private elections and prizes.

- Everyone needs someone to confirm his or her importance, to demonstrate that without them, the life of the other person has less meaning.
- Everyone needs to believe there is someone on whom they can depend for help and support no matter what the catastrophe.
- Everyone needs to have someone with whom to spend lonely hours, times of sadness, and times of joy.
- Everyone needs someone with whom to plan and scheme to win rewards and to complain to when things go badly.
- Everyone needs someone to be with, just in cse.

MRS. A. (age eighty-one):
I wonder about the kids, the way they get along or don't get along. So few of them get married anymore, settle down, have kids. The boys and girls want to fight with each other for money or whatever. They are young and they are tough, but I don't know if they are tougher than we were. We fought a depression and a couple wars, and some of us escaped from other countries by the skin of our teeth. I don't know who is tougher. But I do know one thing. I never had to worry about

who would bring me chicken soup when I was sick. There was always some-body—my husband, my kids. When my husband died and the kids went away, I had to find someone else. I got together with Mrs. L—— and now we do it for each other. You can't be alone. It isn't good to be alone. It isn't human to be alone.

The big question is who should we be with, and how do we get started? Too often we believe in the Cinderella myth, that someday, somewhere, out of the confusion of our daily life, someone will happen to us who will change our lives forever. (If you believe in Hollywood, this occasion will be accompanied by a string orchestra playing from nowhere and by birds singing and bells ringing.) Most of us believe that special relationships "just happen." We believe that it is unethical or silly to search pragmati-cally for a friend or mate. We are taught to expect that the right one will come along and to be noncommittal in our dealings with others until the big moment.

Then we will be, as Kurt Vonnegut puts it, "lonely no more". We will not be bored. We will become important. Like Mickey Rooney and Judy Garland, we will put on a show. We will live in a white house on a tree-lined street (or in a snazzy pad in upper Manhattan), and we will raise Dick and Jane and have a dog that never soils. We will live happily ever after because the same fairy godmother that brought us together will pro-tect us from harm forever.

Our media cater to this myth. The perpetual reruns of Jeannie who

26

"I vant to be alone"

lives in a bottle and protects the young astronaut is the ideal and idol (although Jeannie has been corrupted by Western civilization and has traded her harem pants for red running shorts, and her beloved Tony is now a diabolical Texas millionaire). *Plus ça change, plus c'est la même chose.*

Women often expect to find a mature, helpful, patient, tolerant, cook and child-care specialist who will permit them to have their careers while being perfect mothers and change agents in the community. He should also rise to the top of some profession as well. *The Brady Bunch* and *Eight is Enough* set another model. Men, like *Magnum P.I.,* should perfect their bodies, dutifully devoting them to their women's personal pleasure, while they exercise wisdom and authority like Father Anderson and Marcus Welby (the same person) while being as wise as Mr. Cleaver in dispensing pearls to young "Beavers." He will have a body like "the Hulk" and she like WKRP's Jennifer. Fitting these media models always involves a search for the "real me." Most of us believe that inside we are as brilliant and beautiful as the fictional heroes and heroines we admire.

HARRY P. (age twenty-three)
I usually don't do much more with women than sex. That's all I really want now. I do it well and they like me and it. Every so often one of them wants to get married, but I know that the girl I marry will be the one who turns me down and means it and makes me define myself.

HARRIET C. (age twenty-three)
I didn't get married when I had the chance because I want a guy who will let me grow and be myself. I think being married is part of growing, and if you can't be yourself, there is no point to it. I can do without sex and men. I've got to find the real me. And when I do, then I will be able to make a relationship.

The quest for the "real me" is a major source of defeat in relationships. The popular belief that there is a "real me" residing inside us distracts us from developing personalities. The myth would have us believe there is someone who will be so important to us our real self will emerge, without any effort on our part. We want to be fulfilled and actualized by letting "real me" come out and grow in perfect union with a person of the opposite sex who is doing the same, and thus, between us, we will be rich, famous, contented, talented, fulfilled, with perfect children and blissful simultaneous orgasm whenever we want it.

   "Real me" is a real myth. We form ourselves by developing relatively enduring patterns of interpersonal relationships with others. There is compensation and exchange, expectation and disappointment, and constant change, and what we are amounts to what we can do and what we can talk about. There is no "inner core" or "hidden self." There is only imagination, private goals, unexpected thoughts, regrets, fears, guilts, and tensions that affect our public behavior. We are, however, what our public behavior makes us.

JEFFREY W.
I get into a lot of trouble because people don't know who I really am. I have this tendency to tell people what I think is wrong with them. I don't want to hurt them, though; I just want them to be better. I want to be a helper to people, but I end up hurting them. I wish sometimes that my head was made out of glass so people could really see who I am.

The peril of confusing imagination with reality is very great. Some people seem to believe that others can see what is on their mind. When others take offense at some obnoxious behavior, they complain because they believe the others should have known their intentions were good. Said David Merrick in *Elephant Man*, "Sometimes I think my head is so big because it is so full of dreams." The King Gama sang in Gilbert and Sullivan's *Princess Ida*:

> *If you give me your attention, I will tell you what I am*
> *I'm a genuine philanthropist, all other kinds are sham.*
> *Each little fault of temper and each social defect*

In my erring fellow creature, I endeavour to correct.
To all their little weaknesses I open people's eyes;
And little plans to snub the self sufficient I devise;
I love my fellow creatures, I do all the good I can,
Yet everybody says I'm such a disagreeable man!
    And I can't think why!

The myth of the "real me" is important enough to attract the attention of a number of scholars. Some have argued that people must be "genuine" and "authentic" with one another, that they must "own and share" their feelings and "disclose" to others their deepest feelings and thoughts. There is a branch of the mental health industry devoted to workshops and seminars designed to train people to live this way with one another. The evidence of positive gain through these methods is very slim, but the potential damage very great.

LINDA E.
I've tried some of the ——— workshops, and I don't know whether they did me any good or not. I feel good when I am there, and all the people seem to be so close to me. But when I come home, I feel uneasy. I am afraid to try what I learned on the people around me because I think they will use my secrets against me. I once tried to look up one of the guys I was in a workshop with, but when I saw him, he acted like he didn't know me. I wanted to talk with him about things that I was feeling, and in the workshop he was really close and we spent one magic night together even. But when I got him outside, he really acted like he didn't know me.

Later we will report on how these enterprises work and comment on their record of success.

We must concede, however, that few remedies proposed to improve interpersonal relationships have had much of a record of success. It is, of course, hard to find out how effective any kind of human improvement method is. Sometimes people feel better when they try to improve themselves, even though the people around them can't see any change at all. But training programs in relationships seem fuzzier than most. Therapists often claim the people they treat don't really try. The evidence indicates advice doesn't help much unless it can be translated into specific training in ways to act.

We have resisted our urge to write a how-to-do-it book because we are not at all sure we know how to do it. At the moment both of the writers have stable relationships with their spouses, with each other, and with a few other people in the world. We are *temporarily* out of trouble. We are not sure we know how this came about. We will content ourselves with providing information about people and making an effort to interpret it. The point of view that will guide us throughout this book is that people can only respond to what they see and hear. We can only form our opinions on what we know, and when we respond to private fantasies and dreams, we get into trouble. This almost entirely unromantic point of view helps present a great number of possibilities to you in a way that may be useful to you in your own relationships.

chapter two

How we start our lives together

I wish I'd said that.

All of us at one time or another.

*Good intentions
are far more difficult to cope
with than malicious behavior.*

*If good intentions are combined with stupidity,
it is impossible to out-think them.*

To know thyself is the ultimate form of aggression.

*There are more nitwits than geniuses.
Therefore, think twice when everyone agrees with you.*

The Laws of Disillusionment

*Courtship to marriage,
as a very witty prologue to a very dull play.*

CONGREVE

*If you don't have anything important to worry about,
what you have to worry about becomes important.*

Herman Cohen's Law

STAGES

Relationships have stages of development. Authorities have different names for the stages, and there is no sense trying to memorize them. To explain stages, we prefer to try our hand at creative writing and offer you a fable.

A Fable: The Book of Dreams

Once upon a time, and perhaps for all time for all we know, there lived some creatures known as "Elpoep." They lived pretty much like other animals, grubbing in the ground for goodies or occasionally killing and eating something that ran slower than they did. They also ran about calling each other names and bashing each other from time to time.

One day they noticed a shortage of Elpoep, so they had to figure out how to get new ones. They discovered that if you put two of the right kinds of Elpoep together, a third one, and sometimes a fourth and fifth, would result. The big problem was how to pair them off.

They decided that at a particular time—which they called "the Age of Decision Making," which came when the young Elpoep learned what they needed to know about food, clothing, shelter, and bashing—each Elpoep would refer to a certain book. The elders produced the book, which they called *The Ancient and Venerable Book of Dreams*. (It was not ancient when they produced it, but they knew it would last a long time.) From it, each young Elpoep would select a partner to merge with for life for the purpose of producing young. The selection would follow procedures outlined in *Ye Rule of Review.* According to this rule each young Elpoep would turn the pages of *The Ancient and Venerable Book of Dreams* and select from the eighty-by-ten glossies therein a proper dreammate with whom to merge. There would be a description such as the following examples:

> Skizzwak of Fnertz is 71 gribbles high and eight feet old. He has lasted 111 sleegles, and his signs show him to be good for at least 45,000 more miles. His mother says he is a good boy who brings her Cauliflowers on St. Grinkel's day. Says the chief huntsman, "He is strong and lusty and known as Tosser of the Bull." Says Zelda the Bork, "He is dreamy and dances like on air."
>
> Gruzzle of Glodge has long puce hair and mauve eyes. She is 60 gribbles high and seven feet old. She has lasted 91 sleegles and is good for 51,000 miles. She has lovely, globular gozonks about which Obnok the Critic says, "Wuggah, wuggah, wuggah!" She is built like a brick vomnop.

When two young (originally called "goys" and "birls," but changed later to "boys" and "girls" for obvious reasons) mutually chose, they were merged. They were, of course, prevented from seeing each other in the flesh (since Elpoep flesh, at that time, was not altogether attractive) until merger time. They were only permitted to see the image. They were bound by the following rules:

Ye Rule of Surprise. Young Elpoep are not permitted to learn anything important about each other prior to the merger.

Ye Rule of Separation. Elpoep are merged until death or dissatisfaction do them part, whichever cometh firtht. If one chooses to dechoose, he, she, or it forfeits half the winter stores, and receives a guilty conscience in exchange.

Ye Rule of Second Choice. Dechoosers and dechosens may select only from black and white photos for the second merger.

Ye Rule of Nonchosen Punishments. All who have never been chosen shall be known as "oners" and must live in permanent suspense, knowing that their picture remains in the book, aging along with them.

The fable is not far from fact. In modern times, we "elpoep," backward though we may be, have the real thing to look at instead of pictures, but we are bound in our examination by the social regulation and advice of the great sage Murphy, who invented many laws. For example, we are told:

- Don't worry about what other people say about him/her. Let your heart decide.
- It is just as easy to choose a rich one as a poor one.
- Nothing matters just so long as you are sexually satisfied.
- The important thing is, can you communicate?

- Love is everything.
- Love is nothing. It's money that counts.
- Don't get a fat one, they eat too much.
- Don't get a skinny one, they are too nervous.
- Doctors are the best kind.
- They have to have a big chest in order to be passionate.
- How will you know you're in love? Don't worry, you'll know.

Mothers, fathers, and friends add advice from their own experience. Sometimes the advice is frightening.

- Men are only after one thing.
- All women want is your money and your balls.

Sometimes the advice is impossible.

- Just make sure you don't get into anything where you have to surrender your options or where there are too many strings, and make sure you can be gratified and get out when you need to so you don't have to assume any obligations you'd rather not carry.

Consider the following bit of irony:

The mother of the bride (to her friends)
My daughter has married such a wonderful man. He takes care of her like she is a precious doll. She has anything she wants, she doesn't have to work, she can enrich herself, sit around and listen to music, do art, go out with her friends, and she can hire a maid to take care of the house.
The mother of the groom (to her friends)
My son has married a witch. He has to take care of everything; she can't even take care of herself. All she does is run around with her friends or sits around the house and smears paint and listens to music. And she won't even do the housework; he has to hire a maid.

With advance in technology in virtually every aspect of human life, one would think that the process of pairing people off would be a little less perilous than it is. However, attempts to computerize it have failed, and justifiably so. The method of selection is just as uncertain as it has always been. People (like the Elpoep) make their decisions prematurely based on scant information, and once the choice is made and acted upon, it can be reversed only with considerable pain. The world was somewhat simpler when children were ordered to the altar by their parents and compelled to stay together no matter what, but in those days people were not as concerned about gratification, satisfaction, and avoiding persecution and pain.

FROM FABLE TO FACT: MAKING DECISIONS IN THE REAL WORLD

When people select mates, they have something in mind, although most people are not quite sure what "it" is. One authority on relationships once commented, "People seem to know a good deal more about the cars they purchase than they do about their friends or mates." Most of us are unable or unwilling to make sensible predictions about how people are likely to act when we are with them regularly. Usually, people make the decision and try to justify it to themselves later.

Furthermore, there is no body of knowledge to guide people in how to make their choices. We learn early to base our decisions on our personal experience, whatever that has been, and we must draw our inferences from very limited information. Three-fourths of our respondents said they made the first contact with the person who eventually became their best friend because of his or her appearance.

WALTER D.
When I go to a party, I look for "talent." I look for legs and good big boobs, and, of course, a pretty face, but these days all the girls can do things with their faces. I don't like girls with glasses. If a girl doesn't know about contacts these days, she probably doesn't know about the pill either. I also don't like girls that try to hide on the edges of the crowd. I like the ones that move, bounce around, and are really with it. There are some that stand like they really want to be looked at, and those are the ones I pick from.

SUZANNE S.
I'm not looking for permanent contacts. I want somebody who can show me a good time without getting pushy. I want control over who I do sex with. I sometimes make mistakes, but I know how to handle it. I look for guys in expensive clothes. There's an outlet store around here that sells those alligator shirts, so I stay away from guys wearing those. I don't like big macho studs because I want to be able to win my wrestling matches. I pick guys that look a little weak that I can pressure into spending money on me.

Real-world decisions are made on scanty data, such as the foregoing. Veterans in selecting people for sexual encounters can testify there is no relationship between actual sexiness and looking sexy.

STYLES K.

When you are a semipro stud, you take your chances. As a pro football player, I can usually pick and choose. They come at you and want to take you home largely because they want to say they did it with you. I have to try to figure out which ones know how and which ones don't. After three years, I still can't figure it out. There is one in Cleveland that is built unbelievable and magnificent in bed, but I got it on once with one of those Miss World contestants and she was a stick. And there is this skinny thing with straight hair and no tits in Denver who can send me right up the wall. No, there's something besides looks that tells you whether a woman is sexy, and I still don't know what it is. But can you think of a better research project?

LOUISE E.

Ken was one of those beautiful guys, tall, and he had muscles all over. The bottom part of his arm (the biceps?) just rippled. All of him just sort of rippled along. I had this fantasy of him in a bathing suit walking with me and all the girls looking with their tongues hanging out. He was the best-looking guy there. The others were too fat or too thin and didn't act like they could handle a girl like me. They wouldn't look at me, like I embarrassed them or something. I mean, I want to be looked at. I can get picked up by anyone I want, and I wanted Ken. So we dated two or three times and he never touched me. I asked him about it one night, and he said he was gay. I couldn't believe it. A guy who looked like that couldn't be gay, so I figure he wanted to give me the brush and let me down easy so he lied to me about being gay. That's what a real man would do.

Truth and illusion! Most people do not go to such lengths to rearrange information, but overlooking behavior that might contradict first impressions is common. In fact, people seem to struggle very hard to acquire information that confirms first impressions, while they overlook negative information. If, for example, you think an individual looks gentle and discover later he has brutal moments, it is relatively easy to dismiss them as exceptional. This practice is frequently employed by wives who are regularly beaten.

When things go reasonably well, relationships proceed through observable stages. During each stage people gather information about each other and use it to make decisions about whether to advance to a more intense stage of relationship. All of us know friendly people with whom we relate in various ways, but we become intimate with only a few friends. The stages listed in the following table are composites of those proposed by various authorities. (See references by Davis, Knapp, Phillips and Wood at the end of the chapter.)

The stages can be identified largely by the *content of conversation* between the pair. The first stage is marked by considerable sparring, use of a great many clichés, probes, questions, and answers. In the second stage

Stage	Kind of Information Sought
Meeting and sizing up	1. Is the person clear for contact or too encumbered? 2. Is there anything to talk about? 3. Is there enough mutual interest to continue the contact? 4. Can a "date" be made?
Experimenting with further contact	1. Can the relationship be sustained? 2. Is there some common interest worth pursuing? 3. Is the contact more satisfying than other available or ongoing contacts?
Selecting the basis for the relationship	1. Does the contact have a basis for exchange: recreation, shared ideas, social action, mutual support, information, and so on? 2. If male-female, is it possible to arrange private time and place to explore potential for sexual contact?
Continuation and constitution building	1. Developing the rules for continuing the relationship. 2. Deciding on common goals. 3. Preparing the relationship constitution. 4. Making desired sexual arrangements.
Formalizing the bond (sexual relationships only.)	1. Marriage or equivalent.
Termination: unilateral or bilateral	1. One partner cancels. 2. Partners agree to separate. 3. Details of the separation worked out.

some common topics are considered in depth. The pair try out various activities, and evaluate them. They make decisions about mutual preferences and activities and proceed on a relatively regular schedule or according to an agreed procedure. Perhaps they agree on bowling every Wednesday night, or each may call the other for lunch no more than twice a week. In the next stage the relationship becomes more permanent as rules and regulations are worked out. Couples may decide to marry. Good friends must be content with being good friends, since blood-brother ceremonies are not in vogue anymore. In the termination stage there are a great many options for inflicting pain, the details of which we will provide in Chapter Five.

THE TALENT SEARCH

People learn to meet and greet each other in standard ways. They engage in what Bronislaw Malinowski called "phatic communion," a process similar to animals meeting and sniffing each other to sense intention. Phatic communion is used to stall for time until each individual declares whether to carry on a conversation or return to the bar. When they remain in conversation, they move from phatic communion into "small talk."

Scenario One

SHE: Hi. I'm Lucy Morella.

HE: Good to meet you. I'm Peter Danziger.

SHE: How long have you known Gert and Fred? (The host and hostess)

HE: I'm new in town. We just met. I work at Fred's company.

—End phatic communion. Enter small talk—

SHE: Where did you come from?

HE: Wilkes-Barre.

SHE: That's interesting. I always wondered how you pronounced that. Wilkesbar or Wilkesberry.

HE: Berry.

(silence)

SHE: What kind of work do you do?

HE: It's very technical.

(silence)

SHE: Nice to meet you. I think I need a refill on my drink.

HE: Same here.

Scenario Two

—Same as scenario one up to:

HE: Berry.

SHE: What kind of work do you do?

HE: I'm not sure what I'll be doing here. I train computers to do really rotten things.

SHE: Oh, like what?

HE: Well, like drawing blueprints. I can get a computer to replace three draftsmen.

SHE: What happens to the draftsmen?

—And on they go until he asks her if he can take her home. (Curtain)

During first meetings conversationalists take turns. They offer bits of information, avoid controversial comments, keep a pleasant face, try to prevent long silences. Each can discontinue contact by excusing himself or herself and using a formulary exit, as SHE did in the first scenario. In the second scenario, HE was a bit more communicative, suggesting that he was interested. SHE decided to stay. Each person is required to uphold his or her end of the small talk. If one party lets down, it is usually interpreted as a lack of interest. Even if nothing important is being said, fluency, responsiveness, and attentiveness are important.

Consider the case of a person who is not skilled enough to be fluent, not quick enough to be responsive, and unaware of how to appear attentive. We generally regard these three aspects of contact as intrinsic. However, recent evidence indicates they are *learned behaviors,* that is, they cannot be regarded as accurate indicators of what a person is thinking. A trained person can be uninterested and still maintain a proper demeanor, whereas an untrained person can be very interested but not be able to show it to the conversation partner. Notice the errors in interpretation that can result.

During small talk, conversation partners probe to see if there is a basis for a future contact. If not, they may remain together a polite five or ten minutes discussing weather, the teams, the decor of the apartment, and recent movies, then excuse themselves and move on to try again. If they establish a common reference, however, the conversation may lead to a "date."

SALLY: I was admiring your hair. Is that a new style?

MARY: I think so. I just put myself in the hands of my hairdresser. She's a marvel, and on her behalf and mine, I thank you for the kinds words.

SALLY: Is she a secret, or will you share her with others?

MARY: It's Laverne on Front Street. She's been doing me for years.

SALLY: Is it hard to get an appointment?

MARY: No, tell her Mary Fletcher sent you. Or better yet, why don't I take you in and introduce you?

SALLY: Wonderful, when?

MARY: My regular appointment is Tuesday, 10 A.M. Want me to see if she has time for you?

SALLY: Please. Will you call me?

MARY: (fumbling for pad and pencil in purse): Of course, what's your number?

SALLY: 999-8888.

MARY: (writing it down and writing her number on another sheet): Here's my number. If you don't hear from me, give me a call, please. If she's booked, we'll work out another time.

This is a clear arrangement. Mary was willing to comply with Sally's request. Sally was willing to work out the logistics. Sometimes it is not so easy to work out the details of a "date" because people often have schedules that don't mesh. On the other hand, by the time you get to exchanging phone numbers, you can believe serious business is being done.

Phrases such as "I'll be in touch," "drop around some time," "we really ought to get together," "let's have lunch sometime," or "give me a ring" indicate that serious business will probably not be done. They are discouragement lines. When you receive one, you continue at your own risk. A clear sign that the other person is willing to extend contact is a discussion of specific time, place, or activity. If the discussion does not revolve around something tangible, it must be considered a brushoff.

An important element in early contacts is discovering whether the other person is *available* for some kind of relationship. For example, a move toward someone of the opposite sex may elicit information about a spouse or fiancé. Family, business, and community obligations may also disqualify a person from subsequent contact. Mentioning conflicting obligations discourages further attempts to date. It is not necessary to be specific about what the obligations are.

HE: How about getting together for lunch some day this week? (He knows she is being "hard to get." He is making the invitation open, hoping to get her to set a day and time.)

SHE: I normally don't go out for lunch. I have to be around. (The answer is no, and he should know it, but he persists.)

HE: Well, what do you do for lunch?

SHE: (knowing full well it is none of his business—incidentally she usually sends out or brings a sack): I make do.

HE: Well, how about getting together after work for a drink?

SHE: I am never sure about when I get off. I have to be around to take care of whatever—

HE: (beginning to get the message). —comes up.

SHE: Yes. (One-syllable answers are discouraging.)

HE: (She is very attractive. Time to fire the big gun): Well, how about this? I have two fourth-row seats for the concert Saturday night. How about dinner at a little Hungarian restaurant I know and—

SHE: I'm busy Saturday night.

(That should be it. Time for him to excuse himself to get another drink.)

Only a crude or insensitive person would go on. SHE has given no information, no encouragement. HE doesn't know where she works or what she does. SHE gave no phone number, would set no time. HE doesn't know whether SHE is engaged, married, a lesbian, cohabiting, or what. HE knows his moves have been rejected. It is time for him to move on.

People need not give away personal information during phatic communion and small talk. There was no reason for the woman in the example to explain where she worked or what she did. If you are not interested, your only obligation is to reject the offer within the rules of social decorum. In the example, SHE engaged politely in phatic communion, and usual exchange of small talk, and then rejected the offer. When invitations are extended, you are free to bargain or use an escape line.

Oh, there's Bill Evans. I haven't seen him for months. Excuse me. Nice meeting you.

I need a refill, please excuse me.

(Experts at cocktail parties recommend drinking straight ginger ale and keeping your glass half full. When the others get drunk, you will be in possession of your faculties. Also, note that when escaping, neither party gave any cue that he or she was coming back. For example, "excuse me for a minute" implies that you are returning, but a simple "excuse me" does not.)

Nice meeting you. Excuse me. (This is somewhat blunt, but if you have refilled your drink and were trapped again, it is an almost infallible escape.)

At social gatherings designed to stimulate initial contact, you are not obligated to anything more than expected social amenities. Your duty to the host is fulfilled by your willingness to make phatic communion and not to break the good china. Aside from that, you are not obligated to talk to anyone at length, nor are you obligated to meet anyone you do not wish to meet (unless you have agreed to do so in advance). Be careful of invitations that include the line, "I have someone for you to meet that I just know you'll love." Acceptance of the invitation may obligate you to be a blind date to the host's acne-ridden kid brother or pudgy cousin from Wenatchee.

DATING

When you anticipate the first date, you have no data to go on other than appearance and what you picked up in phatic communion and small talk. Initial dating, therefore, should consist of a simple activity you both enjoy. There should be time for more talk. Moving too rapidly at this stage can be misleading. For example, an invitation to your apartment for a quiet dinner may sound romantic and may be logistically convenient, but it carries the connotation of a tryst. It suggests intercourse. In same-sex dating, however, women may find dinner most efficient. Men usually prefer an activity.

BILL: Have you survived the baseball strike?
TOM: Yes, it got me interested in lots of other things.
BILL: Like what? What else is there in town?

TOM: You're new, huh? Well, there is a local semipro soccer team that's kind of fun.
BILL: I could never figure out soccer. That wouldn't be a substitute for baseball.
TOM: Well, are you into country music?
BILL: Country music? You bet!
TOM: Charlie Pride is playing at the Musitorium this weekend. Want to go?
BILL: Can you still get tickets?
TOM: I can. Two shows, seven and nine-thirty on Saturday.
BILL: Let's try nine-thirty. I'll have to be at the office in the afternoon. Can I pick you up?

They are off and running. There is still some negotiating to do about where to have dinner and who will pay. They need to exchange phone numbers. A date has been made, and they have found two topics to talk about (baseball and country music) and one to avoid (soccer).

There is little difference in opposite-sex dating. The idea is to establish a common interest first, then determine whether both parties are interested in more contact. A specific invitation must be tendered. "We must do it sometime" is not an invitation. If bargaining then takes place, it means both parties are interested in continuation.

One small caution. During the early survey, a questionnaire was circulated. One item was "After providing a woman with a pleasant evening, a man is entitled to expect sexual intercourse." More than half the male respondents agreed with this item, and about 40 percent of the females agreed. If this issue concerns you, make an effort to find out in advance what is expected. The best way to manage sexual presumptions is to make the first few engagements "dutch treat" and public until you establish which way you want to go.

CONTINUING

Once people discover they want to maintain a relationship, they must bargain for a basis on which to continue it. In a simple friendship this means deciding what you will talk about and the kinds of activities you will share. It is essentially a trial-and-error process. If one person is more enthusiastic about the relationship than the other, he or she will offer more suggestions for contact. The one to whom the relationship is *least valuable* will control both the nature and frequency of the contacts.

As relationships continue, friends develop a shared vocabulary, some common references and experiences they can use as a shorthand that shows their connection. They also learn they can depend on specific behaviors from their friends. Building a very close friendship takes considerable time and it does not really flourish until the relationship is tested at least once. A test is a situation that threatens both parties. Once some trouble has been shared and the friends have demonstrated they are willing to take risks to sustain the friendship, their activities may intensify.

Friendships will become regular on various levels. There will be some people with whom you can share activities but cannot count on for service and support. There are some people who will help out in a pinch but with whom you share no common recreation interests. A number of people will move in and out of your life. You can identify a strong friendship by its history and the nature of its talk.

DANIEL A. (age forty-nine)
There are three events that really keep me and Joe together. We were on this camping trip, see, when the blizzard hit. A blizzard in May is bad enough, but we were about three thousand feet up the side of a mountain in a tent. The snow was blowing so hard we thought for a while we were goners, but we managed to keep a fire in the kerosene heater, and we managed to keep the tent up. The canvas was sagging, but the tent stayed up. Now, when things get a little tough, one or the other of us will say, "Hey the canvas is sagging," and we'll both know we have to pay attention to what we are doing.

Another time we were with our families at the beach, and Mim, his little girl, was eating some of the pink goop candy on a stick, cotton candy, and she got it in her hair and she was a mess, and Joe picked her up under his arm, she was about four, and he ran with her to the ocean and told her to take a deep breath, and he dunked her and rinsed the stuff out of her hair and he told her, "Now, all the gunk is going to Europe." That's another line we use, when we get out of a mess, one of us is likely to say, "Hey, the gunk is on its way to Europe." That's always good for a laugh, but we can't explain what we are laughing at to anyone else.

Then, just after Joe's wife had that operation and was in intensive care, and Joe was sitting in that ugly waiting room wondering what it would be like if his wife died, and he started talking to me about this cute little secretary that worked at the office. I said, "Joe, this is a good time to think about it, because you couldn't do anything about it if she was standing here jay-bird naked," and he laughed a little and he said he didn't know whether he could do much about it anyway. "Getting laid ain't as big as it used to be," he said. "Ain't as big as a good cup of coffee." Well, she recovered, still makes the best damn coffee you ever tasted, and when one of us starts getting greedy and like wanting a car that's too expensive or something, we'll say, "Ain't as big as a good cup of coffee," and that brings us back to earth.

Long-lasting friendships and marriages are filled with these kinds of memories. They are like the "commonplaces" of ancient Greece. Brief references to them renew understanding of the relationship like lines that referred to legends that held the culture together. Relationships have no libraries, but they have cultures and an oral history that reminds friends and lovers of the best of times and the worst of times. One way to tell how close friends or lovers may be is to listen for private references they share with each other that outsiders cannot understand.

JOHN H———, PH.D. (marriage counselor)
If I can find the big moments in a relationship, I can usually get the couple talking softly to each other again. Couples may think they hate each other at any given moment, but in order to find out if they really hate each other, you have to find out whether they can remember anything from the time when it was beautiful. If they have no lines that hold them together, it is usually impossible to save the marriage.

Continuing a relationship requires finding out what is impossible. Bad moments must be remembered and not repeated.

HARRY M.
A picnic with her is like going to a goldenrod festival with a hayfever victim. She likes the outdoors about as much as I like subways. When we go to New York, it's taxis for me and no Central Park for her.

SHIRLEY B.
I can get Dick to climb the wall just by reminding him of his stupid habit of feeling his mustache. He sits and strokes and stares off into space and it annoys me, but it isn't that big a deal, so I just go away and shut up.

The idea of withholding a comment you are tempted to make should be learned. Learning is, in part, a process in which you discover what you *can* do to *hurt* the other person, and you decide to avoid doing it. It is not enough to figure out how to support each other. Friendships and marriages must be situations in which people can be reasonably sure they will not be gratuitously attacked. This does not mean friendships and marriages are devoid of conflict. It means they are devoid of unexpected, trivial, and malicious conflict. Once we get to know a person really well, we have all kinds of destructive information about that person's weaknesses. Real intimacy means not exploiting this information.

A major peril in close relationships is learning to rely on the other person for affection and support and feeling secure enough to believe you won't be pointlessly attacked. If the relationship ends, you are vulnerable. Not only do you lose the desirable aspects of the relationship, but you are a potential victim of the other person's attacks. Your only defense is "balance of terror," the information you have at your disposal.

DR. HIGGINS

I remember this one divorce where the husband ran off with a nineteen-year-old. But this was particularly serious because there were children older than the girl he ran off with. His wife was absolutely furious. She remembered a time when he confided in her how attracted he was to his oldest daughter. He called her "sexy, a real beauty." Well, his wife brought this up every chance she got. She would spit, "He is just trying out incest with this new girl. He has wanted to do it all of his life, and now he has a girl younger than his daughter to do it with. I can see him doing it and fantasizing that it is his daughter." There wasn't much he could do about it. He had confided in his wife, and he had wronged her. I mean, it is horrible for a middle-aged woman to see her husband dashing off with a young chick. She was bitter, filled with hate.

To avoid excessive vulnerability, it is sensible to restrict the amount of information you give away. The humanistic, psychological point of view emphasizes the importance of disclosure, but there is no hard evidence that unlimited disclosure leads to better relationships. In fact, we found a large number of divorces (at least thirty out of one hundred) where disclosure seemed to be the reason for dissolution of the relationship.

Certainly, there is something to be said for having a special someone with whom you can let your hair down completely. Authorities such as Harry Stack Sullivan have emphasized the importance of that kind of relationship in adolescence, and it may be essential to satisfactory adulthood. However, as long as there is a risk of a breakup, disclosure is risky.

Husbands and wives often share information, somewhat like best friends. Oddly enough, slightly more than half of the husbands made a distinction between a wife and a friend. They refused to accept their wife as a friend. The role they defined for her included some activity also found in friendships, but there was a good deal they kept from their wives that they would disclose to their friends (in some cases, for example, wives did not know their husband's income.)

HARVEY P

I won't tell my wife how much I am making, and I don't tell her about what goes on down at the shop. It's none of her business. The house gets paid for and the car, and she gets a good allowance for groceries. Whatever the other women are getting, I give her more, but I think I should have some money of my own that she don't know about and don't touch. And she can save whatever she wants to from the house money, if she needs something, or get a job. A guy has to have some privacy, and she knows too much about me already.

MYRNA P

Harvey and I keep separate bank accounts. I knew from the time that we got married that Harvey wasn't going to tell me much, and I knew I had to keep my powder dry and some mad money tucked away. My dad set me up with a ten-thousand-dollar bank account that Harvey doesn't know about, and he'll never know about it. It just keeps drawing interest, for me. I can share a lot more with my friends than with Harvey. He doesn't want to hear about the house or the kids. He keeps telling me to take a part-time job, and he doesn't know that I've been doing some copywriting here in the house for three years. He stays out of my work room and I stay out of his study. Why do I stay with Harvey? He's a good guy. He doesn't commit adultery. He has a sense of humor. He's not bad in bed, and he's a habit. He's not even all that bad with the kids except they sometimes ask why he doesn't talk much. But I won't complain about him to the kids and he won't complain about me. I guess it's our deal and as long as we don't mind it, why should you?

Adapting a relationship to the needs of the couple is important to the maintenance of the relationship. There is no reliable handbook on what adaptations to make. Sometimes changes in people's lives do terrible things to their relationship; friends move away, children grow up and leave, people get sick, there are financial reversals. Even the good times can cause trouble. For example, raises and promotions may alter life-styles to the point where neither partner can adjust to new opportunities. Close friends and loving couples are identified by their ability to handle such changes, even when they have unexpected consequences. If, for example, one friend is promoted, the other may be uneasy about the difference in their position on the organization chart. The question, "Will we still be friends after your promotion?" is similar to the debauched girl asking, "Will you still respect me in the morning?"

PROFESSOR CLIFFORD C

Steve and I both came to this school about ten years ago and we were friends from the time we came. Steve is a go-getter, much more aggressive than I. He'd get excited, I'd calm him down, and he'd keep prodding me to get my important work done. I am low key, you see, and I really don't want to be in this publish-or-perish rat race. I knew I might never make full professor and I didn't care. He and I got through tenure and got appointed associate, and then he got really hot, and when it came time to pick a new department head, Steve was the logical choice. I worked my tail off to get the rest of the department to pick him, and for a while it was like old times. He'd rely on me to calm him down, and he'd keep prodding me to get my work done. But it seemed he got busier and busier. We used to go to lunch twice a week and play some handball, but then he got to playing handball with the other department heads, and then committees would take up his time at lunch. And on weekends, when we used to get together, he'd have "mandatory entertainments" with deans and his "peers" I called them. They didn't invite us over because they said we'd "be uncomfortable with the other people we have to have over." I knew that I would embarrass him, the only associate professor there. We used to drop in on each other, but he stopped dropping in on me and I thought that was a signal for me not to drop in on him. One Sunday I dropped by and they were preparing the house for company, and while I was standing there, couples started coming in all dressed up and I was there in jeans and a sloppy T-shirt, and he didn't know what to say about me except I was his "old friend from a while back" like I wasn't his friend anymore. I don't think we're friends anymore and it's ten years just blown away.

Time, distance, and social position can separate friends and lovers. A familiar cause of separations is "outgrowing each other," a typical situation when wives who put their husbands through college by doing menial work are deserted. People get into the habit of regarding mates or friends as types. That is, they are identified as types (so the executive keeps his fishing friends at the shore and out of his fancy home). When a person no longer needs a particular type of friend, it is easier to throw out a "type" rather than a person.

WAYNE D. (to his marriage counselor)
But she can't do me any good. She can't join the university women's group because she is not a graduate. She is so out of place with the other faculty wives. They are into things, you know, and she has her machinery and her union and that's about it. I mean, one of the guys in my department has a wife who's a doctor. She's in charge of the emergency room at the local hospital, and a guy younger than I am has a wife who's already a CPA. How am I going to tell them my wife is a glassblower. I mean, come on. I think she's the only wife in the department who doesn't have a degree. She suggested going back to school in ceramics because she says she is very good at what she does and she could get to the top with some knowledge of materials. I asked her to fake a degree, some little college in Idaho—I mean, who will check—and she refused. The last thing in the world I can do is explain that my wife is an undergraduate, for God's sake. I don't want to hurt her. She has been loyal and she really worked to get me through, but you'd think she'd want to cooperate with my career after all that.

There are a number of editorials that can be written in response to the foregoing statement. First, who would argue that a good glassblower is less valuable than a person with a college degree? Second, the kind of exploitation exemplified by the statement is characteristic of what is experienced by a great number of women. The rate of divorce by men on their way up, casting off one wife to get another who will give them a political advantage is scandalous. The game of professors running off with their graduate students is a common manifestation of this problem.

Wives of business executives have considerable pressure even when they have their own careers. Industrial executives must entertain like heads of state, and they must have a hostess present. Things must be kept "just so" at home. The image in the community of perfect mother, gracious hostess, civic-minded citizen, and competent professional must be maintained in the community. Some authorities say it requires more skill to be a corporate president's wife than a corporate president.

Friends and lovers must have alternatives at their disposal. When relationships come apart, it is most often unilateral, and the party that wants out virtually has complete control. If the other party does not have some other possible choices, the prospects for social survival are dismal.

DR. H. (marriage counselor)
Once I discover that there is no way to hold the couple together because one partner is irreconcilable, then I become a divorce counselor. The idea is to make the transition without it getting ugly. I need to consider kids sometimes, although kids are hardier than we sometimes give them credit for. I am very suspicious when couples explain to me how they both will benefit if they split up. When they are too rational, someone is likely to be fooled and badly hurt. It is like they are presenting me with a *fait accompli* and they expect me to ratify it like some benign father. I refuse to do this. I think the aggrieved party has some rights, and I try to help them to express their feelings and even show their resentment to the other party who seeks to abandon them. I think they deserve the fair share, and I always make sure they get to a good lawyer. I sometimes pin blame. I think it is heinous for a man to break up a twenty-year marriage because his wife has a wrinkle and has taken on a few pounds so that he can get it on with some young female who is looking for a bit of security. He will, no doubt, drop dead, and his chick will get the money. I think the young women who act as predators on older married men are reprehensible.

Individuals must learn how to respond to requests for revisions. It is impossible to keep relationships the same. Sometimes marriages and friendships come apart because of the inability of one partner to change. In the case of the wife who was a glassblower, the husband provided few options for change. She was locked into a "no-win" situation. Adapting to change is hard enough. When a partner demands a particular change, he or she assumes unreasonable control over the other partner's life. One of the most astonishing findings we had in our first survey was that roughly 75 percent of the women and 55 percent of the men agreed with the following statement: *It is better to stay in a relationship in which you were being used than to face the prospect of having no relationship at all.* It's somewhat like the old Klondike expression, "It may be a crooked game, but it is the only game in town."

The consequences of that belief are enormous. They suggest that one person has the right to demand compliance from the other. Some theorists refer to complementary and symmetrical relationships. In a complementary relationship one person is the authority and holds control over the other. A symmetrical relationship is one of shared authority. It is hard to see how joint management characteristic of symmetrical relationships can be achieved.

HAROLD P., M.D. (psychiatrist)
The whole business of relationship is very Freudian. Even if you reject most of Freud, it is hard to wave off the notion that people will try to replace old relationships with new ones—transference, if you will. When a woman has been dominated by a father, she has learned to live under domination. She is comfortable with it and she will seek it in a mate. She will not be able to adjust to freedom. The same holds true for men controlled by their mothers, although some men will develop a real hatred for women because they were dominated by their mothers. Remember the scene in *Who's Afraid of Virginia Woolf?*, when George complains to Martha about how badly Martha is treating him and Martha says, "You married me for it"? We can't always get upset because we think a partner is not being treated equitably. They may not want to be treated equitably. That's what disturbs me about the notion of symmetrical relationships. I can conceive of relationships where authority is divided but not where it is shared. There is nothing more intricate than the set of agreements that characterize a happy marriage. The people take turns, he in charge of one thing, she of another. It is so rapid, that it looks like joint authority, but it permits people to be adaptable because they can regard themselves as authorities in some ways.

The preceding testimony is very important. In a quality relationship time facilitates development of mutual respect. Each partner knows where the other excels and is willing to concede authority in those areas. When their mates take charge, they do not regard it as a threat to self-esteem. They expect good to come of it, whether the issue is trivial or cosmic. One may be good at picking restaurants, the other at filling out the income tax. One may be creative, the other logical. One may be a good talker, the other a listener. In a sense it is a "Jack Sprat" philosophy, and the Sprats did, indeed, "pick the platter clean." They got all they could out of it, and this is what appears to happen in marriages where authority is shared.

The idea of consensual decision making caused us some concern. As you read the theoretical ideas about symmetrical relationships, you get the notion that somehow, people come to agreement about things, almost magically, and furthermore, they do it consistently. We saw no evidence of anything even approximating this idealistic situation. Sometimes couples came to agreement for no noticeable reason other than boredom with the discussion. It appeared that consensual decisions were made only when one partner cared and the other did not. In general, the relationships in which both partners seemed happy featured shared authority in which control alternated according to the contingencies of the situations.

ENDINGS

One failure can end a relationship. In friendship, endings are not necessarily catastrophic. Because the pair is not locked together by law, they can drift apart and allow each other to save face while auditioning new talent. Hardly anyone confines their friendships to only one person, so there are always other options. Sometimes friends fight. Sometimes a separation brought about by change in residence is very painful, but over the long haul, friends are relatively easy to replace.

The situation is not as simple in a marriage. The Lee Marvin case makes it clear that people have claims on each other, economic and otherwise even when vows have not been taken. The investment of years and emotion build up a backlog of tension that can spill out in painful ways at the time the relationship is ended. The concept of a "no-fault" divorce may be an effective legal device, but it is hardly satisfactory for the partner who has been abandoned by a mate who ran off with someone more desirable. The insult must be avenged in some way. More desirable, indeed! There are simply no formulas for an easy exit.

When children are involved, things can get very sticky. While child stealing is not yet widespread, there are enough cases to illustrate that it is not easy to work out satisfactory custodial arrangements for children. Children complicate matters even more by being unsure of who they want to be with. While the courts tend to favor the mother in child custody cases, more and more fathers are asserting their rights. Divorcing couples often require long and complicated negotiations before they achieve an agreement, and as the children grow, agreements often require revisions.

There are other kinds of endings. For example, major adjustments must be made when a partner dies or becomes permanently disabled. Third parties gratuitously involved in a relationship can often make matters worse. Friends are often used as strategic pawns by partners who want to inflict pain on each other. This book provides no answers to the question of how to end relationships, and the authors really question whether there is one.

WHAT WE LEARNED
ABOUT SOME PRACTICAL MATTERS

This section should not be misconstrued. Its purpose is neither self-help nor advice to the lovelorn. What we have here is a set of statements that seemed to characterize the discourse of some of the more successful couples. We are not prepared to assert the information is a blueprint for successful relationship making. We do think some important insights about self-management are offered here.

People need to learn it is possible for them to make mistakes in the way they relate to their intimates. It is inappropriate to relate to a wife as if she were a mother or to a husband as if he were a fantasy lover. Many respondents advised that it was important to be clear on who the other person was, and to be sure your reactions were to the person and what was really going on, not to your fantasies.

We need to be realistic in what we can expect from others. Some of our respondents said examination of their own weaknesses led them to accept the fact that their partners had weaknesses also. To count on them for more than they could give would put an intolerable burden on them. "You have to give your wife room to fail decently," said one twenty-five-year veteran of a good marriage, "and if you do, she will take it easy on you." Many respondents were concerned about nagging and how to curb it. Their answers revealed that toleration of personal failings is the best way to handle this problem.

We must learn to test our generalizations. People seem to pick up generalizations from a number of places: the media, advice columns, popular magazines, movies, novels, and friends. It is important to make sure the generalizations apply to the given situation. Advice is often based on a unique experience. A vacation at the shore might help one marriage, it might destroy another. Insofar as the private business of their relationship is concerned, couples have to learn to think of themselves as unique. They should not get too excited if they do not seem to meet the standards mentioned in popular articles.

We must understand that people are sometimes not available to us. Everyone needs time alone. Many respondents told us respect for privacy is one of the best ways to sustain a relationship. People need to learn to do for themselves. If you count on people only when it is important and solve your own problems at other times, you increase the chances they will be around when you need them. If you call on them too much, they may get tired of serving you.

Check on whether people need a relationship before you offer yourself. When people are trying to find new friends, they often try to push themselves on the most popular people around. While there may be a good reason why popular people are popular, one consequence of popularity is being busy. Popular people usually have little room for newcomers. The newcomer must hang around the fringes of the circle, taking crumbs of attention. One respondent said, "If you are lonely, go to a party and start talking to someone who looks like you feel. That should get something going."

It is not foolish to take recommendations. The people you know and like usually know other people that you will like. The chances of being abused by a friend of a friend are considerably lower than they would be by a total stranger. In fact, relationships with total strangers are usually tenuous and sometimes dangerous. We tend to make our relationships with people with whom we are most familiar. This is not strange, and there is probably a good reason for it.

Be careful of premature access. Letting people get too close too early is dangerous. Having intercourse early in the relationship or sharing your secrets before you know you can trust the other person reduces your value. If you show too much eagerness to make a relationship, the other person may take you for granted and not try very hard to meet your needs.

Understand the principles of exchange. Said one respondent, "Nothing is free. We get what we pay for. If we don't do for our friends, then they don't do for us, unless they are stupid. Who the hell would want to relate to someone who did for you and never expected anything back?"

Foolishness is inevitable. It is important to keep your sense of humor. People often do silly things, present company not excepted. If you can learn to laugh with someone, you can learn how to love him or her. Sometimes it is harder to enjoy living than to be sad, but some events in our lives deserve to be enjoyed.

ALBERT K.
The first time we met, she invited my wife and me to her house for dinner and she served veal chops. I hate veal chops. I hate them more than anything, but we were new and she was being very gracious, so I gagged them down and told her they were delicious and tried to cover up by eating a lot of potatoes. So the next time we ate there, she served veal chops again, and the third time, because I "liked them so much." I finally had to tell her I hated veal chops. "Well, why the hell didn't you say so?" she said. "You are my most expensive friends. I serve everyone else spaghetti."

OLD JOKE
This guy goes into a candy store and buys a one-pound, a two-pound and a five-pound box of candy. The store owner asks why. The guy says, "I'm going out with a new girl. If she lets me hold her hand, I'll give her the one-pound box, if she lets me kiss her, I'll give her the two-pound box, and if she lets me go all the way, I give her the five-pounder." That night, while eating dinner at the girl's house, he is asked to say grace. He prays for ten minutes. After dinner the girl said, "You never told me you were so religious." He replied, "You never told me your father owned a candy store."

A sense of humor can compensate for social gaffes. Nearly a third of our happily married respondents wrote that we must preserve a sense of humor and avoid taking offense too easily. On the other hand, you need to be careful to avoid insulting people with racist or sexist jokes or offending with bathroom or sexual humor. And some people cannot tolerate wisecracks.

It is not necessary to agree on everything. It may not even be possible. If your friend favors the Equal Rights Amendment and you do not, there is no point to fighting, particularly if he or she makes it clear it may affect the relationship. Trying to enforce agreement can generate a great deal of tension in relationships. One respondent said, "Remember the way the British government set things up in time of crisis by agreeing to disagree? That's what my husband I try to do in our relationship."

Equity is imperative. Relationships demand constant attention. You not only have to be sure that you are getting enough rewards to make it worthwhile, but you have to check from time to time to make sure you are not taking your friend or mate for granted. People will try to get the most they can from a relationship, which means they must concentrate on putting a great deal into it. If people think they are getting less than a fair share, they will strike back in some way. Many conflicts between friends and lovers center around issues of equity.

People operate under a number of myths, beliefs, and feelings about relation-

ships for which there is no evidence. In the chapters to follow we will concentrate on what we observed and we will try to avoid these myths. We will review them here briefly. You may be interested in testing to see how many of them you believe.

Myth 1. Men and women feel and act alike.

Whether it is in the genes or a function of social acculturation, men and women think and feel differently about relationships, and those differences must be taken into account if you wish to understand how men and women relate to each other.

Myth 2. People who do not relate well are psychologically disturbed.

Actually it may be more like: People who do not relate well *become* psychologically disturbed. People often try to excuse themselves for lack of skill at relationship by claiming illness. They may use their illness to blackmail, intimidate, or bribe others into doing what they want. Finding friends and lovers and keeping them depends on technique, not magic.

Myth 3. Romance is possible, and it is good to believe the impossible dream.

Wendell Johnson invented a concept called IFD Disease. IFD stands for "*I*dealization, *F*rustration, *D*emoralization." It refers to the tendency people have to talk about their hopes and dreams in fuzzy terms. When people are not explicit about what they seek, they can never tell if they have achieved it. Furthermore, they cannot distinguished between what is do-able and what is desirable but impossible. People often fantasize about other people and sometimes try to act on their fantasies. Relationships can only be built on realistic assessments of what is possible.

Myth 4. There are products that can improve social desirability.

A major part of the advertising industry is devoted to associating clothing, toothpaste, deodorant, and various other products with desirability. While cleanliness and hygiene are important, they do not substitute for effort and consideration in relationship building. Furthermore, personal appearances or possessions are not a reliable guide to relationship choices.

Myth 5. The idea in relationships is to communicate the real self.

There is no real self. You are only what you communicate to others. The essence of good relationships is to make an honest and productive exchange by talking it out with another person. People fool themselves with fuzzy talk and assault others with egocentric talk. Successful relaters obtain what they want from others by giving others what they want. For practical advice on becoming skillful at relationship talk, see Gerald M.

Phillips, *Help for Shy People* (Englewood Cliffs, N.J.: Prentice-Hall, 1981).

Myth 6. Affection, friendship, and intimacy are spontaneous, and people come together when the vibes are right.

We discovered that successful marriages and friendships are based on carefully developed exchanges between the partners. Throughout our study we found that people who had productive and reliable relationships were able to talk effectively with each other.

Myth 7. People who look alike act alike.

People who believe this are bigots and tend to discriminate in non-productive ways. There is no connection between appearance and the way people behave.

Myth 8. People can agree on what they see and hear.

People often wishfully distort what they see. Many people are disappointed because other people do not meet their expectations, but the problem lies in wishful thinking. It takes real effort to agree on the nature of reality.

Myth 9. People should have a consistent relationship style.

It helps to distinguish between *interaction* and *transaction*. Interaction refers to *public* contact governed by social norms. People must learn to adjust their style depending on where they are. Transaction refers to *private* contact governed by norms mutually enacted. People have the privilege of acting as they choose in private, but they must avoid bringing private behavior into public life.

Myth 10. Relationships make no demands.

Once a relationship is formed, people depend on each other for service and emotional support. If people do not live up to their obligations, their relationships come apart.

. In his book *The New Rules* Daniel Yankelovich points out that Americans seem to seek self-fulfillment. For many, satisfaction on the job or from relationships is more important than financial rewards or possessions. However, this notion is based on the idea that there are enough goods to go around for everyone. We are now faced with an era of real shortages. Maintaining physical comfort will become more difficult in the decades ahead, and we will need people to help us accomplish it.

Above all, we learned that things always change and changes are always required in relationships. You can't resist change, although you need not like it. Very often, our physical, social, and personal survival depend on how well we adapt to change. Distaste for manipulation sometimes interferes with the way we prepare for change. Changing effectively requires conscious action, careful planning, and cooperation between friends or mates. Couples must plan to cope with anticipated changes in society as well as personal changes, with the mundane and the extraordinary. People sometimes seem better able to handle great tragedies and endure great misery than they can mundane change, although both kinds of change can be terribly disruptive.

Consider some of the events in our lives to which we must adapt.

Starting school requires us to learn to adapt to relationship values of people other than our families. Changing schools or neighborhoods teaches us that we must have a repertoire of possibilities for change.

Educational and vocational milestones, such as graduations, starting college, a new job, promotions, or career changes, require that we must change whole complexes of habits. Those relating to us must adapt to the changes that we must make in ourselves in order to cope with situations.

Relationship milestones, such as parents' divorcing, marriage or living together, having children, divorcing, moving away, or death in the family, require us to develop complete new patterns of relationship or to end relationships that were once important to us.

Health milestones, such as development of a severe illness such as diabetes or hypertension, traumas and accidents, or one of the family falling ill, require a restriction on relationship behavior characterized by more attention paid to one person or making greater demands on people for personal care.

Economic milestones, such as major increases or reductions in income or financial windfalls such as legacies, require important decisions about modification of life-style.

Aging milestones require adjustments to diminishing personal capabilities, reduced authority and income, and failing health. The midlife crisis, a recent notion, confronts us with decisions about changes in our vocations and basic relationships, which can have profound effects on everyone around us.

To cope with changes effectively, we must learn *dual perspective* and discover that other people feel what we feel and can be appealed to through their feelings. We must also make what Ernest Becker calls an "Oedipal transition" so that we no longer depend on parents and authorities for our meanings. We must learn to *validate consensually,* to check our perceptions and feelings with others to reassure ourselves that we are not peculiar. We accomplish these goals through skill at communication. We agree with Becker's declaration that *speech is all that is specifically human* and that skill at speech helps us adapt to our families, social groups, and work.

Furthermore, our ability to communicate enables us to achieve maturity in social development. As described by Lawrence Kohlberg, we pass through a series of stages of moral and social development. First, we learn to obey orders about what is dangerous in order to avoid punishment and pain. Next, we learn conformity norms in order to win rewards and the opportunity to make social choices. We learn to be "good" in the eyes of others in order to keep from being rejected and to compete for the rewards of relationship. Next, we learn to do our duty and to obey the law. Doing our duty keeps us employed, and obeying the law keeps us from the various punishments society metes out to those who are dangerous to others.

chapter three

What we learned about friendships

*A friend is a person who will refrain from telling you
he bought the same make of new car two days after you bought yours
and he got a $500 rebate and the five year warranty.*

Law of Contemporary Friendship

*Friends come and go,
but enemies accumulate over the years.*

Tom Jones, HENRY FIELDING

Think twice before you ever speak to a friend in need.

AMBROSE BIERCE

FRIENDS AND FRIENDLINESS

ERIC E. (age fifty-eight)

I came to New England from the state of Washington when I was 45. I had been
raised in the Cascade Mountain region in a town where everyone knew everyone
else and no one locked their doors. In the Northwest people get together a lot, and
when someone says, "Why don't you drop over?" that actually means you would
be welcome if you turned up unexpected. But in this little town in New England
there were two kinds of people. There were second- and third-generation eastern

Europeans and "old residents." Neither group talked to the other, and neither talked to newcomers either, but both would rather talk to each other than to newcomers. My Polish neighbor had the most beautiful lawn I ever saw and a gorgeous house from the outside. In the six years I have lived here I have never seen the inside of his house or got more than a nod from him. The old residents are worse. They treat me like a piece of equipment on the job, and downtown they don't even know me. There was this Englishman that came around one day and when he first came to this country, he lived down South. He reported that someone told him, "Y'all drop 'round an' see me, y'heah?" He took out his datebook expecting to set something up, only to discover it wasn't an invitation at all but a dismissal. It is hard when you go to another region to find out who wants to be friends, and who is just friendly.

Having friends is one of the greatest pleasures humans have, and the ability to make and keep friends is an important skill. Friend making starts in childhood, when we learn to trade with our pals (you can use my ball if you let me play). Whatever the trade-offs are, little kids will find them. The idea that friends add something to our life stays with us throughout our lives. Despite the fact that most of us would prefer to think of friendship romantically, virtually every social scientist who has studied friendship has found it to be a rational process. In friendships people do things for good reasons, even though they may not be consciously aware of them.

We make friends because we need friends. Rollo May believes we make friends because we hate loneliness so much. George Homans, the originator of "Exchange Theory," describes social behavior as a process of exchanging rewards between people. Small children trade doll dresses and baseball cards. As they grow older, they learn to trade advice, support, service, and money for what they need. Friends provide the support that we all need to convince ourselves that we are all right, that our ideas are not crazy, and that what is happening to us has happened to someone else. Friends are essential if we are to grow up sane.

MARK R.
When I was about twelve, I used to look at the advertisements for women's underwear in the papers all the time. I couldn't keep my eyes off it, but I was afraid to look at real girls and women because my preacher had given this sermon on "if thine eye offend thee," and I expected that if I saw a girl's private parts, my eyeballs would fall out. I thought I was going to go crazy, because I'd look at these pictures and get very excited.

One day I finally blurted it out to my best friend, Eddie. Eddie told me to wait till his mom went to the store, and then we went into his folks' bedroom and he pulled this book out from under the mattress. It was one of those sex books they had in the 1940s, where some doctor shows pictures of naked people and explains how to have a happier sex life. Eddie showed me some line drawings of women with no clothes on. They were only drawings, but they were the most important thing I ever saw. I never knew women had hair between their legs. Eddie told me how he would sneak peeks at his mom and he found out. And he still had his eyes. Then he showed me what to do to get my rocks off. I learned how to jerk off from Eddie, and I learned nothing happened if I did.

Then I got one of those magazines, *Beauty Parade,* from New York, with the women in their underwear with stockings and high heels and sometimes bare breasts, and I learned how to pencil on hair. Later on, I got real good with "feelthy peectures." I still have a hard time looking at my wife naked in the light. They scared the hell out of me when I was a kid, but Eddie brought me through. Eddie backed me up almost to the end of high school. Then he moved away. I heard he got killed in Korea.

Much of what we learn about friendship we learn from imitating our parents, from what we read, and what we see. Tales like *Beau Geste* and the standard movie westerns teach us we can have loyal and gallant comrades who take risks for us. Boys are encouraged to become members of teams and work together. Where teams are not available, gangs are common. Men who did not have some kind of intense group association as boys seem to be bewildered by the requirements of adult socialization. The gang or team teaches boys how to support one another, how to choose when and with whom to share secrets, and how to behave in a hierarchy. Teams or gangs also train boys for military life.

Girls are socialized differently. The media do not portray many loyal female relationships. Female situations are more like that in *Turning Point,* where the old friends clash over values of home and family versus career. The idea of women forming protective and supportive units similar to those that come naturally to boys is sufficiently new that a unique term (*networking*) has been generated for it. Oddly enough, our data about women contradicted the way they are portrayed in the media. We did not find women to be generally competitive. Rather, they seemed to sustain long-term relationships with one or two intimates with whom they checked reality and from whom they sought advice. Though women who were strangers might sometimes conflict, by and large we found them much less competitive than men.

Most women reported they sustained close friendships. Virtually all our female respondents had made and kept a very close friend, usually from high school. Consensual validation seemed very important to women, particularly when they faced major events such as marriage and childbirth. We had the feeling that female associations were much more intense, supportive, and loyal in adulthood than those of men.

In fact, one of the most dismal things we found is that almost two-thirds of our adult, employed male respondents discussed their "best friend" in the past tense. They recalled someone from years ago in their hometown or at school. Most adult males reported they were now too busy and had too many obligatory contacts to permit time for a best friend. The data from women were just the opposite. Virtually all had a best friend at the present time, with whom they were in regular contact. It made us wonder why the media and literature seem to neglect the bond women have with other women.

A suspicious finding was that when women entered fields where they competed with men, they often took on the same friending behaviors as men. They abandoned their best friends, made political allies where necessary, and were often very harsh and competitive with other women.

It was clear that both men and women need friends. Grace deLaguna (1963) believes we need friends because we cannot survive alone. Dennis Fry (1977) believes that friendship is the basis for protection of the growing child. George Herbert Mead (1934) and Harry Stack Sullivan (1953) believe that our friends provide us with our identity. George Homas (1974) believes we need friends to exchange with. Philip Slater (1970) believes we need friends as a sign of our own value.

Given the undeniable importance of friendship in our lives, we should have no trouble defining it. Try it. Try, in twenty-five words or less, to specify what a friend is. Here's what some of our respondents said:

MALE (age thirty-six)
Anyone who is not doing me harm is my friend.

MALE (age twenty-nine)
I try to fit in anywhere I go so I can find the people who look like they are popular so I can do what they do, so I can get other people to like me. Friends are the people who like you.

FEMALE (age twenty-eight)
There are different kinds of friends and you are with them for different reasons. I have one really close friend and I try to talk with her every day. Then there are people I go out with or have lunch with or who live in my building and are just around when you want to kibitz.

MALE (age eleven)
See, Billy is my best friend, and when he isn't home, then I go to Glenn and then to Mark. Sam is fifth, and then there's Jerry and Willy, and when nobody else is around, I hang out with Murray. But I can't talk to Murray when the other guys are around, see, because they don't like him because he is too fat.

MALE (age forty-five)
I don't have much time for social life. There are some people in the company who cover my ass and I look out for them, too. I guess you could call them my friends.

FEMALE (age seventy-one)
Susan and I met when we were seven and we have been friends ever since. We tell each other everything. We share everything. We visit now once a year since she moved away. We write every week, and talk on the phone once a month. I love her and she loves me. That is a friend.

FEMALE (age fifty-one)
I went back to my hometown after twenty-two years and I looked up my old best friend from high school, and Edna and I sort of looked at each other like we were strange cats meeting in the alley. We didn't have much to say to each other. She told me her husband owned a dry cleaning and tailoring store on Webb Street. She told me about her oldest boy who was in pharmacy school and how her oldest girl just married the owner of the feed store in Webb Falls, and how her youngest girl was head majorette. I told her about my divorce and how I was an architect with my own firm and how I had no kids. She looked at me and I looked at her, and I left. She was a best friend once, but I don't know what one is now.

FEMALE (age twenty-four)
I'm new in town and new on the job and I haven't made any choices yet, but there are a lot of people who seem to like me and there are people to do things with, so I'll wait awhile to see who becomes my best friend. It'll be the person I want to spend the most time with.

The definition of "friend" seems to be a bit like Humpty Dumpty's: "It means anything I want it to mean, nothing more, nothing less." There are, however, some things our survey indicated that people agree on. (By "agree" we mean that about 60 percent of men and women agreed with the following statements.)

• It is possible to be friends with people who are a good deal older or a good deal younger than yourself and with people of different religions, but it is very difficult to be friends with people of other races.

• Generally, it is difficult to be friends with someone of the opposite sex without the question of intercourse arising. (Men were much more definitive on this issue than were women. More than half of the women believed they had male friends with whom intercourse was not an issue. Nearly 90 percent of the men said they could not deal with any woman without at least thinking about the possibilities of intercourse.)

• Bosses and employees can be friends. (Some hedged by pointing out it was very hard for bosses to figure out which employees were friendly because they liked him or her and which simply because he or she was the boss.)

• Your closeness with another person can be measured by the amount of private information you mutually disclose.

• Friendships are characterized by mutual dependency. If a person does not depend on you for something and you do not depend on him or her in return, then your relationship cannot be called a friendship.

• It is not possible to size people up in advance to estimate their possibilities as friends.

• To try consciously to persuade someone to be your friend is manipulation and therefore unethical.

• Friends are generally not competitive with each other.

• It is not possible to be too close to a friend. The more intimate you can get, the better.

Men tended to agree with the following statements (60 percent or more), whereas women tended to disagree (less than 40 percent).

• It is easy to make friends. They come and go.

• You can only be close with someone who shares your basic values.

• In any relationship one person has to be stronger and in greater control than the other. It is not possible to share leadership in a friendship.

• In any relationship, if a friend hurts you, it is justifiable to hurt back.

• Your friend is obligated not to associate with people you do not like and you must do the same for your friend.

• It is best not to talk about your relationship with your friend. Talking about it might jeopardize it.

Women tended to agree with the following, whereas men disagreed.

• Friendship should be spontaneous and unplanned.

• People should talk about their friendships to make sure they both see it the same way.

• People can be taught how to make friends.

• Closeness is good, but everyone needs some privacy.

There was an incredible range of beliefs about the number of friends one could manage. Some respondents claimed everyone was their friend, they "loved the whole human race." Others said if they had one friend, it would be about all they could handle. In a now-classic commentary on the encounter movement (published as a tape, "Masks and Fig Leaves," by the

Center for the Study of Democratic Institutions), John Silber stated that during a lifetime one could not expect more than three or four truly intimate relationships. In that presentation Silber made it clear that people can have a great many contacts of various sorts, but real friendship involved intense commitment and the expenditure of an immense block of time. We accept Silber's analysis of friendship for our work. To be more explicit, we regard a friend as *a person with whom one has had long-term contact (two years or more for starters), involving sharing of intimate information, exchange of mutual support, and continuing interaction usually involving at least one serious test where a sacrifice to sustain the relationship was required.* This definition excludes all the nice people with whom we have a pleasant relationship, little contact, and who mean us no harm.

We chose this definition because our respondents were not specific in their definition of friends or enemies. Respondents were even more abstract when they tried to provide criteria for intimates of the opposite sex—spouses or lovers. We could not resist the gnawing feeling that the lack of specificity may be at the root of the trouble many of our respondents were having with relationships. Our data were not sufficiently refined for us to test the hypothesis.

The road to intimate friendship, the kind just specified, is not easy. People suffer casualties along the way. Most of the respondents believe kismet will decide who will be their friend and how friendship will come about. Many respondents could identify friends but they could not reconstruct the events that led to the friendship, even though the initial contact had been made within the year. The younger respondents were much more abstract than the older ones on this issue. Most of the younger respondents believed it was unethical to think in an orderly way about their friendships or love affairs. A few confessed guilt because they sometimes found it necessary to reject unwelcome people who were seeking their attention. They felt that not being able "to stand" another person was a flaw in their character.

ALICE W.

Dan and I met the Greevies the day we first moved in. They came over bringing soup. It was the worst soup we ever tasted. Dan almost gagged getting it down while Jim Greevie talked about what a great little soup maker his Donna was. Donna did very little but smile. Donna's been smiling at us without saying much for the last eight years. Dan thinks Donna must be very good in bed because she can't talk or cook and she has those unbelievable breasts that always look like they are trying to escape. And Jim keeps talking about what a great little this or that she is, so she must be good at something. And the Greevies always turn up at the wrong time. They can sense when we are having guests, and they appear. They seem to see through the wall, and the minute Dan and I get into bed for a little afternoon tussle, they are ringing the doorbell. They are always under foot. They never invite us over. They never do anything but sit here. Dan says maybe they don't have furniture in their living room because they spend their money on drugs. And they won't do anything for you. If you ask them to watch the house because you are going on a trip, it seems they are going on a trip too. What a coincidence. They always get back a day before we do. If you ask to borrow something, they just ran out of it. Dan says that if he is ever sent to jail for murder, it would be because he strangled a Greevie or two. I'd like to tell them to get lost, but they'd be so hurt, I don't think I could take it.

The notion that it is not proper to reject advances toward friendship keeps a great many people locked into complicated and uninteresting relationships. Many of these relationships stand in the way of more profitable, compatible arrangements. Sometimes people suffer more pain ridding themselves of bores and leeches than the rejected people feel.

ERICA D.
I still cry when I remember how I got rid of Frieda. Frieda was so skinny she couldn't even buy clothes in the children's section of the store, and she had a little tiny voice that sounded like chalk squeaking. She was smart, though, and I got together with her first when I was in trouble with chemistry in my junior year. I advertised for a tutor and she turned up and said she'd do it for free, and like a damn fool I accepted. She was around for a year, went everywhere I went, no matter who I was with, although she did know enough to disappear when I was with a guy. She paid her own way and she didn't say much, but I really got sick of her looking at me. Her eyes were pale blue and mostly watery and sometimes bloodshot around the corners, and I got this image that she was a creature out of the crypt and finally I couldn't take it anymore and I screamed, "Damn you, Frieda, go away, you aren't my friend and I don't want you anymore." She didn't say a word. She just left. I never talked to her again till last week, I ran into her downtown. She looked the same. She said "hello" and just moved on. It made me feel bad all over again, but does anyone have the right to demand your attention all the time?

The question of who owns the "rights" to friendship is not a trivial one. In our investigations we found people who demanded attention from other people because "they had a right to it." We found some who would give away secrets if they were rejected. Four of our female interviewees reported they had had experiences with men who threatened suicide if the women did not go to bed with them. We also heard such lines as "I'd like to tell Bill to screw off, but he's the only guy in town who remembers the time I accidentally set fire to the auto shop at the high school, and if I reject him, he'll tell and it would ruin my business" or "I know that if I stopped seeing Gina, she would do something terrible to herself."

A particularly interesting response, repeated at least ten times in various forms was, "What can you do? Wendy picks up the checks and does the driving and every so often gives me a book I want to read but can't afford. With my husbanld's income and three kids and me not working, if it wasn't for Wendy, I wouldn't get out at all. Sigh." There is a note of resignation here, and a sense of burden about permitting these friends to make sacrifices. We found Frieda and asked for the other side of the story.

FRIEDA G.
I'm sorry I saw Erica the other day. It made my stomach turn. People like her are all over. They use you and discard you. Let me make something clear. I am a very successful real estate operator. I could buy and sell Erica and her family ten times over. I have always been successful at everything but friendships. I believed that if you wanted to be a friend, you did something and then you could expect a return. When I offered to tutor Erica, I meant it as a friendly gesture, and I thought she accepted it that way. She could have insisted on paying, and then I would have known it was business and I wouldn't have made demands. But she said nothing and acted as if she liked me. I couldn't help the way I looked, and I was angry she found me so repulsive. You know, when I saw her and realized we lived in the same town, I tracked her down and actually worked out a way for me to buy the mortgage on her house. I had this delicious fantasy of turning that bitch out into the street and giggling as she begged me to have mercy for old times sake.

Frieda's story is instructive. Not only does it provide an insight into the kind of resentment and hostility rejection stirs up, it also suggests that people tend to accept what other people do for them without considering why the other people do it or whether there is any cost attached. Most people, it appears, believe they deserve a great deal from other people. Our natural egocentrism sometimes blinds us to the reasonable and conscious efforts others are making to initiate an exchange. We wonder why people are hurt after we accept their favors but fail to accept them as our friends.

We interviewed a few people on these matters and came up with the conjecture that real friendships only emerge when *both* parties understand what they are giving and getting. Our data revealed that egocentric people wanted relationships to be spontaneous. The more self-centered the respondent, the more they tried to avoid discussing the exchange feature of relationships.

A final category of friends are those who make "interchangeable accommodations" when they are together. Corporate employees know the art of instant friend making when they move to a new community. There is a standard social routine of helping newcomers get settled in the community and the country club and working out some casual socializations. All the time these people are being careful not to get too close because everyone knows that everyone will eventually be transferred again. The idea is to *act* like friends without really being friends. If you keep getting close to people who keep moving away, the pain will be very hard to take and will prevent further human contacts. There are five years of Christmas cards and then the people fade into the distance. When you encounter pictures of them in the family album, you rack your brain until you come up with, "Oh yes, that nice young couple in Atlanta we used to play squash with. He was in logistics, I think." (A famous movie producer was alleged to have said, "The most important thing about acting is honesty. When you learn to fake that, you have it made.")

INTIMACY

Most people want more than casual contact. They want someone really close. The urgency for closeness permeates the quest for friendship and the search for a mate. Karen Horney says that sexual relationships are the substance on which male/female closeness is built. People sometimes seek an Occam's razor in relationship, the most intimate privilege for the least effort. There was, for example, a tendency for our respondents to be suspicious of disclosure. They would disclose some things (mostly funny stories about themselves), but reserve a great deal for fear of betrayal. For example, men in the locker room tended to be quite open about whom they were "fooling around" with, but they found it virtually impossible to tell anyone about their weaknesses. (Another conjecture we came up with is the possibility that the male tendency to avoid admitting weakness has something to do with their unwillingness to go to the doctor even when they are sick.) The motto seems to be, "The less people know about you, the less they can hurt you."

Our respondents expected a great deal from their intimate friends.

They should always be around when we need them.
I want someone who will be happy with me when I am happy and not make me feel guilty because I am more fortunate than they are.
You can give him a call and he'll loan you money without questions.

Your best friend has to be able to keep secrets.

They should know what you want, anticipate it, and deliver it without you having to ask.

It's not that you are dependent on them. It is just that they have what you need so you have to keep them around to get it.

I would hate to think he is my friend just because of things I do for him.

She would like me for myself, I mean, she doesn't care about the false me, but she gets beyond it, and I can scream and call her names, but she would know that is not the real me doing it.

My friend would go to a funeral with me and hold my hand while I cry even though she doesn't even know who died.

They bail you out. When you are in trouble they get you out of it.

He would travel for a day to visit me if I was in prison.

Your best friend is around when you need her, but she doesn't pester when you would rather be alone or with someone else.

Your close friend is always interesting and able to make excitement for you, not anything dangerous, but would keep things interesting.

Friends don't make no demands. They do what you want to and they don't do nothing for themselves, but you want to do something for them because they are your friends, see?

These definitions make it seem as though people want their friends to be dumbly obedient and dedicated. It is hard to tell whether the definitions refer to flesh-and-blood people or to subtly designed androids who can act human enough to fool outsiders but who, as robots, serve all the needs of their owners.

The earlier sample indicated that people need a variety of friends in different situations and for different reasons. The current sample shows a considerable reversal, a trend toward the "all-purpose friend." There seems to be some impatience about the difficulty of complying with demands of "alleged friends," as one respondent put it. This may be a function of the narcissism some authorities claim is rampant in the society. It did appear as though our younger sample failed to show a sophisticated understanding of exchange. They believed people should like them and do their bidding simply because they were such intrinsically desirable and delightful people.

About 75 percent of the 1981 sample expressed in one form or another that they were really looking for a relationship with someone of the opposite sex with whom they could relate completely. Their expectation was that this mate would provide not only perfect sex but also care, concern, excitement, wit, advice, social support, and nurturance. In the next chapter we will show how these expectations tend to break up marriages before they have a chance.

Another interesting phenomenon we found was that people spend a great deal of time "running down" their friends, complaining about them when they are not around and bickering with them when they are. People appeared to be polite to and considerate of their enemies, but rude to their friends and mates.

KEN G.
Sometimes Jay is a real pissant. He gets on me and tells me what to do with my life. So Jay got married and he is getting his rocks off, and I am still running around and coming in on Monday morning with a hangover. I am 35 and he is telling me how my wayward life style is hampering my advancement in the company. Shit, I know he cares about me and all that crap, but he can really get on your nerves. Some day, I will tell him to screw off.

CHARLES M.
Greg has been my friend for some time. We have been friends ever since I came to the company on my 28th birthday fifteen years ago. He would call me up any time he wanted to talk. He has a lot on his mind. We would talk a lot because he had a lot to say. We socialized mostly on the phone although we got together *en famille* a few times. We always visited on Christmas eve to look at the trees. Then the calling got really bad. Things were coming apart over in his department and the vice president he reported to was going a little nuts. I know Greg was having a hard time, but he would call me up late at night and talk for an hour. I didn't have time to do anything at home and my wife was really upset, not to speak of my daughter who complained that guys could not call her because Greg was on the phone. One night I had it. He had gone through a real whining complaint, and told me how easy I had it, and I said, "Yeah, we all look at the world different," and he said, "Sure, you look at it like a prison guard and I look at it like a prisoner." That was more than I could take. I said to myself, "It costs too much to have this guy for a friend." I just hung up the phone and never talked to him again.

The urgency in close relationships is for a sense of equity. Equity, however, is not an exact science, and sometimes what we feel is equitable is an imposition to someone else. It is clear people often expect a great deal more from friends than the friends can possibly give. (They do the same with their mates as well, as we will demonstrate in the next chapter.) People have a tendency to develop a fantasy of how the friends will behave and then expect them to measure up to the fantasy.

DUANE H.
It was lousy when Patty got sick. Patty was an old-fashioned wife. She kept things going at home, kept house, cooked good stuff, kept the kids content and happy.

We fought a little because people who live close and love a lot always fight a little, but when she got sick, I came unglued and I was really strange when she was in the hospital. I had a hell of a time with the kids, too, because they missed her a lot. I depended on the Bartletts. They had me for dinner three or four times with the kids while Patty was in the hospital, and Greta came over a couple of times and cleaned up around the place. But Patty was in the hospital for a month, and I don't think I saw the Bartletts more than ten times during that month. You've got to understand, they were close friends. I know what I would have done for them. Well, when Patty came home, they came over to visit, and the third time, when Patty was up and around, Al Bartlett said, "Now that Patty is on her feet, we should go out and celebrate," and I yelled, "Stick it up your ——— you bastard." He looked shocked. "Patty was that sick and you completely deserted me," I told him. Well, the bastard was icy cold. He said, "We did the best we could. You can't expect us to solve your problems, only to help out." I felt terrible after all the years we had invested in the relationship, and I told him, "I hope when your wife gets cancer, people let you rot." You think that a few dinners and stuff can buy me. I mean after all those years of friendship, how could they let me face it alone. What are friends for?

We could not find the Bartletts. It appears that our respondent was asking a bit more than ordinary humans can provide. Like so many of our respondents, he was unable to apply dual perspective to an understanding of what was possible. He could not understand how he would have felt had he been Mr. Bartlett and the demands were being made on him.

We found very few friendships that survived adversity, but these friendships were highly valued. Most people count on support before they have earned it, and they resent it when people do not deliver what is expected. Complaints about friends not being around when they are needed were frequently expressed.

It appeared that many respondents considered it reasonable to expect their friends to impair their mode of living to "help out." What seemed so simple to the people expecting help was often in actuality immensely complicated. Even though people denied that friendships involved exchanges, they regarded their friendships as investments that would bring some tangible return. The idea of long-range return was important in the earlier survey. In the 1981 survey, however, respondents seemed to expect return almost before investment. Younger respondents (we found in nearly half the cases) tended to demand a one-for-one kind of relationship. For example, if someone borrowed a recording, there was an immediate reciprocal demand for something of equal value.

The people who made satisfying long-term intimate relationships were quite different from "mainstreamers." Managers and professionals, for example, were not optimistic about friends. As we reported earlier, they thought of best friends in the past tense and seemed to confine their associations to contact with people who could help them. They stayed together with people very much like themselves, socialized a great deal in organizations and civic groups, entertained customers and important colleagues. Their entertainments were mass projects, and they rarely had contact with people one on one.

NAN U.

I think that it is because we all believe in God the same way that we love each other so much. God doesn't want you to have any best friends but Him, and He wants you to love everyone. That's what we mean when we call Him a jealous God. We all have the same political and religious beliefs, and so we are friends and dedicated to saving everyone else, and if we decided that one person was more important to us than another—except our family, of course—then we would be insulting God, who is really the best friend of all of us.

The people who seemed most successful at sustaining long-term relationships tended to be agnostic. They belonged to few organizations and tended to avoid large socializations. For example, artists and musicians seemed to cherish time alone interspersed with intense one-on-one contact with close friends. People with intense friendships did not seem to be a part of the mainstream. For the most part, we felt that people were very much in harmony with David Riesman's conception of other-directedness to the point where they were *getting along by going along.* Most of them could sense what was expected of them in public, and they provided it. There was very little public dissent and argument but a great deal of grumbling and griping behind people's backs. We conjectured if the people who claimed our society was becoming narcissistic were correct, the pattern of avoiding intense contacts and maintaining a great many public social contacts exemplified their claim. People simply do not want to get too close to people who might make them uncomfortable by making demands on their time and emotions.

SEX AND FRIENDSHIP

We all know there are differences between men and women (praises be!). For the past twenty years there has been an intense effort by social scientists to discover whether the physiological differences between men and women could predict any major differences in the way they interacted. It has been conjectured that women tend to be more creative and have better verbal skills than men, that men are better at mathematical problems and logic. It is commonly believed men make better engineers and women are better in occupations that require sensitive understanding. However, no one seems to be able to demonstrate whether this is a function of social acculturation or a natural outcome of physical differences.

Within the past decade the notion of "androgyny" has become popular. A great many experts (mostly female) believed that if men and women could share the same traits and virtues, equity could be achieved. Men would have to learn to be emotional and tender, and women would have to learn to be tough and aggressive where necessary. Many years ago Alfred Adler suggested the notion of the "masculine protest," a process where women sought the same freedom to express themselves and be aggressive in pursuit of their goals than men used. Adler associated tenderness, apology, and quietness with femaleness and toughness with maleness. Since Adlerian humans were all striving for courage to serve the social interest, learning to be masculine was very important, even for women.

In an androgynous society men and women could simply be friends. Sexuality would present no problem, since androgynous men and women would respect each other for their "abilities." Both women and men could wear comfortable clothing without stimulating sex cues, and they could be alone together without arousing suspicions. In an androgynous world women could be as sexual as men, and they could attempt seductions when they wanted to, just like men.

In order to accomplish androgyny, we would first have to eliminate all sexist references in books and talk (just like we tried to do in this book). Second, images would have to change. Jane would become a star baseball player and Dick would learn to weave fabrics. Sometimes father would be shown in the kitchen making a delicious stew while mother, briefcase in hand, would be going off to work. The ideas of androgyny have not reached the point where wearing unisex clothing is acceptable. Actually, androgyny has not quite caught on.

ARLENE S.

When my husband and I lived in Iran, we really saw androgyny. They put the women in those *chodor* bags because the Iranian men thought that when women showed their "parts," it distracted them from prayer. Women were regarded as filthy, unclean creatures of the devil whose job it was to tempt men from important things like praying and hating Americans. So they desexed them. They put those black things on them and covered their faces, and all you could see is burning little eyes peeking out of the holes. In the dark all cats are grey, no? Of course, women weren't allowed to do anything that society needed because they had to be punished and kept away from things because they evoked filthy thoughts. The country lost about 55 percent of its potential with its little desexing routine.

MAX S. (age fifty-four)
The trouble is, young girls don't know nothing about men. I think that lady is right who says women who get molested ask for it the way they walk about with everything hanging out and nipples showing and those shorts where their cheeks hang out and flop and jiggle. I know I am going to have a car wreck some day with what those girls are showing me. I don't want women to lose their sex, but they should have mercy on us.

There is a vast gap between what is and what ought to be. When we pass a moral judgment and then expect everyone to live up to it, we presume on the rights of people to live their lives their own way. We must apologize for the editorial comment, but as we read the responses to our questions and talked to our respondents, we clearly saw that men do not like women very much. They resent them, they fear being rejected by them, they see them as tests of their manhood, and they find it very hard to react to them as humans. The situation is complicated by the tendency toward prurience in our mass media and in our fashions. There is a synergy of biological urgency and social norms that tends to accentuate the difference between

women and men. This fact clashes with the economic necessity for women to contribute to society.

TONI A.

It's hard to resist the propaganda, but it comes from all sides in all forms. On one side there is ERA and women's consciousness raising and my urgency to have a career. On the other side there is the pressure to be female, to show my sex, and to have good intercourse either with a husband or a lover. I really can't handle it. I feel torn apart a lot of the time. I don't know how I want men to see me. I know that on the job I am sometimes acting like a real executive and then all of a sudden I find myself showing leg and sobbing a little to get sympathy and to get my own way, and then I get really mad when a guy puts his arm on my shoulder and acts like he wants me and I get mad when a guy yells at me and doesn't seem to understand that I am just a girl who needs love and sympathy.

DENISE T.

I got into being sexually aggressive and I started picking out the men I wanted. But I learned how to have sex and it wasn't enough and I knew I wanted some understanding and tender love and maybe a home and husband, but I am so committed to being up front and a little kinky that I can't get out of it. Each time I have sex I think, maybe this time will be better and I will be able to get to know the guy and each time I come away feeling lousy.

KRIS G.

Since I have become a Christian, it has been easier for me to handle sex. I know we were put on earth to be fruitful and multiply and we have to do it within reason. I don't believe in birth control or abortion, but I think abstinence will help us. My husband and I withhold ourselves and don't let animal passion carry us away, otherwise we will commit sin. I want to be a good mother and I expect Parker to make enough money so we can raise a good family. This is much better than the way it used to be when I was working and I used to drink on weekends and end up in bed each time with a different guy.

TIM K.

They brought in this female executive, and the first thing she did was grab for my balls. I couldn't stand the thought of working for a woman anyway, and she made no attempt whatsoever to understand me. She jammed herself in and she found every mistake I ever made and she took me up one side and down the other and finally got me fired. No man would have done that. A man would have taken the time to understand. Men are loyal to one another, but women are bitches. Women shove everybody around—even other women—and then they get you in bed and tell you you are no good there, too.

STEVE C.

I was very uneasy when Barbara went back to work. The kids were in school, but I had a feeling that mothers ought to be home with the kids. When I told Barbara this, she said, "So go home." I couldn't understand how she couldn't understand the pressures on my job, and I didn't think she was going to bring in all that much money anyway. Then I discovered that she had opened her own private bank account and she wouldn't tell me how much she was making. She said that I didn't tell her, and what she was making was none of my business, and anyway she needed to have money in the bank in case she wanted ever to leave me. I think that was pushing it a little far, and I got very angry with her, and she just baited me and baited me until I demanded that she leave. Then she took me to court and got me for child support and half the property and I was so messed up I almost lost my job. I don't think women have any right to break up their homes because of the silly propaganda that they are as good as men. Some women have to work, I know, but my wife didn't have to work and I couldn't understand why she wanted to. All I know is that whatever she got out of it, she sure made life miserable for me, and she had no right to.

PETE O'L.

I am very grateful to the guys who invented women's liberation because all the way through college I could never get any because I didn't know how to ask, but we got this liberated lady in the office, a commercial artist, and she told me she liked my "bod" and she took me to bed and taught me a hell of a lot.

It is entirely possible that the return to religion, characteristic of our present society, is really a protest against trends toward women's equality. Perhaps neither sex can live with the responsibility of having to regard each other as individuals, and both sexes have decided to take refuge in religion to conceal their urge to return to a more secure form of sexuality. Clearly it is the emphasis on sexuality in our society that seriously interferes with the ability of women to be seen as potential leaders and colleagues. Here is what some "experts" have to say about this issue.

CHRISTINE C., M.D.

Masters and Johnson were experts on people who didn't mind being photographed during intercourse. I think people who go to sex clinics are a special population hung up about sex. I do not believe that everyone takes it quite that seriously. We generalize too much about what's right for people and what's good for them. We haven't allowed them to make individual decisions. We really don't know very much about what men and women do when they are alone with one another. We only hear from people who are willing to talk, and even they show a lot of variety. If we want to have equality, it should start in the bedroom and be an equality which will permit women not to be completely dominated in sex by men and to give them the opportunity to say what they like. Then people could work out sex in their own way, without being pressured by the media or pseudoscience.

FRED A., PH.D. (sex counselor)

I'd like to talk about fidelity. You know, part of being with other people is that you owe them a little. People who love one another really are saying that they own little shares of each other. I'm serious about this. You get mad when your friend of the same sex does something with another person and leaves you out. You have lost something valuable, the total attention of someone you care about very much.

It is not quite like friends are property, but almost. And when you have had a sexual relationship, you have shared something very important. This should bind you. I am not giving you old-fashioned conservatism. I think the cheapening of the sex act in our society has cheapened the quality of our life. If we think sex is nothing more than a roll in the hay, a good time, a process of grunt and groans, and when we get involved in making it exciting or kinky, what we are doing is denying the essence of our humanity. Sex is the way we carry on the human species. When we use it for less than that, we cheapen it, and when we do it indiscriminately, we cheapen ourselves.

Philip Slater points out that when men and women work toward intimacy, physical contact is a privilege to be earned. The problem is what people must do to earn intimacy. Young men used to be guided by such adages as "In the dark, all cats are grey" or "If they are old enough to bleed, they are old enough to breed." Young women were taught to believe that "nice girls don't" and "men are all after one thing." To do it the "wrong" way or with the "wrong" person subjected you to the "wages of sin" usually in the form of venereal disease. People were uptight about sex but the world was simple and there was general agreement about the rules.

The notion that admission to sexual privilege has to be earned through a close and loving relationship still prevails, but there are many exceptions. For example, most of our male respondents made a distinction between women with whom they have casual sex and women who are eligible for marriage. For some women learning to say no is the only way to aspire to marriage. Now both men and women are confronted with messages that urge them to enjoy sexual contact for its own sake rather than regard it simply as a means of reproduction. For the believer in the *Playboy* philosophy, sex with beautiful women is an assertion of freedom and manhood. For the readers of *Cosmopolitan* aggressive sex is every woman's right. For couples there is an urgency to do it "right," for satisfying both parties, even for simultaneous orgasm. It is hard to see how men and women can regard each other as anything other than sexual (no matter how androgynous their dress) given the barrage of prosex persuasion.

Furthermore, there continues to be a legacy from the sensitivity movement of the 1960s. People want to say to casual acquaintances more than is reasonable about what they are thinking. As a result, many relationships become intense more quickly than the people conducting them can manage. At least in some cases intimate talk leads to intimate contact before the participants are ready for it. People find themselves engaging in sexual relations without understanding why, except that it seems a natural movement from the exchange of personal confidences.

So—can men and women be friends without sexual intercourse as an issue? Here's what some of our typical respondents told us:

MALE

People have a right to decide what they want to do with sex. No one should have the right to control what they do.

Women want to have it both ways. They give off sex cues and then demand that we admire them for what they are.

We'd better learn to control our sex drives. I am no priest, but I am scared to death about overpopulation and kids brought into the world to be beaten and starved to death. Sex is no casual process.

I cannot tolerate the easy way these women have their abortions. I cannot tolerate the slaughter of innocent infants.

If you can't stand the heat, get out of the kitchen. Men make the demands, and they shouldn't make them if they can't pay the price. I think men who get women pregnant and then won't assume the care of the children should be sterilized. I am sick and tired of paying taxes for welfare just so these inner city studs can screw around.

FEMALE

I don't think anything is OK between consenting adults. Sometimes I find myself doing it when I am not consenting just because the guy thinks we are supposed to consent. Guys just assume you are always on the pill.

I think all men look at my body before they think of anything else, and when they think I am winning, they try to get sexual with me.

I do not understand sex. I don't like it. I think my mother was right, it is my curse and the burden I must bear, but you can't get near a guy unless you give in.

I compete and I'll get control any way I can. If I can, I'll beat a man with logic, and if I can't I'll pussy-whip him into submission. I intend to win and if those bastards only want to fuck me I'll win that way too.

There is considerable confusion. With so many disparate opinions, it is not hard to see that there will be misunderstandings between men and women about the appropriateness of sexual intercourse. The adage that guided sexuality during the 1970s was "anything is all right between consenting adults so long as both parties find it pleasurable." There was some disagreement about what constituted "consent" and "pleasure." The few cases in which women sued their husbands for rape raised those questions, but we were too busy ridiculing the lawsuit to take into account the issue. Our data led us to believe that both men and women acknowledge that men are still in charge sexually and that women are expected to submit even against their better judgment, as a duty to the men they love. How far this proposition can be extended is still arguable.

One development surprised us. That is the widespread awareness of pornography and what could be considered bizarre or "kinky" sex. Most of the older male respondents had something to say about it, and most of their comments seemed to indicate they were sophisticated with it. Casual references to sadomasochistic practices were found in half of the male interviews and in almost 40 percent of the male written protocols. About one-third of the women we interviewed admitted they engaged in some kind of activity their husbands or lovers discovered in pornography. (Most admitted sheepishly that they enjoyed it.)

Our report on the role of pornography could easily be another book (and probably will). The point is that sadomasochism, oral sex, anal sex, fetishes of various sorts, and even some of the more profound aberrations such as incest, scatology, and bestiality have become commonplace in conversation. One must be careful about making a relationship between words spoken and deeds done, but the extent and sophistication of the familiarity was very surprising to us. Our data indicated that, at least for a large portion of the population, sex had reached a commodity level.

In the first study we asked a selected population of 200 people to respond to a series of 375 opinion items to see if there was any modality of attitude that could be established. Some of the items on that survey showed clear trends. Men and women *disagreed* (disagreement = 60% + "no") with the following:

- One partner must have authority over the other for sex relations to be satisfactory. (On the written protocols there was considerable discussion of the importance of mutual satisfaction and simultaneous orgasm. At least 25 percent of the married respondents also commented on the importance of regular intercourse, although there appeared to be no consensus on the meaning of "regular.")

- You have to learn to perform intercourse in order to be effective at it. (On the written responses, nearly one-third of the married couples commented on the importance of spontaneity. Respondents indicated that they could "work it out" if given a chance.)

- Women have the right to refuse intercourse any time they want to. (The negative phrasing of this item made it interesting.) Married men strongly disagreed. In the protocols nearly three-fourths of the men volunteered the information that one of the reasons they got married was so they could have intercourse whenever they wanted it. With women only a bare majority disagreed with the item, and there was little discussion of it on their protocols. It appeared that a large proportion, perhaps a majority of women, bought the old-fashioned notion that women had the obligation to provide sex for their husbands. The following statement typifies many male observations:

CALVIN N.
When I thought about this item [differences between women and men], it finally occurred to me that the biggest difference is that men have to impregnate women, but women don't have to be impregnated. Women are, in that sense, objects to be treated with some courtesy and conserved, but we have to breed them and they are around to be bred. We have to keep looking for the best specimens we can find, but they have to take what they can get. Of course, they want to be bred by the best, so most of them try to make themselves sexually enticing so they can trap the best men they could get into knocking them up. I won't tell my wife about this. Don't you tell her.

The latency of the *Kirche, Küchen und Kinder* school of male supremacy was hard to deny. It accounted for some of the dismay men expressed at the entry of women into the workplace. It is difficult for men who regard women as objects to be bred to accept them as colleagues, reasonable competitors, and friends, much less work for them. While there was considerably more personal consideration shown for women in our sample than is apparent in present-day Middle Eastern nations, there does not seem to be much of a gap between the male attitudes. We do not know whether the male attitude really emerges from a physiological imperative or whether it is learned. We found *no* correlation between political and religious attitudes and the degree of control men thought should be exercised over women. Male respondents who espoused "born again" Christianity justified keeping women in the home on religious grounds. Political liberals defended women in the home on the grounds that working women took jobs away from heads of families and minority-group members.

Some of our male colleagues objected to our findings on the grounds that they did not seem to fit their experience. However, we could find few female colleagues to deny the premise that women are still denied equal opportunity economically and socially. Since hiring in academic institutions is largely in the collective hands of the faculty, we asked about some of the female candidates who had been considered for jobs. We received the following kinds of replies. From these comments, it appears that women are in a "no-win" situation vocationally.

Too flashy, you know, just too glib.
She looked like an iron maiden, a professional virgin. Who needs that around?
She showed too much leg in that skirt she was wearing. She'd probably try to seduce everyone around.
My wife doesn't really trust these single, young women entering the profession.

We are belaboring these findings because we think they are important. We found that the men who seemed to verbalize the androgyny message most vigorously were a group who claimed adherence to "California-style" sensitivity movements. These men felt that when both males and females drop any pretense of careful regulation of sex, it ceases to be an issue. When you can request and receive admission to intercourse from anyone anytime, the value of intercourse declines and other values become more important. The ideas of the communards seemed to add up to this, and those who verbalize the actualization premises of Maslow's psychology appeared to have their sexual business together. It was, of course, not surprising to find that virtually all the people we encountered who advocated the actualization philosophy either had never married, were divorced, or claimed to be gay.

In *The New Rules* (1981) Daniel Yankelovich discussed some of the aspirations for personal fulfillment, sexual gratification, and changed lifestyles, in light of a basic belief in a permanently affluent society. When there are enough rewards to go around it is not necessary to fight over some of the basic necessities of survival, and it is possible to become involved in more philosophic issues such as "quality of life and relationships." In the "Golden State" it is possible to remove the affluent even from the stimulation of seeing the less fortunate; they can develop a lifestyle of personal fulfillment based on sufficient income to purchase the means to gratify both flesh and mind. As recession moves toward depression and less people can have things in unlimited quantities, the tendency to utopian views of interpersonal relations may recede. We felt we detected an association between affluent economic level, and willingness to admit women to equality.

Oddly enough, most women seem to go along with the prevailing view, whatever it is. For example, the number of women who opposed ERA, advocated prohibitions on abortions, agreed with Phyllis Schlafly that if they were molested, it was because they brought it on themselves and indicated that whatever the source of the notion of male superiority, the media propaganda had materially influenced female attitudes. Women continued to be a good deal more romantic in their attitudes toward friendship than men did. When we consider friendships, it appears that women feel they can have both equitable friendships and sexual admiration without causing any problem. We have brought up cases of women being unexpectedly molested by men they trusted. We use these cases to illustrate the importance of using some sort of rational decision-making system to select associates. Many women objected to these issues, not because they deny our main premise but because they feel it could "never happen to them," because they have "this ability" to get the "vibes" and select only safe men.

Women appear more likely to sacrifice their personal aspirations because of their affiliation with a man. Many women in subordinate positions are intensely loyal to the men for whom they work. These men had become like a husband-father substitute for them. Also, women could not comprehend the tendency that men had to form teams and compete, with destruction of the enemy paramount in their minds. The internal ethic of male socialization is very cruel in some aspects, for men tend to swap sex jokes and to demean minority groups. The male who raises an equal-opportunity objection to a joke about a minority group usually loses status in the group. Thus, regardless of protestations made to women, men continually remind themselves of their sexist ethic, reject any androgynous claims, and continue to maintain a wall of exclusion toward women as colleagues and friends.

WHAT WE DISCOVERED
ABOUT MALE-FEMALE RELATIONS

Will you, nill you, this is what we think we found out about male/female relationships.

Women will normally surrender contact with most friends in order to maintain preferred socializations with men. Men do not show a similar pattern. A great many women pointed out how they had to give up contact with old friends when they became engaged or married, although they did retain one very close friend. Men, on the other hand, seemed to maintain their privilege of a team or group connection, which normally was not disturbed by the marriage or intimate relationship.

As a side note to this issue, we confirmed the notion that women are capable of covering up and rationalizing the hostile and sometimes criminal behavior of their "men." Beaten wives (we spoke to seven) were able to find some justification in their own behavior for the way they were treated. Virtually all of the young women we interviewed claimed they could "get along better with men than with women because women were just too catty and competitive." The way we translated that statement was once a woman made a permanent connection with a man, she did whatever she could to keep the man from making contact with other more desirable women. This pattern is confirmed by the treatment of divorcées by their married friends. We report on this topic in Chapter Six.

Men generally agree that they cannot be friends with women without dealing with sexual contact.   Many men offered explanations of how they dealt with their friends' attractive wives or women in the office they didn't dare touch. Many played a theme of sex fantasies, "disposing of it mentally" and then getting on with business or friendship. One respondent argued that it didn't matter what women wore anyway; men were able to remove it in their imagination.

Men still demonstrate considerable behavior that could be called chauvinistic.   The locker-room talk in which we participated indicated that a good way to gain male prestige is to have intercourse with a woman who tries to cover up her sexual capabilities. "Touching" the untouchables is an important game for a great many men, and it is played without concern for either the wishes or the emotions of the women involved.

It is easy to excuse male sexual chauvinism as culturally defined. The close association between religious fundamentalism in all denominations and subordination of women suggests there is an imperative among men to maintain the social order as it always has been. We talked to some of the newly religious people in our sample.

ANDREA MCK. (age nineteen)
In high school I must have been possessed by some kind of demon. I started having sex when I was fourteen. I learned that was how you could get guys. I loved to show off my naked body. I even got money for posing for pictures for some old guys. After my experience with Jesus Christ, though, I felt I had a new body, that I had become virgin and pure again, and that I would never share myself again until I had a husband.

BONNIE J.
I know that God made me beautiful because he wanted me to share myself with those in need. I can use my body to help ease the pain of sexually hungry men and help them come to God, while I maintain my psychological virginity for my marriage. I feel that I am doing what Jesus wanted me to do by giving myself freely because it is charity to give to those who do not have.

MOLLY E.
My hero is Goldie in *Fiddler on the Roof.* For us Chassids, we are to take care of our husbands and our homes. We are to make sure the men have the time to be holy, to pray and to do what God requires. We don't ask questions, because it is all spelled out for us. Those women who run around with their bodies showing are there to tempt away our men, but by maintaining a good Jewish home, we keep them at our side while they are right with God, also.

REVEREND ERNEST P.
The essence of fundamentalist Christianity is that the home is sacred. In the home each person plays a role. It is the duty of the woman to maintain the home as a good place and to raise the children. It is the duty of the man to provide for his wife and children and to spread God's grace in the world. It is the duty of husband, wife, and children to do the Lord's bidding and not to commit the sin of pride by demanding more than their share. The role of women is what it always has been.

We cannot resist commenting that Bonnie was a very popular young woman. We must also warn our female readers that we are not endorsing this trend; we are reporting it. Our sympathies lie with the economist who told us we could hardly sustain sexism considering it implies we demean the talents of more than half the world, talents we sorely need to help us solve the apparently unsolvable problems with which we are faced.

Men tend to regard women as physically and psychologically weak. They feel they cannot count on them as friends and allies. In a later chapter we will discuss the tendency people have to dehumanize their enemies. In a sense men make enemies of women by the language they use about them. Men generally believe that they can handle competition even from very competent women because all women will, eventually, succumb to skillful sexual blandishments. Once women make a commitment to a man, they are under control. We observed that a great many relatively mediocre men seemed to be able to keep very competent women under control by maintaining them in a sexual liaison.

We found this echoed in the tendency of some women to take extraordinary risks with men because they felt they could "handle things." Women were not averse to using sexual attractiveness to move up the hierarchy, to get what they wanted. The use of the body to influence decisions has been a traditional persuasion employed by women. The liberation message seemed to suggest that it can be done with impunity, turned off and on at will. Most women were not aware of the ways in which they could be trapped by their sexuality.

CLYDE W. (personnel director)
I have to be careful about hiring women who use T & T persuasion. You are familiar with T & A on television. In the company T & T refers to "tit and tear." These women forge ahead and some of them are damned good, smart, competent. But when they get backed into a corner, they will try to work themselves out by using their bodies or by breaking down and crying. Both techniques are disruptive as hell. A good body user can get young executives at each other's throats faster than anything I can think of. Some of the secretaries are remarkably skillful at it. I

once suggested that we hire male secretaries. Everyone thought I was kidding. I can see a whole division made up of women, but I really shake when I have men and women working together because there is no better way to get people's minds off the goals and interests of the company.

ANTHONY J. (personnel director)
I disagree. My success lies in picking quality personnel. If my colleagues can't work with women, they should get out. I will not limit my choices by excluding women. A lot of women in power positions in this company do well. They are not as competitive as men. They are loyal and they do not form rebellious cliques. I don't socialize with them or with anyone else for that matter. I won't say that I have conquered my sexism. I still prefer to look at women more than men. I love beautiful women. But for workers, you can't beat a smart, ambitious woman. I take my sex at home, however. My wife is a specialist, too.

In general, our finding is that men and women are not friends in the accepted sense of the word. Women who attempt to maintain regular friendships with men do so at their own risk. Resolving the issue of sexuality is a very important issue. We were startled at how preoccupied our respondents were with sex. They wanted to talk about it and acted as though they thought about it a lot. We would think that having liberated ourselves from Victorian repressions and having learned about the meanings of sex from psychoanalysts and physiologists, we would not maintain a preoccupation with it.

COMPETITION WITHIN FRIENDSHIPS

It seems natural for friends to compete. If there are "goodies" to be obtained in a relationship, then it is entirely reasonable for each partner to want a fair share. We found, however, a genuine paradox in our survey. In their descriptions of friendships most people described competition. In the interviews, however, virtually everyone denied it. We could not understand why it was necessary to deny that competition existed.

AUGUST M. (age sixty-one)
Back before World War II fraternities were important on our campus. They were proof that "birds of a feather flock together." Guys lived with guys just like themselves. We had a jock house and a genius house and a social house and even a thing like that animal house in the movie. We wanted to be around people who thought the way we did. We made it clear to the pledges that if they did not agree with the rest of the membership, they ought to get out. The world was simple, and I wish it had stayed that way. We knew our way around. We had Protestants with Protestants, Catholics with Catholics, Jews with Jews. Once we accidently pledged a Jewboy. His name was Cabot—can you imagine?—and he came from Boston, so

we thought we had something big, but we found out his name used to be Kabetinsky, so we took him across to the Jew house, and he became a member of their house with no hard feelings.

People have a tendency to join groups of people who think alike and act alike. It is simply more secure than running the risk of being misevaluated by someone whose reflexes you do not understand. But the risk of competition under these circumstances is very great. If, for example, you choose to associate only with accountants in your own company, you will find yourself competing with them for available rewards. There is no escaping the freedoms of choice.

In any kind of competitive circumstance there is a tendency to establish hierarchies. There are invariably weak and strong people. Another phenomenon we noticed is the tendency of weak people to group themselves around stronger people from whom they seek favors, much like medieval courtiers sought favors from the "duke." By associating with a power figure, weaker people relieve some of their anxieties. They surrender loyalty in exchange for security. Our data confirm that this behavior still goes on and is very much a feature of life in large corporations, universities, and government agencies. The problem with making such a commitment, however, is that when and if the power figure goes down, you go down with him or her.

The competitive urge is often reflected in gossip. We found a tendency for people to "put down" their friends, to revel in their adversity, and to share stories about them with great joy. In large corporate structures it did not take long to hear wild and weird stories about people we would never meet. Gossip and rumor are weapons used to keep people properly controlled. Among our respondents we found a representative of a foreign country that had a number of agricultural settlements. This person was seriously studying how to use gossip and rumor to keep control over the citizens of the settlements.

Why do people compete? One possible answer is that it is fun. Although schools have recently advocated that competition between people should be reduced and people should cooperate with one another, there is a tendency for most people to think about others competitively. It is hardly possible to contemplate the differences between you and another person without asking whether that makes him or her better or worse than you.

The desire to defeat enemies is very important. If society were permitted to run with uncontrolled battling, people would very quickly wipe themselves out. Therefore, good common sense impels us to develop rules of competition, to derive vicarious kicks out of the Super Bowl and World Series, and to develop norms with which we can battle one another on the job and in the community.

A counterargument is sometimes offered based on the premise that jogging is clearly a solitary activity in which people compete only against themselves. But if this is the case, we wonder why we have all the marathons in which literally thousands of joggers and runners compete against one another. Even more peculiar is the trend toward running for charity, where people pledge money for their favorite runner who will then proceed to run as far as he or she can in order to get money for a charity. It would seem more logical, less costly, and less of a physical strain simply to give the money. Competition, however, provides suspense and excitement and in a way compensates the people who are giving up their cash.

Alfred Adler offered an explanation for competition. Everyone, he believed, needed a *Gegenspieler,* someone against whom to test your strength. Some people compete with their parents long after their parents are dead. It is much more reasonable to find someone in your world who offers you a fifty-fifty challenge to overtly compete as a legitimate test of strength. We all want to be winners. It is clear to us that however much people deny their competitive urges, virtually everyone is competing and usually with their closest friends.

FRIENDSHIP AND PAIN

Sigmund Freud explained that pleasure was nothing more than the absence of pain. Most of us understand the value of having friends; we feel it acutely when we lose one. The pain is most severe when we lose someone of the opposite sex, a love partner, who departed for greener pastures (or purpler passion and potency). People tend to hedge themselves against the pain of losing a friend by playing it cool. More than half our respondents admitted they preferred to stay in an uncomfortable relationship rather than face the prospect of no relationship at all. These respondents gave evidence they could protect themselves from discomfort through rationalization.

Fear of loneliness motivates a great number of defensive reactions. For example, we often tolerate some very unpleasant and boring people for an evening rather than face the prospect of spending the evening alone. Another technique is regularly scheduling public entertainments for weekend evenings, movies, plays, concerts, and so on—anything but face being alone. A third technique is to keep a list of alternate friends so we have some leeway to get angry when an alleged friend does something we don't like. We talk about avoiding getting trapped in relationships and stepping back from people with whom we are getting "symbiotic." We want to "keep our options open."

Another method to avoid loneliness is to overschedule time. By filling in time with shopping, appointments, excursions, child-oriented trips, quick lunches, and an elaborate network of one-for-one entertainments, we can be sure that we will never walk alone. An odd paradox is that despite our insistence never to be lonely, we also want to avoid situations where we must depend on someone to dispel our loneliness. Although logic tells us how important other people are to us, our fear of desertion leads us to minimize our need for others, sometimes to the point where we drive people away.

A great many people handle their close friends by relegating them to familylike positions, treating them like aunts or cousins and feeling obligated to them as if they were family. That way they can be *resented*. Most of us resent obligatory family gatherings, but it is important to us to be able to count on them. We would be discontented if we did not have someone to whom we could be a little hostile with impunity. With family you can always struggle for equity without losing contact. Loyalty to the family would keep you in contact despite your quarrels. Once we have friends in that position, we have created a surrogate extended family.

Many of our respondents who had old friends talked about them in "old shoe," family fashion.

"men do not like women very much"

We always get together with the Smiths on important days—Thanksgiving, Easter, our birthdays. They count on us, you know.

Well, we make it our business to touch base with our plans and our problems and to keep each other posted on how the kids are doing.

They come around to help me start the garden in the spring, I come around to help them get set up for winter. You know, we don't even need the help, but it's been going on for so long neither of us wants to stop it.

Well, with the Goodwins there is always someone to yell at us. I mean they are constantly telling us how to do things, but they are always willing to help out with a buck or two, also.

There is little romance in these statements, yet similar comments were found in most of the responses. Our younger respondents were still filled with wonder and excitement, still searching for romance, still amazed when anyone liked them, but it appears that as you grow older, you want to be more sure of what is going on.

We believe people are defined by the folks around them, and it appeared to us that those with the most certain and specific definitions of themselves were those who had the most reliable relationships. We believe this is a very important finding in light of the flood of popular articles about finding one's "real self." A colleague once said, "Real self may be the place where you go to hide when all your roles break down." Certainly the people who are surrounded by supportive friends are too busy living up to expectations and fulfilling obligations to worry very much about who they really are. They are who people expect them to be, and because of those expectations they feel secure in who they are.

In this sense our data contradict the popular norms. We do not see much hope for the people who seek personal gratification, fulfillment, and actualization, for there is no substance to their quest. In the first place, their ideals are so fuzzily phrased they cannot clarify them. In the second place, there is no way they can count on their perception of who they are if no one else confirms it. People who claim to be somebody other people do not think them to be are customarily labeled "schizophrenic." We had the feeling that a number of the most enthusiastic actualizers were actually on the edge of schizophrenia. *They tried so hard to convince us they were happy that we felt sad.*

Back in 1962 two sociologists studied one hundred "typical" college students. They examined written essays and oral presentations entitled "My Philosophy of Life" in an attempt to describe the students' values. The finding was simple. The students believed that *things would get better as they got older.* Those students are today's adults, and they still appear to believe it. Their counterparts believe it also. Their guiding motif is, "Things will work themselves out, you'll see."

THE ORAL CULTURE

OLD YIDDISH JOKE

SON: (to mother on the phone): Come down to Pier 16 quick. Take a cab. Do I have a surprise for you!

MOM: (arriving breathlessly): What's the matter?

SON: (pointing to a gigantic yacht at the pier): Look, momma, I bought a yacht. That's mine.

MOM: And what's that on your head?

SON: That's my captain's hat.

MOM: Oh, you're a captain?

SON: Yep!

MOM: That's nice, sonny. By you you're a captain and by me you're a captain, but tell me, by the other captains are you a captain?

We share the feeling Daniel Yankelovich expressed, that we are in a time of changing values. Yankelovich somehow makes things look optimistic. We are not so sure. Clearly acquisitive values are changing, since it is getting very hard to buy things. In many places it is not safe to be out alone. People, in some ways, seem to be retreating into fortresses, where they can be alone with their electronic toys. They are fearful of making commitments to people because people demand compensation and maintenance of equity, which interfere with personal, narcissistic, actualizing goals. They are fearful of being alone to the point where they are surrounded by visual and auditory stimuli. Stereos, FM radios, televisions, VCRs, video games, and other amusements are selling furiously despite a receding economy. This may mean people are becoming more self-contained, more able to withstand loneliness. It may also mean that *because of two decades of personal questing and narcissism, people are steadily losing the ability to talk, argue, exchange ideas, and generally amuse themselves by being with one another. Their sensory urges are overcoming their ability to affiliate with one another.* It is hard to explain how our data suggested this conclusion, but we were gratified to find we were not alone in our belief. For example, consider the following excerpt from Jennings (1981):

Though people spend much of their waking hours talking or listening, the status of spoken language as a reliable medium of communication seems to be declining through the industrial world. The problem may be that we are losing our memories—and with them our faith in one another's "word." Studies of cultures where few people read and write suggest that, in general, as literacy improves, the ability to remember information conveyed by sound alone declines. The ability to listen and report accurately what was heard without using pictures or writing may be on the "endangered skills" list as this century ends.

Fewer and fewer important exchanges of information take place by word of mouth alone. Business deals are almost always based on written contracts so complexly worded that even those who sign them prefer to let their lawyers do the actual drafting and interpretation. Rarely does a government leader venture a policy statement without a written text to read from. Even at press conferences, reporters depend on written notes or machine recordings to keep their facts straight. And while the words "will you live with me?" are probably still most persuasive when spoken, modern couples often make the answer "yes" conditional on a written agreement spelling out responsibilities and expectations.

Decreased emphasis on teaching children such skills as careful listening, persuasive rhetoric, entertaining conversation, and even story-telling may have made reading and writing appear more necessary to education than they really are. But without some special effort to teach better speaking and listening, the average citizen of the future may be an "oral illiterate."

Friendships are oral relationships. Friendships are carried on between people who are in contact with each other. They are sustained through talk. In the next chapter we will show how intimate relationships end when there is a shortage of contact and talk. Without capable talk exchanged between relating parties, friendships cannot exist. Ineptitude at the use of language results in alienation from others, shyness, depression, and frustration. The mainstream of psychiatry and clinical psychology demands that people learn to "communicate" what they really mean. This supports the idea that people need to adapt to the oral culture of affiliation and contact on which friendship and intimacy are based. Without skill in that culture very little socialization is possible.

Our notion that the skill of social conversation is disappearing was consistently confirmed by complaints from respondents. Many of our respondents despaired of ever being able to say what was on their minds to anyone. They feared that they were not convincing, that people would not take them seriously. They ascribed their inability to emotional illness or genetic deficiency. The authors of this book are trained in teaching communication skills. It is our contention the state of relationships between living and loving human beings could be materially improved not by mass psychotherapy or religious revival but simply by teaching people to improve the quality of the way they talk with one another.

This position has some serious future consequences. Conditions promise to isolate people more and more in the years to come. With the popularization of word-processing equipment and easy intercommunication through video screen, it will be possible to do most business without bringing people into face-to-face contact. It is hard to conceive of people becoming intimate via video screen. Somehow, people will have to be brought together and trained to talk. Even more frightening is the thought that public defense of issues will be entirely in the hands of the very few people who have capability in skillful talk. The Aristotelian premise that things "good, just and true will triumph over their opposites if given an equal hearing before the minds of men" seems to be doomed. The younger people in our sample generally felt uneasy about committing themselves to ideas or to people (except for the evangelists and single-issue advocates). The trend in the teaching of public speaking over the past five years has been toward presentation of neutral subjects. Students not only do not want to try to argue a point, they feel that argument is distasteful. Carried over into interpersonal relationships, they seem afraid to make an effort to reach out. So many of them are waiting silently to be chosen, and there are almost no choosers.

We talked with many couples who had split up. *They were not skilled in the process of being together.* We train people for virtually everything, except how to be together with other people. We learn the "rules of order" in school and "standard operating procedure" on the job. Some of the skills may carry over to skillful observance of social norms, but our experience argues against it. For nearly twenty years we have been training people to overcome shyness, stage fright, and social apprehensions by training them in communication skills. We find that people have to be educated for specific situations, that oral skill is not a general trait but a set of individual situation-specific skills.

Some estimates place the number of shy people at more than half the population. It may be more. One definition of shy people is that they are people who are not able to handle particular social situations. They are not skilled enough to meet the communication requirements. (For details, see Phillips 1981.)

The shy people with whom we deal report a great number of deficiencies: inability to exchange information, inability to ask and answer questions, inability to state a message clearly and coherently, inability to speak in public, inability to make small talk, inability to handle interviews, inability to meet strangers, inability to carry on talk with friends, inability to talk to healers and helpers, inability to deal with tradespeople and service personnel. However, they are distinguished from their counterparts not by their ineptitudes but by their willingness to seek help for them. In our required oral communication course, we have an option that enrolls over one thousand students a year who are identified as just as unskillful at oral communication as the students who call themselves shy but simply do not care. They do not recognize their inability to communicate as a problem, and they resist training, complaining all the while that their relationships are not working out and that people do not recognize their abilities. Our eyes are prejudiced, of course, but we cannot resist concluding that relationships come apart when people can no longer effectively talk with one another.

People don't just "drift" apart. There is usually a reason, and the friends or lovers are simply unable to talk about it. The idea of "owning and sharing feelings" is not important with casual acquaintances, but it is important to be able to say what is on your mind to people about whom you care very much.

Sometimes people cannot communicate because they do not understand the problem. When relationships are plagued by outside temptations unknown to one partner, it is hard to talk. Another problem is that people feel generally tense and ill at ease when they have to talk about something important. Even more important is not knowing how to phrase what you want to say or how to say it once you have it put together.

These are *skills* deficiencies. People can be trained to organize information and feelings and say them sensibly to other people. Furthermore, they can be taught to overcome their anxiety if they want to. Based on our study, if we had to propose a remedy to the problems we see in friendship and intimacy, it would start with skills training in the kind of talk on which relationships are based.

chapter four

Lovers: What people say about their mates

I love steak,
Joe loves whiskey, and by the same token,
a cannibal loves his neighbor.

MAURICE SAMUEL

Friendship is far more tragic than love.
It lasts longer.

OSCAR WILDE

I can resist anything, except temptation.

OSCAR WILDE

Handsome woman—lovely bust.
Fine young fellow—stirred up lust.
Babies' diapers,
Bottom wipers,
Years of struggle—coffin—dust.

1888 bit of British doggerel

THE VOICE OF LOVE

Go on, say it! *I love you!* Three little words. Hardly takes a full breath to get through it. Once you get through the words, however, you may need a whole lifetime to assess the results.

People in love want to talk about it and hear about it all the time. It is as though they believed there were some relationship between words and love. The protestations of affection and undying fidelity seem important, as though the words themselves were protective amulets. When the words don't come, a great many people believe that love is gone.

The psychiatrist Richard Rabkin (1970) suggests that verbal statements of love are not necessarily signs of love. People who love are supposed to act in loving ways. It is easy enough to say "I love you," but for the most part it is a ritual employed to get someone to permit intercourse or do some tedious task. Thus, the man who can say "I love you" convincingly enough can get a woman to go to bed with him and, later on, to do his laundry. The woman who can say "I love you" convincingly gets a man to "love, honor, cherish" and support her relatively permanently.

The word *love* is a genuine abstraction. It is a Humpty Dumpty word. It can mean whatever we want it to mean—nothing more, nothing less. The only problem is, if everyone has a different definition, how can we talk about it at all?

How we talk about our lovers is also very important. The person we call lover may not love, but he or she may talk of love and/or make love. It doesn't matter whether there is a connection between words and deeds. The logic of love is neither inductive nor deductive, but *seductive.* We can use love words as inducements, verbal ploys, little promises, presents, and pretenses.

"Tell me how much you love me." Love questions have no answers. They are not designed to be answered, merely to solicit. Love cannot be measured. The questions we ask each other demand a response according to the accepted ritual, which is always regarded as "good" even when it is "bad." Love talk can often be a substitute for love. The clichés "You are mine forever," "I'll never let you go," "Love, honor, and cherish [obey] till death do us part, for richer, poorer, sickness, health" are as valuable as oaths as the people who make them are truthful.

But, what do lovers talk *about?* When lovers talk about loving, what do they say? What is important to them? What is vital to their relationship? What do they fear? In essence what we wanted to know was how the language of loving was spoken both by people who stay together and by those who don't. This chapter reports what we found.

IF YOU CAN MAKE THE STATEMENT, YOU CAN COMMIT THE ACT

In part, Adolf Hitler was so powerful because of his ability to get people to say things out loud. There is a tendency for people to try to believe the words they say when others can hear. Thus, to say "I love you" tends to create a mood. The ritual generates expectancies.

Recent publications claim to reveal womens' secret fantasies. Most of the fantasies are bizarre, somewhat violent, and a bit like Hollywood scenarios. It is hard to believe women generally think that way, but who can deny their public reports? The same is true of men. What they say about their desires and the fantasies they conjure up when they see an attractive woman may very well represent what is on their mind. It is hard to tell what people *really* think about love, but it seems reasonable to take their word for what they think. We have no other way to get an answer. We assume that they believe at least some of what they think (although orthodox psychoanalysts would argue they think a good deal that they are unaware of). It is questionable whether anyone ever reveals all they have on their mind, and sometimes we are likely to say what we think is acceptable in public rather than what we really believe. With all of those reservations, we forged ahead and asked people what they expected from a person who said, "I love you." We received some interesting responses.

MEN
She will do her best to satisfy me sexually.
She will bear my children.
No one else can touch her, only me. I own her.
She will do whatever kind of sex I want her to do.
She will always try to be beautiful and make me proud to take her out.
I can count on her to be loyal and do whatever I want her to do.

WOMEN
He will be there to comfort me when I am down.
He will not touch other women and he will be a good father.
He will never ask me to do anything I don't want to do.
He will make sure I have a fulfilling life-style.
He will respect my desire to have a career and we will be partners.
He will gratify me sexually and not get up to eat after sex.

We can infer what people consider important by listening to what they say. Jules Henry (1971) once noticed a man playing with his son, cuffing the child while saying, "I love you." Henry wondered if the child would learn that love meant hitting and hurting, and how would his wife fare, if that was what he expected?

The word *love* is commonly used to express passion. When we "love" someone, our possibilities for action expand to include physical intimacy. Mutual love usually means sex, although sex is possible without love. Mutual love also implies pairing. Even though there are now more single than married households, most of us persist in seeing people as part of pairs. The norm is for singles to anticipate marriage, and married people expect singles to succumb to marriage sooner or later. Actually, approximately 95 percent of the American people will marry during the course of their lifetimes.

The word *love* has become synonymous with intercourse; it no longer expresses emotional intensity and commitment. People who are deeply involved with each other now look for "authentic" contact, or "mutual caring and sharing," or struggle for some other vocabulary in which to express their feelings. They *have* sex. They *make* love. The verb *to love* has become a noun and has lost its power to convey emotion. We

wondered whether the change in meaning of the word meant a change in the way men and women saw each other.

Many who talked to us about love seemed naive about it. Regardless of their socioeconomic level, they seemed to believe in the movie version of romance. When they met the "right one," bells would ring and life would be blissful. There would always be love talk and perfect sex.

FEMALE
Like, in the movies, they kiss and there is this music, like in *Silent Movie*. Even though it was a comedy, there was a beautiful scene with Mel Brooks and Bernadette Peters running through the grass with music playing. It'll be something I never felt before. I sometimes feel good with a guy, but it isn't love because I know it is my glands acting up, not the real thing.

MALE
Your orgasm is so good you freak out. It's not fainting like in this porn novel about a guy who made women faint he did sex so good. I don't want her to faint, but when it's over I just want to lie in bed and remember it and hope that it will happen again and I want to keep doing it with this woman over and over again because I know it can only happen with her.

FEMALE
I think of sacrifice. My husband will make a good home for me and the children: two girls and the first a boy to be pals with my husband, and he can grow to be a man just like his dad. I'll raise the girls to keep house and be loving and caring and do good in the world. Me and my husband will be together a lot and we won't make love too much, but he'll kiss me and tell me how much I mean to him, so I will always know that I am safe and protected.

MALE

She'll be so beautiful that when I'm out with her, people will look and wonder what she sees in me, but only I can touch her. She'll do anything to make me happy. And people will know I'm a real man because *she* loves me.

The contemporary definition of "love" has become so physical that we find it difficult to express our emotions. The value assigned to intimate contact seems deflated. It is easy to make love. Many women, convinced of their right to seduction, have become more aggressive. The pill and abortion have reduced the risk and consequences of "accidents." The act that used to symbolize relationship is now *the relationship itself,* whereas couples struggle for a feeling about a relationship for which they have no name.

FIRST TALKS:
WRITING THE SCENARIO

Let's get married.

No, we'll live together first, then decide whether to get married.

I want two children. A larger family is nice, but impractical.

Kids are too much trouble. Who wants to raise them in the kind of world we live in today, anyway? Do you know how much it *costs* for just one kid?

Maybe we should buy a big house with Chip and Beverly. We could all live together and share expenses.

We'll have to work out a way for both of us to have careers.

I want to keep my own name.

The choices people make about their life-styles are based on what is familiar and on their ability to think about goals and what it takes to attain them. Individuals from lower socioeconomic levels seem to select more traditional life-styles than do those from the middle and upper classes. Alternative life-styles seem to be issues among professionals and intellectuals, who have the ability to pay the price for their choices. People who decide to become a couple must, at one time or another, decide how they wish to live their lives together. Once the goal has been selected, the hard part begins: accomplishing it.

ANNE W. (secretary)

Chuck and I decided to get married while we were still in high school. Chuck got a job with a contractor, and I took a job in an insurance office. We put our money in a joint bank account so we could buy a place to live when we got married. We thought if we worked a few years, I could quit work because Chuck would be advanced enough so we could have kids.

CHUCK T. (carpenter)
I was taught that it was my job to support my wife and it was her job to take care of the home and raise the kids. That's the way both my parents and hers did it. Neither of us wanted to go to college. We thought it would be OK doing it like everyone else around here did it.

MAUREEN W. (account executive)
I was thirty-three when Wendell and I decided to get married. We had lived together for three years. Prior to that I had lived with an actor for about five years. Wendell and I met at a convention and we discovered we had common commitments and interests. We each were making enough money so we could afford to get together and make a permanent connection. I'm established enough now so that I can free-lance part time and keep my name current while we have our child.

WENDELL K. (commercial artist)
I know our marriage looks like a merger, but it's not going to hurt when we get it together and form our own agency. We'll have two kids and move to some New England town where we can work Boston and New York and some of the adjacent cities. There will be enough money to care for the kids, and we'll have the best of all worlds.

The issue is broader than a choice between living together and getting married. In each case the couple must figure out *how* they want to live together or be married. The first decision is usually made about how they want to handle sex. However, couples can have sexual relationships without being married or living together. The choice to live together or marry is often logistical. Sometimes the decision is designed to please relatives, and sometimes a decision is made purely for career purposes. Despite the publicity given to living together, marriage is still more popular. It attracts millions each year, for better and for worse.

People have various reasons for pairing off. Some seek marriage for security. Their goal is to find someone with whom a less threatening and chaotic life can be managed. In unromantic terms, this means that the woman usually wants economic security and the man wants to escape the pressure to find sex on the open market. It is an exchange of convenience often accompanied by an emotion that could be classified as love but could easily be interpreted as relief. However, when people marry for mutual security, if one partner suddenly becomes stronger, the marriage usually comes apart.

SUZANNE G.
When Bill got sick, I had to go to work. I put Peter and Lucy in a day-care center and got a job as a secretary. I won honors in the business course in high school,

and I was still pretty good. I was reliable and learned to handle the equipment and solve problems without harassing the boss, so I became valuable. I got raises. I took a night school accounting course and got an A. I discovered that I could have made it on my own. Now I was saddled with Bill, who was boring and going nowhere in *his* job. I had two kids that hadn't started kindergarten and I discovered I could have been independent. I guess the frustration about my dilemma made me decide to compensate by getting it on with the boss, which in turn got Bill to ask for a divorce, which in turn forced me to be alone. It's rough and will be for a while, but it's better than just leaning on Mushface Bill.

Others form alliances. In this scenario marriage is a kind of feudal partnership forged out of a need for satisfactions not available from their careers. Skilled professionals will often get together to share ideas, pool financial resources, make themselves less available, and—most important—provide themselves some moments of warmth and affection. Such arrangements are often childless, or the couple may adopt. The idea is that mature adults ought to be enough for each other.

KURT W.

There comes a time when being irresistible to women is boring and you want the full attention of one good woman. There comes a time when you want to be concerned with the real issues of your career and not have to worry about your image all the time. There comes a time when you want to be able to give up running around and enjoy your living space. When that time comes, you find a woman to marry.

COLLEEN W.

Kurt and I have different careers in the same town. He is attractive, witty, warm, and considerate but needs to let his hair down and confess his fears. I have a reputation for being a tough woman executive, but I need to be secure that someone cares about me as a woman, a human. Kurt does that. So we married and are learning to love and be loyal. It is not necessary for us to have affairs; we have each had our experiences. We can discuss our career problems because we do not compete with each other. We have fun when we go out. We do not fight, although we sometimes quarrel. I think we are a good couple.

Some couples join together for regular sex. In this hedonistic scenario the individuals involved see life together in relation to genital satisfaction. This coupling seems to predominate in teen-agers and the recently divorced. According to this scenario, life is extended foreplay punctuated with episodes of less than satisfactory orgasm. Such relationships tend to be short-lived. Either the partners discover that sexual gratification is not enough to hold them together, or they discover they have to revise their sensuality to accommodate a number of other, more pragmatic issues.

However, a great many people believe in the magical power of orgasm. Advice on how to achieve good sex abounds in both men's and women's magazines and on daytime television. Men exercise, seek muscle tone, and buy their women clothing from the Frederick's of Hollywood catalog. Women learn "techniques," accommodate to "variety," and engage in activities their mothers would have universally regarded as sinful. They seek an orgasm so beautiful it will make the rest of their relationship transcendental.

The popularity of birth control devices for both sexes increased greatly in the last few years. Clearly a great many people indulge in sexual activity. Many form semipermanent alliances to protect their possibilities for sex. The major problem with arrangements based on sexual urges is that they rarely develop enough commitment to be permanent. When one partner discovers sex does not measure up to expectations (or to what is available elsewhere), the couple breaks up.

KEN D.
Myra was the sexiest woman I ever met, so I married her. We spent three years trying everything imaginable, and it was great. But when she got pregnant, it was not so interesting. I got this book on open marriage and we discussed how I needed sex to keep me going. I thought I talked her into something, but when the baby came, she told me to settle in or get out.

CYNTHIA N.
All the girls at college were doing sex. Some of them got into lots of trouble fooling around with people of, you know, other races or classes, like one girl was sleeping with this ex-convict and he used to slap her around and she said it aroused her. I didn't think much about sex; I just slid into it and it was fun, except I got uneasy about what was going to happen when I got out of school. I got real interested in Gus, but he doesn't seem to be too tolerant about fooling around. In fact, he isn't so good in bed, but I think I really care about him. But I don't know whether I can marry him because I think I will always keep trying to get it on with somebody anyway.

DICK P.
It was good when we did it before we got married. We were living together and we didn't feel obligated to anything but what we were doing. It was sensuous and we worked at it. When we got married, there were all kinds of other things. I don't know what happened because we certainly didn't change our living conditions or anything. It was just like we had suddenly gotten older and had to be more responsible. It may not last.

The big question seems to be: Doesn't anyone just "fall in love"? What ever happened to the old romantic notion of "a marriage of true minds" or at least of "true hearts"? We concluded from our talks with couples that romance is very important during the initial stages of a relationship, but as the couple spends more time together, they talk more about practical goals and possible outcomes of staying together. Love, when it works, seems to progress through stages of development, from the euphoria of initial sexual discovery to the carefully planned development of a life-style, to building a history of reliable and considerate support over a long period of time.

TOM H.

I have this joke: "We've been married fifteen good years and that ain't bad out of twenty-seven." That's about the proportion. It was tense when I was messing around with Gordon's wife back in 1960, and then Cathy got real depressed after she had Sally. She was thirty-five when Sally came, and another kid was almost too much for her. I lost my job twice. Cathy went back to work and had to adjust a lot. When I had the accident, she stood by and made me do the therapy so I could walk again, and she needed me for the mastectomy. Sounds like a soap opera, don't it? But, we have three kids pretty well on track, and we have a little money, and we travel together, and we have our moments. Sex in the golden years? I don't know. Maybe it isn't worth the effort. But it's worth the effort to have what we have, I think.

We encountered rare cases of romantic obsession that reminded us of the recent novel *Endless Love,* in which a young teen-ager pursues an elusive nymph (played by Brooke Shields in the movie version). In the movie he sacrifices his hopes for an education and career for his one-sided love. No one seems to understand his obsession. In the novel, his desire drives him to insanity and ruins his life.

Some people seem to live their lives in an endless quest for the unattainable. They appear to be "falling in love with love . . . falling for make-believe." Obsessive and idealized love is often the beginning of neurosis, since it is usually directed at an unattainable person. If the love object becomes available, he or she can seldom live up to the expectations.

People who claim to be in love often do not seem able to explain what they feel. They act as though they were the only ones who ever felt that way. Their "true" love preoccupies their time and thoughts. They are distracted from duties and obligations. They sometimes impose themselves on the person they love, and they bore their friends and relatives with incessant talk about their love object. Whatever the feeling, however, success in love usually results in the formation of some kind of relatively permanent relationship.

SECOND CONGRESS:
THE MAKING OF A
RELATIONAL CONSTITUTION

Talk is the substance of a loving relationship. Talk enables lovers to exchange feelings and make agreements about their day-to-day life. In this way each couple develops their own unwritten constitutions, agreements about how decisions are to be made and carried out, how disputes are to be settled, how rituals and ceremonies will be conducted, and how they will deal with each other and everyone else.

These arrangements are negotiated through serious talk about goals and how to reach them. Before making a permanent connection, couples often play with unattainable, romantic goals. The success of a loving relationship depends on selecting attainable goals and abandoning the impossible. Couples who believe their problems will be solved the minute they leave the altar are doomed to disappointment. The agreement to commit permanently only provides the couple with an *opportunity* to work things out.

SANDY U.
I thought after marriage we'd take a long honeymoon in Bermuda, buy a home, furniture, a new car. We got about five thousand dollars in wedding presents, and I had two thousand in the bank and Fred had a little more than that. But ten thousand dollars doesn't buy much these days. It didn't make a down payment on the home we wanted, and even if we made the down payment, we couldn't have afforded enough furniture. We took a deep breath, had a short honeymoon at Ocean City, and put the rest in savings certificates.

Most of our respondents found it hard to handle the ordinary business of living. Some could respond to tragedies and extraordinary demands made on them by those they love, although sometimes tragedies tore them apart. We found most initial relational trouble came from time schedules and work conflicts. Before marriage it seems all that is necessary to reach goals is working together, saving money, and planning. Most couples seem to feel the routine difficulties of everyday life will take care of themselves. Simple disasters such as missing a bus or burning a dinner can escalate into real disasters because romantic couples find it depressing to think about details.

JERRY S.
I always used to laugh at Blondie and Dagwood, but about three months after our wedding, I was lying on the couch and Marilyn screamed and I ran to the bath-

room and water was pouring out of the sink pipe. I got on the phone, and it was harder than hell to get a plumber on Sunday, but I got one to come while Marilyn diverted most of the water into the toilet. When the plumber came, he started to take the faucet off, and I said, "Don't you think you should turn off the water first?" He looked up at me and handed me his wrench. "You do it, buddy," he said, "and send yourself the bill. I'll just charge you rent for my wrench." And he walked out and left us with that mess.

Our respondents seemed to encounter these basic issues.

Decisions must be made about how to cope with such economic issues as fluctuations in income. Couples found it hard to adjust to economic adversity as well as unexpected increased income. For example, couples could come apart over conflict on whether to invest the money or enjoy a vacation.

Economic decisions include such ordinary expenditures as food, clothing, transportation, and so on, as well as choices about such major expenditures as housing, cars, and vacations. Investments were not quite as sticky. Couples with enough money for investments to become a major issue usually found more exciting topics on which to exhaust their argumentative energies.

It is difficult for new couples to merge their individual interests. His and hers expenses must become "theirs" expenses. Personal wants must often be subordinated to purchases from which both can benefit. Some working couples reported it was very bewildering trying to manage separate and joint bank accounts so that each partner contributed equitably to the marriage. Such arguments are hard to handle because they suggest the partners do not have much confidence in each other. Couples tend to feel more secure when common tastes reduce arguments about expenditures.

Couples on limited income feel the crunch when a major household appliance needs replacing or the car breaks down. About all that can be given up is six-packs and cosmetics. Middle-income families feel the most pressure when one of the children is ready for college or the time comes to purchase a better house. Even those in the upper-income brackets have difficulty figuring out where to invest and how to spend the proceeds. There is an old adage that "prosperity is always about 10 percent more than income." Thus, even though it is reasonable to believe that high-income families will have no problems, they manage to create them.

"There's something very wrong here," said Suzanne Owens, a 34-year-old assistant administrator of employee relations, at a Denver energy company. She works hard to earn her $27,000 salary, and together she and her husband earn $70,000 a year. When the hot-water heater in their three bedroom suburban home blew up, she broke

down and cried "because I didn't know where the $1600 to fix it would come from. We're not living high on the hog," Suzanne said, "and we're making more money than we ever thought we would. I get angry that I have to pinch pennies."

(ARRINGTON, 1981).

Economic matters seem to be the major issue in most marital disputes. Couples with one income often bicker about privileges for the main wage earner, who, in turn, carps about unnecessary expenditures in running the household. Husband and wife in two-income families often squabble about joint versus private bank accounts and what proportion of the joint expenses should be paid by each partner. The literature of marriage counseling gives minimal attention to ways and means of solving financial problems, but our evidence indicates battling about earning and spending can interfere with even very strong emotional ties. There is something essentially unromantic about balancing a checkbook, and when couples fight over that issue, it affects the way they relate about many other matters, including sex.

CAROL C.
It's very simple. We have fifty lousy extra dollars this month. He wants a goddamn golf club. I want a night out on the town. He says a golf club will last longer than a night out on the town, and I say I won't get anything out of a golf club. He says he earns the money. I say I ought to bill him for the work I do around the house. I don't think our marriage will survive this silly little argument, but if I let him get away with this, I will never have a fighting chance to get anything for myself.

MATTHEW C.
What does she want from me? I work hard for my money. She stays home. When the kids are off at school, she does as she pleases. I give her house money and she can take her recreation out of it. I don't get any recreation; all I do is work. I have a right to demand something for myself now and then. If I give in to Carol, I'll be a financial martyr for the rest of my life.

This dispute is typical of those fought in millions of homes. If there is no synthesis of values, there is no possible settlement. It is hard enough to settle a financial dispute when times are good and resources unlimited. Those of us born during the baby boom, from 1946 until 1964, grew up taking wealth and abundance for granted. We believed that everyone had a chance to join the upper class. We were taught that we would be rewarded for hard work with a house in the suburbs, two cars, neat and clean children, exquisite sex, and togetherness.

Today the message is different. With interest rates around 20 percent, buying one car is difficult and a house virtually impossible. A great many people who would like to work hard can't get jobs, and in many households two people must work just to break even. Affirmative action, ERA, CETA, and equal-opportunity employment have given way to bankruptcies, imports, and federal spending cuts. Tensions have gone up accordingly.

Add to all that the ordinary sources of argument in intimate relationships: how to make love, how to handle friendships, and what to do with leisure time, and it is not hard to understand the divorce rate. In general, we found people fight because they cannot meet their own expectations. Most of our society has learned from the media that everyone can be physically attractive and intelligent and find loving partners who will cater to their needs. They seek to "actualize" themselves and be fulfilled in their careers and their relationships. They believe that if they "live right," somehow, they will never be old or poor. Because the media messages are directed at those who can afford to buy advertisers' products, people with inadequate funds are doomed to economic discontent.

The third major decision point is sex.   People who marry expect to have intercourse. They do not expect that they will have to work it into their regular routine. If they try to make sex the center of their life, disappointment is inevitable.

ART W.
I like that country song "I Get Daydreams about Night Things in the Middle of the Afternoon." Sometimes I think about Connie all day. I have to struggle to pay attention to the customers. But I handle it. I get home and I have this picture of grabbing her and feeling her up and then we go up to bed and have a hell of a time. But by the time I get home, I'm limp and she's worn out from changing diapers and cleaning the house, and we sort of look at each other and sigh. I haven't touched her for three weeks, and I've pounded off twice during that time, and we've only been married five years.

Activities once considered aberrations or even crimes are now considered ordinary. The relational norm is "anything is OK that gives pleasure to consenting adults." Couples have to decide what consent is, and sometimes they have to argue about what constitutes pleasure. In the early days of a marriage, partners might try very hard to please their mates by acting as if they enjoy activities they really find unpleasant. After a while the hypocrisy begins to grate. In order to achieve a satisfactory (or barely tolerable) sex life, couples need to find a way to handle "kinkiness," including such matters as oral and anal sex, the use of fetishes, and their attitude toward sex with outsiders. While the "double standard" still appears to be in force, each couple must work out the penalties for violating the bond.

Sociobiologists explain male infidelity by ascribing it to the urge to impregnate as many women as possible, whereas women seek the security required to rear the young. Accordingly, men and women may be biologically incompatible on matters of fidelity. True or not, the issue of sexual relationships outside the marriage are very important to both male and female.

CHRIS D. (to the marriage counselor)
It's true I get a little on the side now and again. But it's "nooky," not really making love. I only make love with Karen. I mean, it's different with your wife than with a "one-night stand." When I'm away from home, in a motel, all alone, I sometimes need to "get my rocks off." I pick up somebody and buy her a few drinks, and she goes to my room and leaves in the morning. No strings. I don't even learn their last names. And I have never paid. I never used a prostitute in my life.

KAREN D. (to the marriage counselor)
When we got married, he agreed that I was to be the only one. I get lonely, too. What if I got myself some "nooky" while he's out of town. Women don't even have a word for "nooky." We know how to remain faithful to our marriage vows.

CHRIS D.
Men and women are different on that score. I'd be mad if Karen did it outside the marriage because women don't need it like men. Women are aroused by loving, not by the nature of their sex. But men are built to want every attractive woman they see, so it is something when they stay in a marriage with a woman. Karen has nothing to complain about. She gets it regularly and it is good sex.

KAREN D.
It is not good sex if I know you are doing the same thing with another woman. I don't care whether you know her last name or not.

The battle of the sexes goes on, and on and . . . on.

Foreign policy is another issue about which decisions must be made. Foreign policy includes all of the people outside the relationship with whom the couple comes in contact. For one thing, when two people become a couple, they discover that they must present a common face to the world. She cannot keep her friends without involving him, and his cronies become part of her life.

BERNICE K.
We have to share our friends. I have two girls that I've been friends with since elementary school. We kept contact even when we went off to college and we still

keep in touch now that we are all living in the same town. I want to invite them over and visit them, but all Al wants to do is go bowling or sit in the neighborhood bar with the guys. He doesn't like to entertain or visit and he really doesn't seem to have any friends.

Work associates represent another bone of contention. One of the most interesting findings in our study was that regularly employed adult males report very few friends. Most reported they had no time for friends because they have obligations to their allies and political associates on the job.

CRAIG P.

I have no choice. When executives come to town, I have to entertain them. I expect Tammy to provide. It costs too much money to take them to a fine restaurant. Most of the account executives I know use the "how would you like a good home-cooked dinner?" strategy. When I do this, I don't have to provide female company for them. It's not so bad. They don't stay late because they want to get to the hotel bar to see who they can pick up. Tammy complains that they work on her, touch her unnecessarily, but she shouldn't worry because I'm around and nothing is going to happen to her.

Couples must make decisions about who, when, and how to entertain, whose invitations to accept, and how to meet new people. Some couples prefer having a few guests at a time; others prefer to pay off social obligations with one large reception or cocktail party. Although the whole issue seems very simple, entertaining is often a logistical nightmare, requiring much planning and considerable scurrying about on the day of the event.

A sticky matter for men is keeping contact with old teammates and friends. Male socialization commonly consists of activities that exclude the mates. Thus, most formal entertaining and socialization usually involves the wife's friends. Activities such as the weekly bowling match or Kiwanis meeting are often mysteries to wives, who often seem unsure of what their husbands are doing when they are out.

Lionel Tiger (1970) argues that males socialize like a hunting pack. They develop strong loyalties to their group and compete with outsiders, unlike women, who socialize for consensual validation. Women have very close friends in whom to confide, whereas men tend to use their friends to set competitive norms. Because of sex-based differences in socialization modes, many couples have serious disagreements about socialization.

PETE W.

I can't stand it when Terri has friends over. The husbands are jerks. The women get together and chatter, and I am stuck with some bastard who doesn't understand anything I say to him. I tough it out, but I hate it.

TERRI W.
Sometimes I think I'd rather have Pete be unfaithful than to keep running out nights with his "team." I don't know what they do when they are out. They are always having matches or banquets or honor award things or practice sessions. I have this vision of them with a cake and a girl jumping out of it. I don't understand how a bunch of grown men can always want to be together. They never have time alone to get to know one another.

It is clear most husbands do not consider their mates to be friends. The response was overwhelming. "A wife is a wife and a friend is a friend." Furthermore, most men think it is impossible to be friends with a woman without having sexual contact. Women, perhaps wishfully, believe that men and women can be close friends without sex being an issue. The result seems to be considerable disappointment and frustration.

SHEILA N.
I thought Eddie was a good friend. He'd take me home from work and drop me off, and occasionally we'd have a drink together after work. I knew he was married, but we were friends, see, and we didn't do anything that his wife would object to. One night we worked late and he took me home. He looked tired, so I asked him up for a cup of coffee. He said, "I thought you'd never ask," and he came up. I should have suspected something with that comment. Then he said, "This is the first time I've been in your apartment, and we've known each other for two years. You sure are a hard one." Then he said, "Aren't you supposed to get into something comfortable?" At that point I knew something funny was going on, so I asked him to leave. He said, "Come on, honey, don't get cold feet now." I tried to get to the door to open it, and he stopped me, and the next thing I knew I was on my back on the couch and that was it. I didn't know what to do. I couldn't scream. I couldn't do anything. It's not like I was an innocent little virgin. I have my guys and I like to do it, but not with Eddie. I really did think he was my friend.

Experts on the topic claim that most rapes are by friends like Eddie.

When two people become a couple, decisions about friends must be made early in the relationship because outside entanglements can pose real threats to the security of a marriage.

The relationship between work and home is another issue requiring major decisions. Couples must discuss financial matters, the use of leisure time, and accomplishment of household routines. They must become familiar with and adjusted to each other's work schedules and the demands of the job. It is very difficult to adjust to another person's schedule. Egocentrism and the urge for privacy are very difficult to overcome. Anyone who has had to share a small space with a roommate knows how annoying the other person's habits can become and how important it is to have agreements about such activities as cooking and cleaning. Married couples must not only make these initial decisions, but they must keep revising them to meet external demands, taking into account that each partner will regularly meet new people who must be included.

MEG V.

When Mark and I got married, we had an agreement that supper preparations and cleanup would start at six P.M. If either of us got home earlier, we could do our share or we could wait for the other. We blocked out time on Saturday to take care of heavy housework and left Saturday afternoon and evening and most of Sunday for recreation and personal time. It worked. It was like I had it at home with my brother and sister. We all had our chores and we did them on schedule. Mark's upbringing was a little looser, but I got him involved and we made a habit out of it. When I got promoted, though, there were a couple of nights a week I had to work, and those nights that bastard Mark would do his half of the work and make sandwiches or go to a fast-food stand and I'd get home exhausted and he'd be on me to do my share and there'd be nothing to eat and it was pure hell.

MARK V.

I don't care about her promotion. We made the deal and we'll keep it. If I ever had to work late, I wouldn't expect her to make my supper and I'd expect to do my share of the work. Who said her job is more important than mine? I still make more than she does, even though she has to work longer hours. If it's too much for her, she can quit and get another job.

It was customary in virtually all the marriages we examined, despite protestations of liberation and equality, for the female partner to do a *major* share of the housework, including food preparation and laundry. Males were expected to do major repairs and yardwork. The problem is that few couples can afford a house with a yard, and in an apartment the heavy work is done by the custodian (if it gets done at all). When the wife demands equity, life can get rocky. Husbands seldom accommodate to their wives' careers unless it is worked out in advance. Even so, in most cases, the wife is expected to be more considerate of the man's job demands than he will be of hers.

Leisure time is another major issue.   Someone estimated that a career woman needs to spend nearly 40 percent of her income on clothing and requires nearly two hours a day in personal grooming in order to keep herself properly uniformed for work. In addition, everyone needs private time, to read, to think, to write letters, to talk with relatives and friends. Too much time together can be disastrous.

BILL Y.

When I first met Denise, I was flattered that such a good-looking woman would want to be with me so much. I was no bargain, because I was overweight and a little shorter than her, but I was proud to show her off. In the first year or so after our marriage she and I were inseparable, walking in the park on warm Sundays, skating at Rockefeller Center, museums, shows. We both had good jobs, and she'd call me twice a day at work to tell me she loved me. At home after work we'd talk about our day and about the news broadcast. She'd read the paper and pick out things she thought would interest me. By our first anniversary it dawned on me that I was a captive. I had no time to myself. I tried some "men only" activities, but when I got "interested" in fishing, she learned to tie flies, and when I decided to try bowling, she found a couples league. I tried talking to her about how I wanted time alone, and she didn't understand. She couldn't believe I would want to do anything without her. She couldn't understand how I would want time to myself. She didn't think I was fooling around with other women. She just didn't want me to be without her.

Some couples can't find anything to do together. Leisure time becomes more important as the couple becomes more affluent and sex becomes less important. More leisure time and increased income afford greater opportunity not only for day-to-day recreation but for vacationing. Thus, these issues become very pressing.

ARTHUR F.

Every time it comes to vacations, there is a fight. I always wanted a camper. We can afford it, but Ruth doesn't like to camp. She says she has to do all the work and she doesn't like scenery. She wants to go to the city and visit museums. I hate museums. I get sore feet. We compromised for the past four years. Two years we rented a camper and went camping and two years we went to the city. Neither of us is satisfied. She ruins my camping, I ruin her museums. Maybe we should take a trip on the Q.E. II.

Other major decisions must be made about holidays, religious observances, and who takes the children to church. When should we spend time with your grandmother? What should we do over the Fourth of July? Unless couples work out ways of making satisfying decisions about these crucial issues, minor conflicts can become wars fought in divorce court. Arguments about child rearing are very important. Children can polarize parents by favoring first one parent, then the other, in order to get what they want. Decisions about how to relate to aging parents and how much contact to have with relatives become extremely important.

VIVIAN Z.

I will never go to another of Irv's Cousin's Clubs again. I can't stand those people, all those uncles pinching me, people showing off, babbling, shouting at one another. I'm from a small family. I know it means a lot to Irv, but I'll get a divorce before I go again. I mean it.

THE REQUIREMENTS
OF A RELATIONAL CONSTITUTION

In our sample, marriages that lasted looked like mini-governments with unique constitutions. Each relationship had some method of making decisions and carrying them out; some way to complain and settle complaints. You could compare them with legislative, executive, and judicial components of government.

We found five distinct formats used for governing intimate relationships:

Autocracies usually place the man in charge of everything. The wife takes orders and carries them out with little right to complain. The husband manages the money and gives the wife a limited allowance to spend on the household. Infractions are often punished by physical abuse. A recent study noted that 25 percent of all wives reported they were hit at one time or another. In an autocratic management system, physical punishment is usually part of the relationship. The wives expect it and the husbands use it as a way of releasing tensions caused by impotence in other aspects of their life.

Another type of autocracy is the one-person family (or the single parent household). There are more of these in American society than ever before. The increasing divorce rate and the desire of many people to remain single have made single households a fact of contemporary life. When you are alone in a living unit and have no responsibility to anyone, you are in complete charge. Aside from observing the terms of the lease, you can leave newspapers where you choose, spend the money any way you like (or any way you can get away with, given the state of your credit), eat what and when you like, and entertain whom you please. The major problem confronted by singles is the difficulty of merger when they choose to marry and combine their efforts.

Single parents have a particularly difficult situation, since children, at best, are difficult to control, and as they grow older, they demand a greater share in government. Single parents face a number of threats to their authority. A great many battles in single-parent households are about such ordinary business as use of the phone, mealtimes, guests, and hours.

Limited monarchies are households where some authority is granted the wife, usually in domiciliary operations. For example, the husband may grant the wife full authority to operate the household within a fixed budget. He may allow consultation regarding the size of the budget, but he retains control over other decisions. The wife may be authorized to spend on herself what she can save from the allowance. Male authority seems to prevail in these marriages. Giving the wife responsibility for the operation of the household is a tradition. She usually has control over scheduling social life and day-to-day management of the children, menus, and household logistics. The husband usually controls the purchase of vehicles, vacation choices, and his personal recreation. Working couples usually fight about these issues, but in the end most assign responsibilities traditionally. (There is a commercial in which the wife sings, "I bring home the bacon and cook it, too.") The husband commonly reserves the right to register complaints if the operation does not meet his standards. This type of relationship has been the source of husband-wife cartoon humor for several generations.

The paradoxical aspect of authoritarian control is that if the wife accepts the authority her husband delegates to her, she concedes that he has the right to grant it. By the same token, if the wife tells her husband to dominate her, his acceptance of the role is a concession that his wife had the authority to grant it. These latent fundamental conflicts over the source and nature of authority can spell considerable trouble. Things may work very well until there is a real crisis. Then the fundamental issue of who is really in charge may destroy the marriage.

LEE W. (to the marriage counselor)
I can't turn down this opportunity. Moving to Houston means a forty-percent raise right away, plus a responsible position in the company. It is the career move I have been waiting for all my life, and Bonnie has no right to object to it. I'm in charge of earning the income, and what this does for her is give her more to spend.

BONNIE W. (to the marriage counselor)
Lee doesn't understand how important stability is to the kids. To pull them out of school and away from friends and family now would ruin them. I don't care how much it increases our income, I think it is more important that they stay in familiar places. And I don't want to live in Houston. It is a terrible place.

LEE W.
She has no right to say that. I know what's best for us. A husband in a second-rate job is no asset to a family.

BONNIE W.

A husband in a second-rate job isn't necessarily a second-rate husband. A husband who gives a damn about me and the kids is what I want. We're getting along all right on what you're making. If you want the damn job, take it, but I'm staying here. I'll get a job and mom will help out, but I am not going to uproot those kids.

LEE W.

You are being completely selfish. You are pouring me down the drain for some foolish reason. Kids adjust. I think you are afraid to leave your mother.

Problems such as this are often not possible to resolve because the fundamental issue of authority is never addressed. Settlement depends on whether one person gives in or one decides to call it quits. If there is no method by which to resolve such conflicts, they simply continue till the bitter end. Because the issue of authority is not resolved, any demands by the wife for more authority are met with resistance by the husband. These kinds of marriages are most susceptible to splitting up "after the kids are grown."

Constitutional governments are arrangements in which the partners have fixed the lines of authority. They are what theorists call "symmetrical relationships." In such relationships no authority can be granted, since no one has it to grant. Authority is established by consensus. There is understanding about the rights and interests of each member of the family. Issues like job versus kids that plagued Lee and Bonnie would be resolved in advance by such constitutional provisions as "We will not make any major moves while the kids are in high school" or "I will look around for some other kind of work as soon as my pension rights are vested" or "When the kids are all in a full day of school, I will return to work." New problems are dealt with as they arise.

While these kinds of arrangements are usually very effective, they are very hard to make. In the first place partners must have respect for each other and understand how difficult it is to divide responsibility down the middle. The person who controls accounting, for example, has considerably more power than the one who decides on entertaining. Both must be willing to surrender authority; otherwise the constitution of the marriage is constantly eroded by dissent and sometimes quiet sabotage.

Constitutional arrangements do not spring into existence from the start of a marriage. The fad of writing marriage constitutions in advance has not been terribly successful. Constitutions arise out of mutual respect; they cannot bring respect into being. If you consider the history of the United States, the original colonies could not bring themselves to trust one another sufficiently to form a central government until after they had built a record of loyalty tested in the Revolutionary War. The same appears to be true in marriages.

SANDRA N.
Our marriage was chaotic in the early years. We fought all the time about everything. Little things like who should pick up the laundry were as important as big things like changing jobs or buying a house. But gradually, I learned that Quent was usually right in his decisions about the kids, and he learned to trust my judgments in capital investments like housing and stocks. It was a weird reversal, but like he said, there's no reason not to bet on a winning horse. I remember, it was after Buddy's graduation from junior high that we sat down together and talked over how well things were going. We discovered that we had pretty much stopped fighting long ago. We still argued, but it was real argument, with facts and reasoning, and even footnotes, sort of. We were like two proud Tartar princes that night, dividing up our universe. You work with the kids, Quent, I said, and I'll ask you questions about what you do with the bucks, he said, but I won't interfere with your final judgment. And if something goes wrong, we've learned no one's perfect. We've been married thirty years on our next anniversary. The kids are all married and working, and we are grandparents three times over. I've gone back to work, and Quent is gearing down for a career change. We're reshuffling the finances so Quent can buy the craft shop he's always wanted to own without interfering with my position as an office manager. But it's working. If illness spares us, we'll have a lot more good years.

Elected leaders characterize the political brawling in large households. When there are several children, it is like a political crazy quilt complicated with the intrigue of a small-town courthouse. This is not necessarily bad. When there is goodwill, the political shenanigans usually result in serving the interests of the greater number. It is not easy to resolve such issues as which of several eligible children gets to use the family car on a given night. The mythology of *Eight is Enough* or *Father Knows Best* is that warmth, love, wisdom, and kindness will prevail in families of this sort. It is not necessarily true. On the other hand, you can't have a democracy unless there are some voters.

The counterpart to the Robert Young syndrome is the Machiavellian intrigue that often takes place when children attempt to manipulate parents into combat for their own personal gain. Couples on the verge of divorce often find their situation materially complicated by the struggle by the children to keep the couple together or to derive particular advantage from the split.

Shared government is the regulation characteristic of roommates or the Articles of Confederation. It is based on the principle that the people sharing the household are sovereign individuals united only in a limited number of activities. Some marriages between employed professionals use this sort of government. The system works until the couple is confronted by a major problem such as pregnancy or loss of job. It appears difficult for confederated partners to adapt to change. Success depends on how dependent and loyal the partners are. As we pointed out before, constitutional government depends on shared goodwill and trust. Sometimes the act of living together and respecting each other's rights is sufficient to build up the requisite trust. Sometimes, however, the thread of relationship is so frail, it separates the partners.

NICK S. (to the marriage counselor)
I told her to take precautions. We can't handle a pregnancy. Our house payments are fifteen hundred dollars a month without utilities. That requires a common effort, and her sick leave will not cover her share. We can't keep the house unless she pays her share.

NINA S. (to the marriage counselor)
It wasn't like he didn't have a share in this baby. The odds failed us but he is still obligated.

NICK S.
I may be obligated and I'll pay my share of the abortion, but I won't support a kid. That wasn't part of our agreement.

There is no hope for that couple. Nina will become a single parent, and Nick will look for another partner. Trust was insufficient for a permanent connection. Anarchy arises when a confederated couple discovers they have no common interest.

SUMMARY

Lovers need to develop mutual agreements about how to define goals, ways and means of attaining them, ways to settle disputes common to shared lives. The difference between success and failure in marriage seems to lie with the ability of the couple to find methods to organize their relationship. The process of thinking through government and working out the details is unromantic, and we encountered many couples who evaded the issue. They paid the price in unresolved conflict later on. It is virtually impossible to measure the degree of order that exists in a relationship, but most of the marriages we encountered in which both husband and wife expressed satisfaction seemed to be characterized by mutual agreements on a way the mundane, daily business was conducted.

We have discussed love and loving and the government of relationships. These days, however, couples do not relate "till death does them part." They relate until they feel too uncomfortable to stay together, and then they avail themselves of the loosened divorce laws. In the following chapter we will examine the dynamics of couples coming apart.

chapter five

How love ends

*If there is a wrong thing to say,
someone will say it.*

Law of Divorce

Take my wife, please.

HENNY YOUNGMAN

Divorces are made in heaven.

OSCAR WILDE

*Did you hear about the woman
who divorced her husband because of habitual adultery?
I wouldn't call adultery a habit,
but it sure beats nail biting.*

Catskills resort MC monologue

*Communication is boring.
Why don't people just talk?*

An anonymous Communication instructor.

Divorces and separations do not "just happen." They are as intentional as couples getting together. When one partner (or both) becomes sufficiently dissatisfied so that life alone looks better than life together, the decision is made to split up. If the decision is unilateral, the partner with the most interest in staying together is the most vulnerable. The one who wants out has the power.

In the *Ballad of Reading Gaol,* Oscar Wilde said,

> *Yet each man kills the thing he loves,*
> *By each let this be heard,*
> *Some do it with a bitter look,*
> *Some with a flattering word.*
> *The coward does it with a kiss,*
> *The brave man with a sword!*

Ending a relationship is never pleasant. Recently, there has been a wave of literature about "friendly" divorces. Certainly, when children are involved or when the couple has other interests transcending the marriage, it is important to try to avoid jeopardizing other aspects of life during the process of divorcing. A divorce is an admission of failure—nothing more, nothing less. Both parties must admit they have failed to work things out and they have either made an error in deciding to marry in the first place or they were inept at getting along with each other. No matter how much blame can be heaped on the other partner, the person initiating the divorce usually carries considerable guilt about his or her failure.

There are three basic reasons for divorce.

1. The marriage failed to live up to the goals and expectations of one or both partners.
2. There appear to be more desirable options on the outside for one or both partners.
3. A traumatic event pushed one or both partners to a point of no return.

In any case, there is a good deal of communication (or lack of it) that signals discontent and malaise before talk about endings begins.

COMMUNICATION IN AND ABOUT THE RELATIONSHIP

Communication has long been suggested by counselors as a panacea. If couples could only learn to "communicate," they could work things out—such is the popular wisdom. There are few advisories about *what* to communicate about or *how* to do it. There are some inept suggestions about family councils or consensus sessions, and during the early days of the sensitivity training movement it was assumed that authentic and spontaneous communication, in which each person disclosed what was on his or her mind, would solve all problems.

None of this wisdom appears to work. Marriage counselors who confront fighting couples discover that much of their work is like that of a labor mediator. They are constantly trying to compromise, make agreements, correct the facts, and arrange equitable distributions. Often couples come to a marriage counselor when it is too late to get back together. Their hostilities have driven them so far apart that concessions that could have cemented the marriage had they been made earlier have no effect at all. When bitter words have been said and the fighting has been for keeps, it is hard to come back together. People hate to admit defeat, and they rarely discover that they need help until it is too late.

One of the dismal factors in divorcing is that most marriage partners do not develop techniques for problem resolution. Although marriages operate like little governments as far as executive and legislative functions are concerned, it is hard to get a judicial system going when there are only two people involved. When children fight, parents can serve as third-party resolvers of conflict, but when parents fight, they must find their own ways of working things out. Talk works best when both partners want to agree. If the desire to agree is present, there may be harsh words, but eventually one party will concede something and start a trend toward compromise. If the battle goes too far, however, there is no chance of reconciliation, even in the hands of a skilled counselor.

A well-worn but seldom heeded truth abut communication is that problems occur because of *assumptions* people make about its power. We *assume* that things are OK because we have communicated. We *assume* we have an understanding, whereas all we have done is exchange words. We *assume* we understand the reasons why the other person made a particular statement without ever bothering to ask him or her what the reasons were. We *assume* people understand our meaning even when the ideas we are presenting are complicated, personal, and subtle. We *assume* the meanings we have for our relationship are *equally shared* by the other person. Paradoxically, when problems arise, we blame them on willful deceit. We refuse to concede we have made faulty assumptions about each other's communication.

An important point to remember is that communication is purposive. People may not know precisely what they are after all the time, but communication is not accidental. We reveal both our satisfactions and discontents by the way we talk and what we talk about.

For example, facial expressions and tone of voice often signal approval or disapproval of what a partner is doing. We are vaguely tuned into interpretation of subtle nonverbal behaviors with strangers, but we know the moves our intimate partners make. We know the unique and idiosyncratic ways they signal to us what they think and feel. Couples who have been together a long time can carry on an argument in public without anyone else knowing what is going on. The problem is that even when we know our partner very well, we cannot tell precisely what he or she disapproves of. Sometimes, disapproval is annoying and we respond with our own nonverbal signals. When this happens, the argument can be well into midstream before words are spoken.

Most people avoid stating specifically what they expect from their partners. They assume the partner "ought to know" despite the fact that no questions have been asked nor expectations stated. We are more prone to talk *about* our relationships than we are to talk *in* them. We tell our friends and associates about our problems despite the fact they can do little, if anything, to help us solve them. We rely on support from family members instead of arguing our own case with our mate. We confess our sins to bartenders, priests, and casual strangers we encounter in waiting

rooms or on jets. They may listen, but they really do not care. They regard it as a license to share their own discontents. The latent assumption in many relationships is that we have communicated. We have unburdened ourselves, and despite the fact the object is of our concern knows nothing about it, we believe our problem is solved.

Good talk seems to be the substance of any lasting relationship. When a couple can develop verbal techniques of sharing joys and discontents and use their understanding of each other to negotiate equitable solutions to problems, the relationship lasts—in spite of anything else.

GREGORY K.

Milly and I have had a strange relationship. She never liked sex much and I wasn't very good at it, so we didn't do it much. We had three kids, so when we did it, we did it well, but it wasn't big with us. Lots of other stuff wasn't important either. We never fought about families. We went together to her folks and mine once a year, and then we were free to visit alone as we saw fit. We had the whole gang in on Thanksgiving and Easter, and that was that. When we moved east, we permitted one visit every other year. It was our life. And we had this logic going. We talked. We talked about everything. We discussed politics and religion and our friends and what we did on our jobs and how the kids were doing. It was fun to talk, and we agreed there would be no lies, no deceptions. We had to talk, you see, because that was the way we lived our life. I don't know that I would recommend it to everyone. It could get a little boring. But it is now nearly twenty-one years. She looks good. She is the best looking forty-year-old I know. I'm no bargain, but I must be doing something right to keep her around.

The words we exchange are important. The private languages we develop separate us from the crueler world. We can carry on our own business in our own way. We can change our world or we can change the way we adapt to the world. Couples who understand the notion of "united front," for example, and use *we* and *us* in juxtaposition to everything outside the relationship seem to have a private language going. It helps them interpret experience in their own way. Most couples who return home from work exchange words about the events of the day. Communication about what happens in our lives is important in two ways: First, talking about the events of our day allows us to share both meaningful and puzzling experiences with someone else who can help us understand them. Second, talking about what we have experienced provides a common history for the relationship. We each know what the other has been through. Having the ability to appreciate mutual experiences contributes to the successful operation of the relationship. Finally, talking about a good or a bad day helps the partner adapt accordingly. However, the data show people tend to react to their partners as if their partners were filled in on both trivial and important events, and they are frustrated when a partner asks questions and does not seem to understand.

Another important kind of talk that seems to characterize successful relationships is when each partner *validates the identity and integrity of the other*. Our research shows this does not happen very often in marriage, although it is an important part of the intimacy of courtship. It appears that people seek validation in their intimate relationships. They select the person they think will enhance and encourage their identity. The fact of the matter is, a great deal of time is spend by marriage partners attempting the "Pygmalion" task, trying to make the other person over. It is almost a cliché in marriage counseling that it is unwise to marry an alcoholic believing that you will be able to reform him or her. The rule is generally applicable. It is a most unpleasant surprise to discover that your partner is trying to make you over.

One of the most important aspects of intimacy is finding the kind of support that is not available in the public world. People who have to spend their work lives in contact and competition often look to their mates to restore their spirit and strength. When the support system fails, it engenders suspicion and begins to pull the relationship apart.

DENNIS V.
You really have to be on top of it to make it in our company, but the rewards are worth it. We do the exterior design for various kinds of innovative household products, you know, like food processors or those new buffet servers. If your design is accepted, you get a royalty share of the profits on the sale of the product. It's not easy. It's more than just art. You have to know something about the materials and about manufacturing processes. And there is usually at least two of us working on the same project, so the client can have a choice of designs. The boss feels it keeps us on our toes to compete.

When I come home at the end of the day, I am tired. I want kind words and strokes from my wife. When Kris and I were engaged, she really kept me together, you know, from flaking out because of the stiff curriculum in engineering. But now, all she does is ask questions and correct Billie. She doesn't listen to me at all. And if I don't have a really positive report about the day, she is on my back about how we are going to pay the bills and why I don't look for another job. She doesn't understand and she won't even try. She wants me to be a financial winner and that's all. And I can do it, eventually. I can be a winner, but I need some help from the grandstand now.

Another kind of communication characteristic of successful relationships is talk used to build a private world for the couple, complete with a unique language, myths, nostalgic stories to repeat to each other, techniques for reminding each other of past joys and victories, ways to say "I love you," and words to use in public to communicate private understandings. For example, the novelist and short-story writer Mark Helprin often composes letters to his wife written in their shared secret code. In the play *Who's Afraid of Virginia Woolf?* we encounter a couple who have created an intensely private world in which they can live even in the presence of others. Even though they fight with fury they are able to rebuild their lives because of the shared privacy of their joint fantasies. They create an imaginary child, kill it amid furious explosions against each other, and then proceed to begin a new myth as the play ends. It is these kinds of shared worlds that represent the strongest aspects of steady-state marriages. Even something as mundane as pet names show commitment to a private world.

MARY N.

I've been married for twenty years to a cop. He just made sergeant. When we first got married, he was going to be the chief inspector. Now I hope he makes lieutenant before he retires, but it is not likely. But so what? He is the inspector to me. When we first got married, I called him Dick Tracy and he called me Tess. I'd say, "Hey, Dick Tracy, what evil monsters did you put away today?" And he'd answer, "Well, Tess, we got the notorious Sammy the Sidewalk Spitter and Julian the Jaywalker. The world will be a better place because of it." We'd laugh and go eat dinner. When he got shot at a bank holdup and won a hero's medal, we had the same joke. "What evil monster did you put away today?" I asked him when he was lying in the intensive care ward, and he said, "Constantine, the Cute Cop-shooter, the world will be a better place." He could barely talk, but he could smile, and I knew the world would be a better place. You can't stay married to a cop if you take things too seriously, and that's the way we built our world.

Most important of all, successful couples have a practical kind of talk they use for resolving difficulties. We have pointed out that if one partner wishes to split, there is really very little the other can do about it. In the next section of this chapter we will discuss the kinds of talk that lead to irreconcilable hostilities, *even among couples that want to stay together.* If the couple does not have a language to get themselves out of some of the talk traps they can build for themselves, they will find it very difficult to stay together.

Couples in our survey sample that had been together for many years and reported that they were satisfied, even happy, with their relationship had a variety of techniques they used to interrupt a trend toward disintegration.

WANDA T.

I have a hot temper, but fortunately Jerry is very mild. We learned very early in our relationship that I had to take the initiative to end quarrels. When we first got married, I would stay on Jerry's back for a day or two until I provoked him to real anger. But we learned that once he was provoked, it was hard to calm him down. So we made the agreement that he would hear me out once and only once. I could call him names, blame him, make my case, yell and scream—but only once on any issue. Then I had to leave the room and not come back until I was ready to hear his side of it quietly without comment. It was tough, but I knew I had to do it or I'd lose my man. I didn't think I'd get a better one and I couldn't understand why he would put up with my anger even once, so I learned how. Gradually, over the years, I got calmer, and we could just get to work settling our differences without the ritual.

RICK A.

Like all people, me and Susan have topics we don't like to hear about. I can't stand it when she talks about her cousins. I hate her cousins. She doesn't like locker-room talk—you know, bad jokes and stories about what the guys do. So we agreed we get phone pals. She found a cousin willing to talk about cousins all night, and I got one of the guys who would swap yarns with me almost any time I wanted to, and when one of us brought up a forbidden topic, the other one would give a signal to get on the phone, and then that person would leave the room so he or she wouldn't have to listen to the phone call. Learning that little trick taught us how to be very honest with what we could tolerate. I think it saved us a lot of pain.

BARRY J.

Melissa likes to talk about her feelings. I like to clam up. I hate to hear Melissa talk about her feelings, but if I don't listen she will get on the phone with a girl friend and then I'll hear about it anyway. So I had to take a deep breath and listen for while, and she knows how much I hate it so she makes it short. And she learned not to ask me about how I feel because she knows it makes me mad.

These techniques may sound trivial; however, they seem to work. What we discovered was that couples who are making it developed their own private and unique way to keep things together. We could find no conclusions about their techniques except that they had them, and we can't generalize about what they are and how they work. But we did discover some common features and trends in couples who fought a lot, were discontented, or were headed toward divorce.

Discontent at Expectations
Not Being Met

Most people live at least part of their lives in a fantasy world. They sometimes speculate about what people close to them will do. Sometimes they rehearse scripts about how they will act in particular situations. Controlled fantasies are useful because they help us prepare to cope with difficult events. However, when fantasies get out of control, we sometimes put dangerous expectations in our heads.

For example, one phenomenon we noted among dating couples is the tendency of the male to fantasize sexual intercourse with the female and then act as if he should have it "again" when they meet a second time. Very often, the women are bewildered. The quiet and courteous young man they met had turned into an insistent lover, becoming pesty in his demands for sex. We were also bewildered by this behavior until our research revealed that some people fantasize, ingest the fantasy, and act as if it were real.

To add to the difficulty, men are socially pressured to think sexually. Their urge to have sex is equaled only by their expectation of what they will get from it. Many of our male respondents confessed they knew very little about the woman they married, and cared even less. They married because they were excited about a particular sexual experience. Six months into the marriage, when sex began to become relatively commonplace, they woke up to the discovery that they had married a complete stranger.

ANTHONY K.

I don't want to get you all upset, but when Lucy and I first started going together, you wouldn't believe it. The first date she let me feel her all over and she gave me oral sex. It was eleventh grade. I never did that before. The first time I got laid it was bad. I came too early and we laughed, you know, it was a gang bang. Lucy said she never did it before, but she did what came naturally. So we went steady and I was at college two years, but we got engaged, and every chance we got we would try something new. We tried ticklers and vibrators, and one night she even got a girl friend so three of us could do it. You wouldn't believe it! I can't remember when the fun started wearing off. It was after we were married, about six months, maybe a year. I guess I stopped wanting it so often, but she didn't. She was always on me, fondling me and kissing me and telling me to say I loved her, and she told me how she sacrificed her innocence for me, and I didn't even want to touch her. Then I began to notice what a creep she was. . . .

Our female respondents were somewhat less mystical, although they were idealistic. They tended to believe the security and stability of marriage would change unpleasant mannerisms and modify bad habits.

MARILYN O'B.
Wally was a compulsive with women. He had to have a different one about every week. I knew that when I married him, but I chalked it up to youth and inexperience, and he didn't know how good I was. I didn't know how bad I was. I couldn't handle it, and I couldn't handle him, and by the beginning of our third month of marriage, Wally was out three or four times a week. He was doing it with everyone. Neighbors would smile funny at me, and I knew they knew. It didn't take long before I had to give it up. Less than a year. And now I know that if I ever do it again, I'm going to have to be sure of the guy's qualities and not expect that I can make him something he is not. I see Wally every now and then. He's still good for a wild night in bed—but not much else.

People pass critical judgments about their friends and intimates. They have one set of ideals they develop internally and another set of standards by which they compare their intimacies to what they imagine people outside the relationship have. Neither set of standards is reliable. Internal comparisons are usually based on unattainable utopian states. Outside comparisons are usually based on shadows or fantasies. In our own minds we can make people do whatever we want them to do. When we know someone well, our knowledge tends to limit the possible fantasies. With an outsider there is no limit to what we can imagine. Thus, it may be impossible for the partner to meet expectations even if he or she wanted to.

When talk turns to such topics as "I wish you would try to . . ." or "I am sure that Steve (or Stephanie) would . . ." things look pessimistic for the partner who is being compared. There doesn't appear to be an antidote to this kind of talk. Sometimes the partner who suffers from invidious comparisons tries very hard to compete, with no tangible results.

RUTH L.
It was about the beginning of our fifth year, after two children, then Ken started comparing me to people. First he commented on the effects the children had on the tension in my vagina. He believed that the babies had made me loose. So I checked with the gynecologist and tried some exercises. Then he talked about how some women faked orgasm, and so I tried very hard to come when he did. Then he talked about fetishes and how this girl at the office turned him on with the way she let her hair hang loose and her boots and bare legs. So I read Krafft-Ebbing and then I got a copy of Maribel Morgan's book. One night I dressed up. I got black patent leather boots with spiked heels and gun-metal fine mesh stockings and a black garter belt, and I dressed like that. I even did the Saran Wrap thing.

When he came home, I greeted him at the door in my housecoat, slipped it off, and stood there. I really wasn't all that bad. I could have made it in your everyday eight-dollar porn magazine. Ken was so shocked he couldn't talk. I started coming on to him, and he actually pushed me away so hard I fell down. "What the hell are you trying to do?" he screamed. Well, what I was trying to do was please the son of a bitch. I was the one that filed for divorce, and by the time I got through with him I got everything and he couldn't even see the kids. I don't know who he's comparing to whom these days, but I'm sure better off.

Belief in the Magical Healing Powers of Talk

Popular magazines have emphasized "communication" in marriage. The idea is to talk about things, endlessly if necessary, and after enough talk, things will work out. In the final analysis there is little good advice about what married couples should talk about. Many people have the idea that talk alone can solve anything.

There are two problems with communicating inside a marriage. First, if talk is not purposive, it can stir up trouble that really doesn't exist. No one is perfectly contented. The idea is to be as contented as possible and reward your mate for behaviors you appreciate. Constant talk about what could be not only stresses some egocentric issues that are harmful to marriage, but it tends to take attention away from behaviors that are working well. The alleged authorities tell married people to remind their partners constantly how much they care. Sometimes the result is bizarre.

RICH W. (to the marriage counselor)
You know, Selma, I don't really think it's possible to love anyone the way I love you. You are the only woman I ever cared about. That's why I think it is so important that you learn to appreciate some of the important cultural things that I find important, because it is not like you, you being almost perfection in so many things, to be so, well, you know, ignorant in your taste in music.

SELMA W. (to the marriage counselor)
I don't know what you're talking about. I'm not a musician. I listen to whatever is on. What the hell do you want from me?

RICH W.
I have this emotional thing, Selma, about how your beauty and personality synthesize with just the right music, you know, and you don't even think about it.

SELMA W.
So you mean I should stop listening to Tammy Wynette and George Jones? Ok, so what do you want me to listen to?

RICH W.
Selma, you are so beautiful when we talk like this, and I care so much about you and how much you mean to me.

SELMA W.
I think you're full of crap, Rich.

RICH W.
That's another part of it, Selma, the way you sometimes slip into language that—

Rich suffered from an overdose of popular-magazine advice giving. He really did not know what he wanted from Selma. He *did* want to talk about his choices in music and everything else, and apparently he wanted his wife to sense his preferences and select them even before he had made them known. Whether he cared about Selma as much as he claimed he did is moot. By the time he finished confusing Selma with alternate protestations of love and irrational criticisms, she was turned off. By the time Rich got a grip on what he was doing, Selma had made other choices, none of which were to continue talking to him.

Some of the more "effective" marriages we encountered were characterized by *negative spontaneity*. The partners carefully avoided saying anything they knew would offend the other. They treated each other like valuable business clients. While it is often a relief to get things "off your chest," it seemed to us that catharsis in a marriage relieved tensions in one partner only to stir them in the other. Effective marriage partners seem to be able to find other ways to release their tension.

GREG T.
When Marlene and I have to fight, we fight, but we try to make it on some issue, like what show should we see, or how should we invest the money, or what should we do about Thanksgiving, your mother or mine. We try to spell out the issues, you know, to be rational. Aside from that, anger and hostility should be reserved for enemies. Marlene and I know a lot about each other. We use that information to help us avoid getting on each other's nerves. It is very important to me that Marlene likes me. I know she loves me, but I want her to like me. She is fun to be with when she likes me and she likes me so long as I stay off the sensitive areas. You know, sometimes we sit quietly doing our own thing. She likes to read. I like TV. Sometimes it is better to be quiet and to save our talk to resolve important issues.

It is hard to know when to talk and when to remain silent. However, egocentric talk, selfish talk, ambiguous talk, and critical talk tend to stimulate discontent and trouble. Silence, on the other hand, is sometimes very reinforcing.

Changes in Goals

One of the most destructive forces in marriage is a unilateral goal change. When two people decide to marry, each one has some expectations for the other. Mostly the expectations are based on both experience and talk during earlier stages of the relationship. Expectations might include career choices, life-style, orientation toward relatives and friends, and so on. If the couple is not aware of how their life may change, they can make serious errors in goal setting.

When one partner discovers the other has changed in an important way, the entire relationship is disrupted. Though it is necessary for couples to find ways to adapt to changes both outside and inside the relationship, fundamental changes on which the relationship was originally based are very hard to handle.

CAROLINE H.
We sort of had an understanding when we got married that Bix would graduate from med school and intern and I would work until he did a residency in internal medicine, and then we would find a small town where he would practice and I would be official mother and head of the household. I never wanted a career doing anything other than being a small-town doctor's wife. It was one of those silly childhood dreams, but it looked like it was going to come true until the last year of the residency, when Bix got persuaded to join this research team at a big university in a big city. I can't handle big cities and I don't understand research, and it just didn't look like the place to bring up children. I tried it for a few years. I tried to talk to Bix about it. I tried going to school. Then I discovered I had to work because a researcher's income isn't anywhere near a doctor's income and a city costs more than a small town and there were no children and I cried a lot and I finally left him because he could never understand, no matter how I tried to talk to him about it, that I couldn't handle this change in goals.

Goals change for a number of reasons. Sometimes people make their commitments before their ideas have had a chance to crystallize. For example, men are often surprised when they discover their wife wants to continue working or, even worse, their wife must continue working to make ends meet. Economic contingencies and major changes in society, such as recessions, require goal changes. If the relationship does not have a means by which the partners can understand why goals are changing and through which adjustments can be made, no amount of talk can keep the relationship together.

Another characteristic of solid and satisfying relationships was the existence of mutual goals, shared ambitions. Though each partner might have some private accomplishments in mind, by and large, there was agreement on such matters as homebuilding, investment plans, career ambitions, and retirement. This kind of understanding does not guarantee the quality of the relationship, but a common purpose can often generate cooperative behavior.

WINSTON K.

Cornelia settled into that retirement community in New Mexico as if it had been home all her life, but inside of a week I knew it wasn't going to work for me. I liked golf, all right, but I liked it when I had to sneak it. When I discovered I could play every day all day, it lost its value. I liked fishing, about once a year. I wanted to paint, but only on Saturday afternoon while Cornelia listened to the opera. And I hated eternal sunshine. I needed a little rain in my life, in a lot of ways. Age sixty was a little too early for me to become a vegetable and they needed my kind of engineering, so I took a job with a small company in Montana, and I told Cornelia she could come or stay, but I was going back to work. Believe it or not, I don't miss Cornelia at all. I found a friend, a tough lady accountant who understands the business. She has enough money, she doesn't want to get married. We are living together up here. Cornelia is getting a lot of sympathy down there, and so far the bills are being paid. When I really get too old to work, I don't know what'll happen, but at least I won't waste five or ten years waiting to find out what it is like to be senile.

Appeals to Outside Parties

Talking too much to too many people can often end a relationship. We have already mentioned that people tend to talk about their relationships with outsiders rather than with their partners. People who have solid and satisfying relationships develop the facility to talk about important issues in a sensible and problem-solving way. Talk to bartenders or even psychiatrists sometimes does little more than reinforce discontent and help the aggrieved partner become more resentful.

It is even more disruptive to talk about the relationship with family or well-meaning friends. When outsiders try to intervene to "save the relationship," they document betrayals. It comes like a bolt from the blue when one partner discovers that he or she has been the topic of conversation with outsiders.

GWEN C.

She said, "I know you'll think I'm a busybody and this will hurt a little, but Fred has been talking to George about your frigidity since the baby, and since George and I went through it after Winky came, I know I can help you. After all, you don't want to lose your husband to some heavy-breathing fox who—" She was really happy about it. She had me. She knew I was inferior to her because she was humping with her husband and I wasn't doing it with mine. She didn't know anything about what was going on in our house, and I didn't know Fred was advertising it, but that silly bastard really did it this time. I told her to get the hell out. I knew she'd go away feeling sorry for me, but I didn't want to see her again, and I didn't want to see that lying, sneaking husband of mine either. I packed my clothes and important things, and I got a cab, and I left, and I didn't leave an address.

Generally, it does not help for one partner to try to save the relationship. Most marriage counselors urge both partners to be present when discussing problems in the relationship. When both parties are not present, alternate interpretation of events and feelings can get very confusing. Furthermore, friends and family usually want to become involved. Most of the time their actions are at best upsetting and more often destructive. Once the confidentiality of a relationship is broken, there is little possibility of rebuilding trust. Virtually all our divorced informants mentioned betrayal of confidence as the beginning of the end.

Violation of Privacy

Intimate couples should not spend all their time together. Each person needs private space and aspects of their life that are confidential. Humans are, to an extent, territorial animals. They may not need much territory to call their own, but if they do not have a space over which they can exert control, they become discontented and disrespectful of the space of others. Reserving a favorite chair or leaving the room when the partner is on the phone can often be enough to show respect for privacy.

Prurient curiosity about the small details of the partner's life can be very annoying. The broad events of the day either on the job or in the home are better topics of talk than each sharpened pencil or changed diaper. Fumbling through billfolds or household papers may be innocent acts, but they connote deceit and suspicion. Questions such as "Why did you take so long shopping?" or "What did you do at work so late?" imply suspicion. "Who did you see?" or "Who was working with you?" accuse.

It may be relatively easy to brush off the first invasion of privacy as a sign of intense interest, but small acts add up and create a mood of uneasiness. Everyone has something to hide, even from their most intimate partner. It is seldom productive for one partner to cross-examine the other and intimidate him or her into disclosing hostilities and suspicions. Once a hostile matter is revealed, the next step is blackmail and intimidation. Once the first breach of confidence takes place, the descent from suspicion to contempt to hostility is very rapid.

The right to privacy is paradoxical because it is important to know whether you are being used or abused in a relationship. Extended absences from home without explanation, strange phone calls, and locked file drawers may suggest mischief is taking place. It is difficult to know when to probe. However, we can learn from the successful relationships we encountered. All the people involved in long-term, reliable relationships talked of the intense trust they had in their partner. Of course, these relationships had lasted a long enough time for trust to be earned. There is little advice on how to survive the earning years.

Trivial Discords

Intimate relationships make people vulnerable to many sorts of attacks. The basic structure of an intimate relationship can be eroded over time by an accumulation of trivial offenses and insults. We will let some of our interviewees testify to these statements. Each of the following statements represents a kind of communication assault reported by at least one-fourth of our respondents.

STEVE P.
I can never understand what Carol is complaining about. She acts as if something terrible is going on, but I can't seem to get her to name names or tell me where or what. She hollers and cries and accuses and then gradually simmers down. I usually apologize, but I don't know what for.

SALLY R.
He always says "always." I mean he *always* says it. He never reacts as if something happened for the first time or happens occasionally. If I am late coming home from work, he says, "How come you can't ever get home on time?" If I burn something for dinner, he says, "You'll never learn to cook, will you?" If I am gloomy about something that happened at work, he says, "How come you're never happy?" If I complain about something he did, he says, "How come you are always on my case?" He always, and I mean *always*, responds the same damn way.

LINDA Z.
When he gets on a roll in an argument, everything comes tumbling out. He can start complaining that he needs a dress shirt to pack for a trip and then he gets on me about doing the laundry, keeping house, spending too much at the store, not raising the kids properly, and then he will start on my not finishing college and not taking a job and not managing money and being jealous. He remembers everything he ever complained about in order, and with every new complaint he recites all the old ones, too. Even if I wanted to do something to make up for it, I wouldn't know which complaint to react to, so I usually tell him just to screw off and I leave the house till he settles down.

BOB H.
She really gets emotional. Anytime something comes up between us, she gets

emotional. I wouldn't mind it, you know, when there's an argument you feel a lot of emotion, but she gets as emotional about me spilling something at dinner as she did the time she caught me fooling around with Jackie at the office Christmas party. I can't tell how important things are to her because she is usually crying and sobbing so much she can't make herself clear.

NORA O'M.

He really can't keep anything to himself. He lets me know what is on his mind all the time, whether I care or not. It comes out in an endless stream of talk, "Nora, how about fixing a drink, I sure am tired, Bill did something rotten at the office, why did they put Dan Rather on instead of Roger Mudd? what are we having for dinner? I don't like those pants you're wearing, did you hear from your sister about when she is coming? someone took my parking space in the lot this morning, did you pay the electric bill? I don't like the new kind of mouthwash you got," and so on.

GUS W.

Our arguments don't seem to follow any pattern. We jump to solutions before we have the problem, and we talk about causes and conditions at the same time. I make a proposal and she gives me more details. I try to provide some details and she's arguing for a proposal. The long and short of it is that our arguments end when we get tired of jawing. We never settle anything. The same issues seem to keep coming up because we just don't have a way to get out of the trap.

WENDY T.

I think Walt is more interested in his one-liners than he is in the issues that come up. When we get into a fight, he sort of waits for the right moment and then he delivers the slam or the insult or the pun. Sometimes I'll say something that doesn't come out right and he picks right up on it. I'll be madder than hell, and he's laughing about the way I talk. I haven't ever been able to get him to talk seriously about anything. Before we were married, I really thought it was cute the way he laughed his way out of everything. What I didn't notice was that he never gave in. His laughing was just his way of saying that he's going to do it his way no matter what you want or how important it is to you.

ELAINE M.

We often don't use the same language. He is so darn complicated in the way he talks I don't understand him most of the time, and I talk, you know, like a normal person, and I use slang a lot, and he doesn't understand me when I talk. We go round and round and neither of us understands. If we could just take a minute to make sure we understand, we could probably settle things.

Most of the people we talked to knew how to settle an argument. The problem was that in the heat of battle they were too interested in winning to worry about resolving. It was hard to tell what the net effect of problem communications was on relationships. A great many people seemed to feel that if they could have improved the way they talked, they might have saved their relationships. Those who cherished their relationships felt that good talk had a lot to do with it. But both concepts were elusive. We could not draw any conclusions about what good talk was and what kind of talk seemed to have a negative influence. For some couples it was important to shout and emote and "have it out." Other couples feared noisy arguments. Some couples seemed to work things out systematically, something like a trouble-shooting conference in industry. Other couples felt that systematic problem solving was not sufficiently deep and emotional to handle their problems. Thus, though everyone could identify what kind of talk they found useful and what they objected to, it was very hard for them to explain it to us, and sometimes even more difficult to educate their partner.

Blackmail, Bribery, and Intimidation

One last important point remains. We encountered some couples (confirmed by the literature) whose relationships were based on one party brutalizing and humiliating the other. Most frequently, a male had taken total possession of a female. She was completely submissive, a virtual servant. He ordered her about, punished her when she did not meet his expectations, and ignored her most of the time. The problem of battered wives gained our attention as a result of publicity provided within the women's movements. Most of our respondents tried very hard to avoid the topic. A recent study conducted by a major national publication stated that one-third of the wives in this country had been struck by their husband at least once.

There is no question that some marriages are based on intimidation. The physically stronger party, usually the male, keeps the weaker member of the relationship in complete subjugation. We encountered a number of women who reported little or no contact with anyone outside the home. Though they did not complain of intimidation, their pattern of response at least suggested that they were kept under close control by their husbands. The play *Lysistrata,* in which the wives kept the husbands under control by withholding sexual favors, seems more mythological these days, given the consistency of reports that nearly three-quarters of the husbands have had intercourse with someone outside of the marriage. Women held under control appear to have little recourse, even less chance of escape, and few agencies of society to which to turn.

The issue of physical violence in relationships is very much a part of the contemporary ethic. The issue of marital combat and discord constitutes a great part of our culture. A large proportion of our serious and comic literature is based on it. Though couples ostensibly marry to find harmony, security, and love, the prevailing belief is that marriages are characterized by a wide variety of tensions. Couples must establish an orientation to sexuality, personal growth, career, finances, logistics, and relations with people outside the marriage. Questions about whether to have children, what life-style to have, and what goals to pursue preoccupy the orientation of the couple, while each individual continues to retain idiosyncratic urges for vocational, social, and personal growth. The dream is that marriage will facilitate personal growth through shared commitment and activity. The reality is that couples find it very hard to relate to each other.

The idea that we can only become people when we interact with others pushes us toward what the ethologists call pair-bonding. Some animals practice pair-bonding to produce and raise young. Humans seek something more from their bonds, although they are hard put to say in words what they are seeking. Harry Stack Sullivan said humans seek *security* and *satisfaction*. Security comes from knowing that someone cares enough about you to consider your personal needs. Satisfaction comes from someone providing comfort, pleasure, and concern without demanding immediate returns. Relationships in which both parties derive security and satisfaction are characterized by equitable exchanges. One person is not dedicated to the welfare of the other with no hope of return. Martyrdom or altruism does not appear to be a good basis for a healthy relationship. Martyrs and altruists are resented sooner or later. Our urge to get together with others is sometimes so great we idealize the potential of marriage far beyond its ability to provide rewards. We endow the state of marriage with magical powers. We believe matrimony alone is sufficient to meet our relationship needs. But our personal problems often get in the way of effective pairing. We have just reviewed some of the kinds of discord that prevent equitable bonding. We will now examine the process by which couples dissolve their unions and individuals return to a single, and often lonely, state.

LOVE AND DIVORCE

We begin with the premise that processes create change, and we must accept the fact that, almost without exception, all things (good and bad) must pass. Viewed this way, it does seem remarkable that some humans who contribute to and are affected by these processes manage to remain friends or lovers over a lifetime. We have already discussed the rarity of lifelong friends; we are now ready to discuss the rarity of lifelong lovers.

Most people marry believing they will remain married. Either they believe the sanctity of matrimony will make it work out, or they believe their love is so perfect that nothing will ever come between them. They believe divorce or separation happens to others. If your marriage fails, it is your own damn fault. You knew what you were getting into. You blew it. Your relationship will fail, but ours will remain eternal. The mystique of young lovers is based on believing that no one has ever felt the way we feel.

When we asked people who had never divorced about divorce, virtually all seemed to rule it out as an alternative. Those who had divorced parents were a bit more realistic, although they claimed they could benefit by contemplating their parents' mistakes. People who had divorced and remarried were almost cynical about the possibilities. They had learned that they could try again. People who had divorced and never remarried appeared to be almost conditioned against marriage. Many seemed to go to extreme lengths to develop relationships that did not obligate them to make a permanent commitment. This, in turn, had a serious impact on the people with whom they related.

DENNIS K.
By the time you are forty, you know you want something permanent in your life. I like women and I like to go to bed with them. I have spent a great deal of my life searching for the perfect lay. I think it has interfered with my career. I married twice, to very good women, both of whom divorced me because I couldn't keep from testing new flesh in bed. Gradually, I discovered that not only was I not getting pleasure out of sex, but I was not even able to do it well anymore. I went to the doctor and discovered that I had a prostate condition. Now I had a real problem because I discovered that I wanted the closeness and the companionship of a woman, but I didn't know any way to come at them other than sexually. I have had a couple of connections recently that ended because the woman wanted to go to bed and I couldn't. One of them threw me out, literally, calling me a "diseased bastard" and accusing me of trying to pollute her. I don't know whether they can cure my physical condition. I am even more concerned about my psychological condition because I am going to have to learn now what I should have learned before I got married the first time. Maybe if I had learned it, I wouldn't be in the mess I'm in now.

About 40 percent of the people who get married get divorced. This rate is higher in some regions of the country than in others, and the rate varies according to age. If you live in California and are in your late twenties, there's a good chance that you have already been divorced once and are considering it a second time.

There are several important ways of interpreting why the times we live in make separation and divorce commonplace. For example, we know our increased mobility contributes to the fact that we will encounter more people in our lifetimes than our parents or grandparents did. We also know the more people we encounter, the more possibilities for relationships we have. Divorced people tend to report similar patterns of falling in and out of love—a "serial relationship phenomenon." You meet someone and marry them; if it doesn't work out, you drop them and find someone else. Because we do not want to be lonely, we prefer having serial relationships to having no relationships at all. If we are a known loser in our hometown, we can always pack our bags and move somewhere else. As long as both men and women buy into this ethic, divorce will be both commonplace and cheap, although not painless.

Thus, a second reason for the increase in the divorce rate is its more general acceptability. We all know people who have been divorced. They seem to be perfectly all right. They do not exist in a state of moral depravity, although sometimes we must be very careful of them because they do pose threats to our existing relationships.

VANESSA C.
The general rule is that when one of the girls you hang around with gets divorced, you don't invite her into your home anymore. You keep seeing her because you know she needs your friendship, but divorced women are a real threat to you because your husband will think they are available and they are usually so lonely they are willing to have sex in order to get a man to pay attention to them. Don't get me wrong. I am not insecure about my husband, but he is a normal, red-blooded guy, and he gets a hard-on when he sees a good-looking woman, and I know if he had a good opportunity to do it, he would. I suppose I have to put up with the idea that he may be doing it with strangers when he goes on business trips, for example, but I don't think I could take it if I found out he was doing it with one of my close friends. Listen, if I got divorced, I'd get it any way I could, you know.

A third reason for divorce involves our preoccupation with ourselves. Our society is characterized by narcissistic messages. We are told to look out for ourselves, to fulfill ourselves, to achieve to the limit of our capabilities, and to get over anyone who might stand in our way. If our relations with others do not consistently reward us, we abandon them. At an early sign of trouble, we start to make contingency plans for escape. After all, you only live so many years, right? The fantasies start. Why be unhappy? Why not "grab for all the gusto you can get"? Many writers, including Richard Sennett (1978) and Christopher Lasch (1978), have railed against the tyrannies of intimacy in the latter half of the twentieth century. We have, essentially, been taught to be selfish in our marriages and our friendships and to demand that our friends and lovers do for us what we want done.

Narcissistic exchanges are largely accidental, not planned. When we encounter someone for whom we can provide and who also provides for us, then we have a relationship, so long as the rewards retain their value and keep coming. In essence, the notion of looking out for the other person and of working out exchanges with him or her seems to have been abandoned. The question of whether easy divorce has led to selfish marriages or whether the urge to be selfish has led to easy divorce cannot be answered, but the connection between the two is undeniable.

These three reasons—mobility, acceptance, and narcissism—all induce us to look at the problem of divorce and separation as something created by mysterious forces beyond our control. After all, we can't change society. We can't help it if we meet more people than our ancestors did, nor can we help our biological programming for self-interest and protection. Nobody is advocating a return to viewing divorce as a disease affecting only the sinful and inept. But these three contributing causes of the problem do not account for what happens in a marriage when it begins to end.

Individuals are responsible for divorce. It is not social pressures, but individual responses to social pressures that make marriages end. In the first place, not everyone divorces. Some couples (in fact, probably a majority) stay together because it is the best available alternative. That does not mean the marriage is euphoric, filled with unbroken joy. They have ac-

cepted "for better and for worse" and discovered there would be more "worse" outside the marriage. There is a sizable minority who stay together in unutterably painful relationships either because of religious commitments or because one partner will not let the other escape. We are not trying to make the case for either marriage or divorce. We are trying to point to the issues people must face to make productive decisions about which path to take.

When we discussed divorces with divorced people, they did not talk of mobility, the acceptability of divorce, or narcissism. These reasons are assigned by outside investigators for purposes of convenient explanation. The reasons they offered were personal and specific. They were filled with charge and countercharge, despair and hopelessness, resentment and hostility. They blamed themselves and each other. As far as they were concerned, their divorce was a unique event, shaped by their personalities. No matter what kinds of generalizations "experts" could make, they saw themselves as exceptions.

They were not exceptional, however. The statements they made grouped neatly into categories. We made no effort to figure out what proportion of divorces was accounted for by each category. What we present are reasons given for divorce by at least one-fourth of our sample. Of course, it all adds up to more than one hundred, because virtually no one had just one reason for divorcing. To understand them we will let typical representatives of these categories speak for the others that presented similar ideas.

JENNIFER N.

He cheated on me. I guess the old words were "he done me wrong." Someone else was "getting all his best." Every one of those damned pop songs described what he was doing "behind closed doors." Look at me, dammit, I am a good-looking woman and I know what to do in bed. I am thirty years old and in my prime, and he was picking up high school seniors and doing it with them. That was intolerable, and I will not be insulted that way.

KEN D.

We could never settle an argument. We'd get something started—it didn't matter what it was—and each of us had to have the last word. I think I tried giving in from time to time, but she never even noticed, and she never gave in, ever. We could argue about what kind of ball-point pen to buy or how to invest several thousand dollars, and the result was always the same: an endless brawl. We just never settled anything. She did what she wanted to do and I did what I wanted to do and we never did anything in common. I'm surprised we stayed together for five years.

MARTY J.
Everything she did surprised me. When we got married, she was going to work for two or three years so we could get some equity; then we would start a family. But she decided to go to night school and then she got a good job as an accountant and she was making more than I was and she decided she didn't want children and she didn't seem to want me either because our marriage really was a trivial part of her life.

HARRIET W.
We didn't have any fun. It wasn't that Joe didn't love me. He loved me a lot, but everything was so serious. When we had someone over, it was three, four days of planning, and when we took a trip he had everything logged and worked out in detail. There was never anything spontaneous. We couldn't just get up and go out to eat. He had me planning the menus a week in advance, and every Saturday he was on my back with the coupons and he mobilized the kids into such a schedule that it seemed like I was driving all day long. Then Sheila graduated and went to college, and then William graduated and went to college, and my old roommate, Susan, turned up in town all neatly divorced, and she wanted to take a trip around the world, and I had enough money saved from my household budget in an account Joe didn't know about, and I got my passport and took off and left him a note and when I came home, I started divorce proceedings, because now it was time for me to have fun.

GEORGE P.
It was like we slid into it. There were several of us who hung around together at the country club and parties on the weekends, you know, like a clique. The first brawl was up at the Harvey's cabin on the lake. Dennis and Jane got into a battle about something or other and a week later they were separated. That sort of triggered something, I guess, in all of us. I know I started bickering with Mary, and we got to talking about whether it would happen to us and we were so aware of the possibility of divorcing that I guess we talked ourselves into it. We were the third couple in our group to go, and now out of the five of us, only Art and Marilyn are still together.

DAWN D.
He didn't want much, just everything. I worked, he worked, but when I came home, I had to take care of his needs and do the house and listen to him talk about his problems and pat his aching little head. I never got a kind word or any kind of a hearing. He wanted kids, and I would just as soon go to hell as have kids because he wouldn't hear of me not working. I don't know what he thought I was made of, but I wasn't made of it. It took me two years to get up the guts to walk, and then I quit my job, came home, packed, and moved out. I took every stick of furniture, every dish, everything we owned in common. I left him a damned empty apartment and a note that dared him to come after it. I thought if the bastard would at least take a day off from work and come and talk to me about it, there might be a chance because before we got married he was a pretty good guy, but he didn't take a day off from work and we fought it out in court, and it was a mess, but I got him good, and I am going to be damned careful before I do it again.

JANE L.
He hit me once and I refused to let it happen again.

JANE T.
It took me three years to learn you couldn't stay married to an alcoholic.

PAUL R.
She laid there like a stick when we had intercourse. She didn't make a sound. She just laid there. She refused to believe she could have any fun with it, and I couldn't have any fun with it, so I found someone else.

The days when you could not get divorced unless you had an eight-by-ten glossy picture of your "beloved" in the sack with another person are over. Divorce laws allow a great many reasons and excuses, and no-fault divorce makes it a matter of mutual consent. The net result is that people do not stay in unsatisfactory relationships. The unwelcome result is that a great many people do not work very hard to make their relationships satisfactory because it is so easy to escape.

HOW PEOPLE RESPOND TO THEIR DIVORCES

In one scenario the theme seems to be "relief and mutual good riddance." In many ways this is, perhaps, the "best" kind of divorce, for neither party is particularly sorrowful nor are they excessively charged emotionally. It is not likely that the mate will want to come back or commit suicide. In fact, with this kind of attitude, there is some reasonable possibility of mutually working out the details.

This ideal scenario may be what the writers in women's magazines have in mind when they discuss "friendly divorce." It was our experience that none of the fifty-odd divorced couples we talked to were particularly friendly. Some kept contact because of the kids or some other common interest. The majority appeared to be perfectly willing to keep away from each other.

In a second scenario the theme is "the desperate escape." Very often the scripts for these scenarios seem to be drawn from bestselling novels or movies.

It is a sunny day and we are driving down a beautiful street without a care in the world or an evil thought in our mind. Suddenly we turn in the driveway and see our beloved locked in a horny embrace with a recently separated neighbor. We are dazed and confused and filled with betrayal. We deliberately move the gearshift from neutral to drive and just keep on going. In El Paso we sell the car to a shifty character for bus fare to San Diego. In San Diego we avoid mentioning our name, and do not accept long distance phone calls. We join a self-help group and try to work it out. . . .

The desperate escape scenario may also result from a sudden violent outburst. A simple family argument can become a fight, and the last one standing (or living) may beat a hasty retreat from the scene of the crime, escaping from what may have been an imagined prison to a real one. If the fight merely ended with a bloodied nose or blacked eye, the injured party may run away from the relationship, leaving only bad memories and bloodstains behind.

ALLAN E.
We fought all the way back from my parents' place. It was a wonder I didn't wreck the car. Anyway, we got back to our apartment and I couldn't get the damned door open, so I just kicked it down. She started yelling at me and I hit her too. I never felt so much anger in my life. I really wanted to kill her. It was the look in her eyes that stopped me. She had been really angry, but now she was totally frightened. She looked up at me like she never knew me before that moment. I felt it too. It was awful. I reached down to her, you know, like to help her up, but she just crawled away like a scared animal. I went outside and vomited in the snow. I had done something I never believed I was capable of doing and there was no way to "take it back." In a way I felt worse about me than I did about Ellen. So I just left town. I wrote her a letter about a week or so later and told her I was sorry and to keep everything we had. I just had to be rid of her and the things in our life. She never answered the letter.

The unilateral divorce is particularly painful. When one party is consumed with hostility or hatred, it is difficult for the deserted party to adapt. Sometimes there is depression and self-deprecation. It is clear that in any marriage all the power is with the person who cares the least. But the tendency is for the aggrieved party to be tolerant and understanding and to blame him or herself. Many marriage counselors advise developing a healthy hostility in order to help adjust to the "desertion."

WILLIAM J.
There will never be an other woman like Carol. I miss her. I am living with a beautiful creature and in a month we will get married, but I still miss Carol. Carol split and I still don't know why. She won't talk to me. It was a bad divorce for me, but she seemed so relieved. I don't even know where she is, but every so often I find myself looking at her picture and Susan sometimes reminds me that she is not Carol or tells me that I should stop talking about Carol. I don't know how my marriage to Susan is going to be because the shadow of Carol is still with me.

There is a sense of newly discovered "freedom" for the escapee. This kind of split is usually the result of a relationship in which one partner perceived himself or herself to be exploited. There was usually some activity or goal one partner wanted that the other partner could not understand or would not tolerate. The escape was often sudden, with the departing partner plunging into the previously forbidden activity.

Neighbors are usually surprised when the separation occurs; these were always such wonderfully happy people, they say. Friends and family usually sensed something was wrong but hoped things would work out. After the divorce the departing partner may feel guilty, but the guilt diminishes fairly quickly. For the one left behind, bewilderment is immediate, followed by guilt, which turns into resentment after a while. Neither is immediately ready for another marriage.

HARRY D.

I guess we both saw it coming for a long time. We had this silly notion that the kids would be better off if we stayed together, so we stayed together and we were careful only to fight when the kids weren't around. But she had Lenore really hostile to me, and I suppose I said nasty things about her to Kennie. Little Anne was just completely bewildered. She was really too young for this kind of battle. The whole thing came to a head when I discovered that she was actually getting it on with a friend of mine. She knew I kept a mistress, and I wouldn't have minded if she had done it with a stranger, but this was one of my closest friends and I looked like a damned fool. When I confronted her with it, she was cold as a clam. She just said, "Let's divorce." And then she ordered me out of the house. From then on it was war, and not cold war either.

MARY D.

Harry and I turned off after Lenore. We had Kennie to keep the marriage together. We had Anne by accident. We each had our real experiences outside the marriage. We learned to hate each other, and even though we never yelled, everyone knew. Friends kept telling us to split, but we agreed on one thing: The kids needed both a mother and father. Well, screw that crap. The kids have a mother now, and their mother makes damn well sure they never see their father. At the hearing I brought up everything, his mistress, his addiction to prescription drugs, his gambling, and I even brought up the time I found him in bed with Little Anne, "comforting her" he said. And he could never tag me for intercourse with Dan. Dan stood up for me and comforted me, we never had intercourse, and after the divorce he and his wife were my best friends.

This kind of scenario can get very ugly. Often the theme is nihilism and mutual destruction. Neither party seems content to separate and let bygones be bygones. Both people are interested in hurting each other, sometimes physically, usually psychologically and socially. When children are involved, they often bear the burden of guilt, believing, somehow, they were responsible for the failure of the marriage. In extreme cases, this kind of divorce features childnapping and various sorts of blackmail. Individuals who have come out of this kind of marriage are often unfit for remarriage, because they have a tendency to make their new partner carry the sins of the old one.

There is a good chance for divorce in second marriages. The probability is based on the inability of divorced individuals to understand the role they played in the first divorce. Often, the same problems that characterized the first marriage were carried into the second marriage. In some cases the new partner was able to resolve issues that defied the efforts of the first partner. Mostly, however, second and third marriages are risky gambles.

IS LOVE BETTER THE SECOND TIME AROUND?

As children we learn not to touch hot objects. Inevitably we do touch them, however, and usually we receive a burn. The next time we know better, and before picking up an iron skillet from the stove we wear a protective glove.

The human tendency to believe we have learned valuable lessons from being in unpleasant circumstances applies to both friendships and love affairs. What we have learned is debatable. The debate becomes more intense when we examine the longevity and reported satisfaction of second marriages.

We have found that divorced women tend to live in reduced financial circumstances. Unless they have a college degree and some work experience, many learn to live on limited income: welfare or alimony. Often the adjustment to single life is painful. Most single men regard divorcées as available sex partners. Women who divorce after age thirty-five have fewer chances to remarry. Men on the marriage market prefer younger women less sophisticated in the possibilities of being harmed.

Many divorced women are almost gallant in the way they try to keep their lives together. The media honor them (*One Day at a Time*). People have sympathy for their problems. When children are involved, they are often regarded as inconveniences. Problems of custody and visitation are not easy to solve. The typical ex-wife resents the fact her ex-husband seems to have more choices, whereas she is locked into child care and support problems. The presence of children makes her a less desirable companion. Her social encounters are marked by sexual crises. She often sees her ex-husband as receiving all the advantages.

Divorced men usually fare a little better. They usually keep most of their income. Most divorce laws no longer provide for automatic alimony, and child support usually amounts to less than it costs to maintain the children before the divorce. But emotional strain shows. It is often as hard to be lonely as it is to be poor. Guilt and fear of failure often press them into working harder. They wonder what's happening to the kids, and the nagging loneliness drives many of them to prostitutes, singles bars, or other places where they think they can find easy women. They believe that a "roll in the hay" will solve their problems, but they discover that sex in their marriage meant more than physical satisfaction. Making new relationships is complicated by the memory of problems in the first marriage, and the irksome feeling that the divorce should never have happened. Some keep going back, trying to maintain contact with their ex-wife. They resent it when she finds a new partner.

We found divorced men often develop elaborate rationalizations for abandoning their wife and children. Many will tell you their children are "better off" without them around. They say that as fathers they were less than they should have been. Others claim children are too protected and need to feel the sense of independence that comes from knowing you either make it in this world or you don't. Some claim they hardly knew their wives and children anyway. Or didn't want to.

It is no secret that both men and women frequently become alcoholics or drug users when their marriages fail. Many spend considerable time trying to "sort out" their lives or "find themselves." Whatever the reason for the divorce, it is seldom pleasant or easy to adjust to single life again. Many divorced people find they have lost basic social skills and find it hard to make new relationships.

For this reason many newly divorced individuals seek to become newly marrieds again. There may have been someone waiting in the wings to whom a commitment has already been made. Being alone makes you vulnerable, and a warm and sympathetic human can be very enticing. Most people who remarry are aware that the odds of a split are higher with the second arrangement than with the first. Most feel their need for a meaningful and rewarding human relationship outweighs the odds. They also remind themselves that what they learned in their first marriage will help them handle the second one more effectively. Sometimes, it works.

FRED O.

Linda and I divorced when I was fifty. The kids were grown. It was kind of a despairing divorce. I had had a good career and I always thought Linda was dedicated to it, but she made it clear she wanted a career of her own and she felt it was not too late. She planned to go back to graduate school. There was enough money, there was no real problem. I was very sad for a while afterward, and I had rather painful relationships, not sexual, with a couple of women. One was very religious and wanted to make me over. One was very pretty and wanted to be displayed. Finally I met Anna. Her husband had died in the second year of the marriage. There were no children, and so she became very good at what she did. She had a satisfactory career. We could both retire early and we did. We talked over very carefully how we were going to live, what we each wanted, and what we wanted together. Would you believe that we will celebrate our silver wedding anniversary this year? I learned a lot about being considerate from Linda, and Anna knew a lot about what it meant to be lonely, and we really did well together.

What do we know about second partners? Men often seem to seek a younger edition of their first wife. Women tend to seek a smoother edition of their ex-husband. It is almost as if they want to repeat the mistakes they made. More men remarry than women. The number of divorced women is increasing steadily. They would, if properly mobilized, make a powerful political force.

For both men and women there are special problems associated with "blending in" with old friends and family members. Alan Alda's film *The Four Seasons* gives an accurate description of what happens when a middle-aged man falls in love with a young lovely and then attempts to act as if she had been part of his life all along. Simply put, his friends do not know how to treat the new mate. Nor do they know how to respond to statements made about the old mate. Very often the new couple tries too hard, causing divisions between and among friends that lead to lost friendships and hard feelings. Many divorced people who remarry discover that they must make all new friends, since their old friends may still be relating to their former partner. This creates some serious problems in families, particularly when grown children decide to marry and need to work out the politics of having their natural parents at the wedding with new mates.

So is love better the second time around?

According to our research, the answer would be a definite "it depends." Women seem more satisfied with second marriages (or living together) than men do. Women also seem more urgent about remarrying though less able to do so. Men seem to become more romantic the second time around. Middle-aged divorced men, particularly, seem to want to recover their youth. When they marry a younger partner, there is often a brief glow and possibly offspring. Disappointments occur when they discover how hard it is to raise children when they are in their mid-forties. Both men and women defy easy generalizations. In a few cases they report being happier than ever before, and in a few cases they admit to being more miserable. More often than not, they simply do not know whether their life is better. There is just more of a need to make it better.

THE VIRTUES OF LOVE, REVISITED

We all know life without love is hardly a life at all. We need to be needed, to establish some form of permanent relationship to buffer us against the constancy of change in the world. We need the feeling that accompanies love, the sense of timelessness and common purpose, the sense of excitement about our partners.

We are reared to believe that love will happen to us, and something is wrong with us if we are not loved. We grow up to believe that we deserve a perfect love, despite all our shortcomings, problems, and woes. We want love so badly we are willing to risk heavily for it.

The excuses we give for remaining single are usually feeble:

I haven't found the right one.
My job interferes.
I have obligations to my mother and dad.
I am ambivalent about my sexual preferences.
I am too set in my ways.

We offer excuses, but we usually do not really believe them and we are prepared to discard them when we have an opportunity to make a "relationship."

How much do we really know about being in love? How much do we know about what makes one love affair last a lifetime and another fail after the first few months? "Scientific investigation" has revealed very little information. We probably know less about love than we do about the nature of the universe (which is hardly anything at all). We probably know more about hating than loving, for we often hate with great success and love with only limited talents. As the philosopher Eric Hoffer asked: "Why is it that we always believe there is strength in those we hate, and only weakness in those we love?" Perhaps it is an unanswerable question.

We may need to begin at the beginning in our attempt to draw some conclusions about love. We need to go back and look at how we learn about loving or—more to the point—how we *don't* learn about loving. We are raised on myths about love without even being told they are myths. Our myths are fed by the media. We think we will live our lives like the people we see in movies or on soap operas. We are barraged with advice on how to be a "real" man and a "fulfilled" woman. We are instructed in sex as if we are all priapic athletes.

The instructions we are given about loving are usually personal conclusions based on one person's limited success. Sex education is largely concerned with the proper identification of genitals, not the proper identification of a suitable mate. In the end we seem to be a society of prowlers and alley cats, stalking the streets and downtown lounges for others, who, like ourselves, are hoping to be "discovered." We will settle for being fed and needed, probably in that order.

We emerge from our study of couples a little saddened. We have heard and recorded what people say about their present and former mates, and we sense a great deal of despair. We hear a lot about communication, but we have found few people who seem to know how to do it. We hear a lot about "love" but very little about *loving acts*.

Most people we talked to were surprised when we suggested they had some control over the outcome of their relationships. We found a great many people believe in fates and furies and are really unwilling to take responsibility for their behavior toward others. We found a great many people who were careful and considerate in their public dealing with their colleagues at work, with tradesmen and strangers and social acquaintances, and absolutely unfeeling or uncaring in their relationships with the ones they allegedly loved. We arrived at the opinion that somewhere in the area of applying public rules of consideration to our private relationships, there may be the secret of successful intimacy. The couples who seemed satisfied with their relationships provided the consistent evidence. The crucial questions are: *Can* we learn from the mistakes of others and is it really possible to modify our own style of living and relating? At this time we cannot answer the questions.

chapter six

Enemies: Hatred and other emotions we have known and loved

If you want to make someone into an enemy,
first do him a favor.

Murphy's Laws (Revised)

He hasn't an enemy in the world
and none of his friends like him.

OSCAR WILDE

If you have no enemies,
it is a sign fortune has forgot you.

THOMAS FULLER

If you are looking
for a better love affair,
it's a sign you are probably having a bad one.

Old Fraternity proverb

Somewhere in the world,
there must be a place that is occupied by only the front halves of horses.
Considering the population of our country,
that's the only way
I can account for the absence of them here.

The authors

THE SPECIAL PROBLEM
OF HAVING ENEMIES

Standard procedure in an old-fashioned mystery is for the great detective to ask the widow of the murder victim, "Did he have any enemies?" "No," she replies and then begins to enumerate them: the old lady he dispossessed, the artist whose paintings he destroyed, the colleague he insulted in a public place, the ward whose money he embezzled, and possibly, the inventor whose patent he stole. Given this delectable array of suspects, the detective would find someone with an even greater motive: perhaps the butler, once a noble, whom he was blackmailing, or even his wife, whose chastity he took only to spend his seed with women of easy virtue in Soho.

What answer would you give about your spouse or loved one if the great detective asked you the question? If you are like the people we spoke to the answer would be, "No, he [she] had no enemies, except, maybe, well . . ."

For the most part, we like to think of our enemies as abstractions and we pride ourselves on being able to control our emotions about them. These two myths are perhaps the most destructive findings in our study of friendships and intimate relationships. Because people tend to deny the possibility of having enemies, we are bewildered when we are attacked. Because we tend to deny having unpleasant emotions, we cannot deal with some of our important reactions to others.

Most of our respondents had trouble defining the word *enemy*. Some said it was "the opposite of friend." Others thought "acquaintance" was the opposite of friend. Some wiseacres said, "My wife" or, "My husband." Several replied, "The boss." When we asked whether they could conceptualize a state of affairs in which someone disliked them intensely and tried to do them harm every chance they could, virtually all said no.

However, at one point or another, all of our respondents expressed hatred. Some hated communists, atheists, or homosexuals. Many embarrassed themselves by expressing hostility toward some racial, national, or religious group. Some did a double take when they recognized that Polish jokes signified hatred.

Vietnam veterans had no trouble identifying enemies. They hated "gooks," "the congs," or the "slants." Some World War II veterans hated the "krauts" or the "nips." Some black respondents hated the "honkies" and several white respondents hated the "niggers" or "coons."

The "kikes" and "hebes" came in for their share of hostility, as did the "dagos," "spicks," "micks," "rednecks," "queers," and "hooligans." The pattern was clear. Enemies did not have names or identities. They were stereotypical representatives of groups.

We *fear* our enemies' ability to harm us and change our ways of life. We assume their evil intent is caused by a lack of ordinary human virtues. It is easier to admit feeling this way toward a "hostile" nation, more difficult to admit feeling this way toward individual humans.

LIEUTENANT H.

When I first got to Nam, I used to sit around the officers' club and listen to the men talk about their scores of the day. "I saw this gook running through a paddy and I sprayed all around him to make him dance, then I shot him in the head." "We played this game, we had to hit every third gook who was running down the road. The yellow little bastards were running away from us, so they had to be commies, see. And we got up high enough so it was a contest. All they had to do is hit the ditch and we wouldn't kill them, unless we missed. But they kept running and we kept picking them off." I couldn't understand it. I felt sick. So I went up with them one day to see for myself, and by the time I came back, I had piled up quite a record. Seven in one day, just like the fairy story about the tailor who killed the flies. That's what it was like, killing flies. When I talked to the chaplain about it, what he said was, "War is war, and you have to expect soldiers to be proud about their skill at killing the enemy."

We fear what people can do to hurt us, but we try to deny they will act to harm us. In this way our enemies control us. They stimulate us to behave in irrational and often stupid ways. They get us to reject people who might help us and insult people who will hurt us. This is why people do not like to admit they have enemies. Because we won't admit having enemies we simply don't know how to act when we come under attack.

We seldom admit to anyone, even to ourselves, that we harbor such fears about anyone. We prefer to think we are capable of handling other people's infringements into our mental, emotional, and physical territories. When the "creep" at the next desk chews gum so loudly it interferes with our work, we make a note of it, and when the time is right, a proper insult comes out. Eric Berne compared our tendency to store up our hostilities to collecting trading stamps. We store them up for the time we can cash in with a tantrum or a deliciously hostile act. But we pretend enemies do not exist, and we tell ourselves they play no important role in our lives.

In our first investigation, involving nearly five hundred people, we asked two questions about evil acts committed in relationships:

1. Have you ever been used and hurt in a relationship?
2. Have you ever used and hurt anyone in a relationship?

When the data came in, we decided we had a very unusual population. More than 90 percent of our respondents (91.6 percent to be exact) reported they had indeed been used, abused, and hurt in a relationship. Virtually all were willing to give details. The average response for this item ran to three paragraphs. However, only 4.4 percent were willing to admit they had ever used anyone, and none of those respondents provided more than two lines of explanation.

The first problem is to get people to admit the possibility of having enemies. To admit having enemies means facing the possibility that we may have done something to cause someone to become an enemy. People tend to have excellent rationalizations for their trespasses against others. Consider some of the following interview responses.

It was not easy for me to flunk him out of law school. But there will come the time when he will know I did him a favor. There is nothing more painful than letting a person graduate from law school who will be unable to pass the bar.

Of course she had to get the abortion. We simply weren't able to fund a kid. I'm sorry the surgery made her sterile, but I told her when we were ready we could adopt just the kid she wanted.

153

We had grown apart. She had kind of become a drudge while I went to grad school, and she just didn't fit with the people I was meeting in the firm. I mean, it was a favor to her to get the divorce because she would have been terribly unhappy living the life I was getting into.

When he went overseas, I just didn't have the heart to tell him that I had married Freddy, so I waited until he came home to break it to him.

These statements were typical. Comments like these are made so matter-of-factly it requires sober reconsideration to discover how destructive we can be to others. We think primarily of our own welfare and assume what is good for us is also good for the people around us. Consequently, the inability of most people to admit error is what prevents them from admitting they have enemies.

ALLEN W.

Wendy was the best secretary I ever had. I really liked her and so did my wife and the kids. We had her over a lot and she was really one of the family. That's why I got very concerned when I came in one morning and found her crying. She told me about this guy, the mail room supervisor, who had been playing up to her and laying her regularly, promising he would marry her. She really loved the guy. She'd talk about him and even mention his name, but I never connected. We have a lot of employees. I always wondered why he would never come over when we invited Wendy. When Wendy told me how he had dumped her, telling her that he wasn't good enough for her and he had decided to stay with his wife, I was furious. I called him in. He wasn't running that mail room well anyway. Things were misrouted a lot of the time and mail got delivered late. I watched him for a while and gathered "the goods" on him and called him in and fired him. I told him I would have worked with him and given him another chance if he hadn't been so rotten to my friend Wendy. He couldn't understand. All he could say is, "Holy shit, are you the guy who's getting into her now?"

People being surprised when they are "blind-sided" by a friend of someone they have hurt is not uncommon. Virtually everyone had "socked it to" someone or other, but they did not recognize it as injury. After all, it was "us" or "them," and it was all right for "us" to do it to "them." Thems should not be surprised; they had it coming. We got the impression most people maintained a kind of tribal linkage with their friends and allies so they could break the world down into our guys and their guys. Once we identified someone as "their guy," we could hurt them without worrying about it.

Even more dismaying to us was the pattern of sexism resulting in considerable injury to employed women. We should have gotten an insight when we discovered that most men do not consider their wife to be their friend. As the evidence accumulated, however, we got the distinct impression a great many men did not even regard women as human. "Seminal spittoons," one individual called them. "We keep them around the office to decorate the place and give the guys something to compete for." Decisions were made about employed women with absolutely no regard for their personal interests or qualifications. It was the rare supervisor who considered his female employees in the same serious way he considered the men who worked for him. Women were usually hired and promoted because of their appearance. Some employers preferred attractive women; others rejected attractive women for fear they would "disrupt" the work force.

Referring to women as "chicks" or "girls" reduces their ethos. Worst of all, we could not resist feeling that those who gave the most lip service to equal opportunity employment for women used their advocacy to gain trust so they could hustle women into sexual relations. Most chilling of all was the impression we got about female executives who bought into the sexist ethic, and instead of supporting their female subordinates, joined their male colleagues in pushing them around, guaranteeing they would not be able to offer them any competition. Said one female executive, "It took me awhile to get up here and there will only be a handful of women on top in this company. The last thing I need is some cute, well-built, little prodigy after my job."

Our conclusion: Making enemies is a common, often malicious, and conscious activity, but people will rarely admit to it. When people injure others, they use their rationalizations as reasons, and when the injured people complain or fight back, the person doing the injury is bewildered.

The second problem involves the lack of a common language to use to discuss enemies. It is relatively easy to get people to talk about their friends and to make fine distinctions among them. They have a great number of common expressions to use; we used only the single-word expressions from the following entry for *friend* in Rodale (1961, p. 439):

FRIEND, n. . . . intimate, companion, comrade, chum . . . confidante, buddy, pal, bunkie, crony, sidekick, mate, bedfellow, playfellow, shadow, associate, acquaintance, partner, co-worker, ally, confrere, frater, colleague, fellow-member, neighbor, shopmate, roommate, schoolmate, messmate . . . paramour, sweetheart, concubine, mistress, girl friend, boy friend, well-wisher, advocate, supporter, backer, defender, patron, protector, benefactor . . .

Notice the difference when we talk of enemies:

ENEMY, n. . . . opponent, adversary, assailant, attacker, rival, competitor . . . [Rodale, 1961, p. 349; the listing also includes anarchist, Red, traitor, and rebel, among others].

Clearly, we do not have much versatility when discussing enemies. Enemies tend to be all-or-nothing propositions: We generally do not differentiate between or among the ways we conceptualize them. An enemy is a person who is *completely* evil, capable only of inducing hatred in us, a source of potential, real, or imagined violence. We tend to want to *destroy* our enemies, *if* we admit we have them at all.

Because most of us like to see ourselves as civilized and respectable, this lack of options in our language clearly puts us at a disadvantage in our thinking. It is hard to think about total destruction of people who have human identities. Because we do not have accurate categories in which to file them, we try not to think about enemies at all. When we encounter them, we are usually bewildered by the fact that they seem to want to *hurt* us, whereas we only want to get them on the right track. If we had a way to talk about the people we "brush block" on our way to the top (a language like that used by interior linemen or linebackers on a professional football team to refer to their opponents), we might get a sense of the necessity involved in doing injury. We have already discovered that people, in general, do not like to admit the existence of competition. It is small wonder that they prefer to disregard talk about people who might possibly be hostile to them.

The third problem in discussing enemies is getting people to disclose information about people they oppose. It is pleasant to discuss our friends, or to talk about people liking and respecting us. But even when we are aware that people don't like us, we prefer not to discuss it or them. Most of all, we do not want to think about what we might have done to cause the hostility, nor do we want to speculate on how they might "get us." In the early 1950s William White's book *The Organization Man* showed how important it was for a rising executive to be a bit paranoid (Murphy's law of executive neurosis: Being paranoid is no guarantee that you won't have real enemies). People who won't admit they might be hurt are usually taken by surprise when it happens.

The fear of making enemies gets us to perform some strange acts. We are respectful of, even obsequious to, powerful people who could harm us. We may gripe a lot at home about how the "boss" takes advantage, but we rarely confront the boss with our objections and our hostilities. Strategists who know how to make these confrontations seem more secure in their relationships.

KEVIN G. (research chemist)
It takes a lot of time and trouble to actually go out and hurt someone. Most people do it inadvertently. I want people at work to keep clear of me, and I think terror is the most productive technique. So, when someone is getting on my case, I will call them aside privately and say, "Someday, when you least expect it, I am going to hit you from the blind side. And if you tell anyone about what I said, I will call you a liar." Then you go off and never worry about them again. When anything bad happens to them, they will credit you for it, talk about it with their friends, and people will learn to fear you. I haven't been bothered by anyone in authority for the last ten years.

When we asked people to talk about their enemies, most of our respondents tightened their jaws, squinted, and remained silent. At first their emotion was so intense they could not talk about enemies at all; then, with encouragement, they burst out tales of injury and harm going back several years. (On this subject we interviewed twenty people, all over age thirty-five and in responsible positions. We also interviewed twenty college students. Their responses did not differ: silence, contemplation, then quietly furious attacks on people who were clearly enemies, although they were not so identified at first.)

Most punishing was our respondents' obvious inability to deal with the emotions stirred up by their enemies: jealousy, envy, anger, resentment, fear, and hate. These emotions appeared to be part of their personalities, although they did not seem to be aware of them and probably would not have admitted to any of them without prodding. We do not purport to be psychoanalysts. On the other hand, we have read a lot of books and talked to a great many people. So much of our fiction is about enemies and negative emotions; the fear Mr. Sammler has of black people (Bellow, 1970) and Othello's urge for revenge on Desdemona are but two examples. Our soap operas and major video dramas are filled with prime-time scenarios of hostility and hatred. Heroes avenge villainy with little concern about how it might affect the wives and children of the scoundrels. There is little equity in our media and a great deal of bloodshed. We live close to hatred and hostility, yet, the people in our sample—perfectly ordinary people,—found it virtually impossible to find any malice in their own lives. Perhaps violence succeeds so well as a theme in fiction because so many of us are on the fine edge, suppressing our hatreds and hostilities and needing some kind of vicarious outlet for viciousness we might prefer to direct at the people we think are harming us.

These three problems associated with the study of how people think and talk about enemies prevented a "hard data" survey of the issue. What we report in the following pages is drawn from interviews we conducted with respondents who wrote like they might have something interesting to say on the topic. Because we are interested in the study of human relationships, how people deal with the dangers posed to them by other people was as interesting and informative to us as our data about friendship and love. We believe we need to know more about hostile relationships, and the rest of this chapter is about what we discovered when we asked people about their enemies.

THE QUESTION OF MOTIVE: WHY WE THINK PEOPLE WILL DO US HARM

Maybe it's the pheromones. People may do us harm because they have been biologically programmed to see us (or smell us) as an adversary. Someone passes by while we stand waiting for a bus on a street corner, leaving a trail of invisible odors that wrench our nose. Suddenly we are seized with hatred for the individual. But the passion subsides as the person moves farther away, until we are left wondering why we are feeling so tense; something must be wrong. Maybe we need a massage or a day off.

We do not know whether or not pheromones or similar chemicals predispose us toward hostility against individuals or groups with whom our chemical composition clashes. Perhaps they *did* at one time during our evolution, but with the effects of pollution and the myriad antiodor devices we use to bathe and pamper our bodies we may well have lost the sense of scents. We may have numbed it out. Pheronomes are relevant factors with animals, and they are part of the mythology we have developed to explain our contempt for minority group members.

ERIC G.
I said to my wife, "I don't like Shirley. She is the worst student I have ever had. I can't even stand being in the same room with her." But the next week, when I graded the papers (with no names, to keep me honest), Shirley's was in a pack by itself, a truly outstanding paper. "I don't know what it is I hate about that girl," I said. Then, one day, I can't remember why, she had to deliver something to the house. My wife invited her in. She no sooner came through the door and I moved

to the farthest corner of the room. "You twit," my wife laughed, "she's wearing ———— perfume, the kind you are allergic to. You don't dislike Shirley, you can't tolerate her perfume."

We have already referred to animals sniffing each other when they meet and explained how humans use phatic communion for the same purpose. We have socialized ourselves out of the sniffing stage. So, in most cases, we must look for answers elsewhere to the question of how humans decide they have enemies and whom people chose as objects for their hatred and hostility.

If our biological makeup cannot account for our propensity to do harm to others, perhaps it is the way we are reared. Culture may be the culprit. In 1941 we knew our Japanese fellow citizens were very decent folk, yet we had no problem putting them into concentration camps. Today it is very difficult to tell a Protestant from a Catholic in Belfast, yet somehow both Catholics and Protestants know the difference and kill each other because of it.

Catskill joke: This fellow was walking in Belfast one night and he suddenly felt a gun at his back. "Are ya' Catholic or Protestant?" whispered a voice. The man thought, "If I say I'm Catholic, he's likely to be a Protestant and he'll kill me, and if I say I'm Protestant, there's a chance he's Catholic and he'll kill me." Thinking quickly, he said, "Neither, I'm Jewish," and the voice laughed and said, "Aha, and who's the luckiest Arab in Belfast tonight?"

"You've got to be carefully taught," they sing in *South Pacific* and most of us are taught early on the identities of our abstract enemies. We may learn about the "melting pot" and "equal opportunity" in school, but at home and on the streets we learn about "kikes" and "coons" and "spicks" and "dagos" and "rednecks" and "eggheads" and "polocks" or whatever the locals consider to be the inferior people around and about. We hear our parents complaining about the people they know, and our street cronies teach us about "four eyes" and "fatso" and "skinny" and "knobnose" and about "nerds" and "jocks" and whomever they hate. It is not hard to learn to hate and it is not hard to have enemies. Hate is easy, in fact, so long as our enemies do not have names and faces and can be identified by terms rendering them less than human. We noted with some dismay that virtually everyone we interviewed referred, at least once, to some group they found detestable. Furthermore, when our rational side finds the identification false, we do not revise our generalization; instead, we say, "You're different, you are not like the rest of them." Most of our respondents had a "pet" black or a "tame" Jew whom they cherished, while they cheerfully hated the rest of the group.

MARSHA S.
The thing I could never understand about yankees was the way you all talk about how much you love the black people but the minute one comes close to you, you all try to escape. In the South, we make no bones about saying we hate blacks as a race, but we certainly know how to get on with them as individuals.

The big problem comes in getting a grip on hating a human being, or allowing for the possibility that a human being might hate you. We are not trained to deal with these emotions. We are, in fact, trained in constructive narcissism: to believe that our habits, our values, our behaviors are so correct that anyone who disagreed with them was somehow inferior, and all we would have to do is to show them the truth and they would accept it and love us. Unfortunately, the world does not turn so peacefully, and every one of our respondents eventually told us a story about someone they had injured who now "had it in for them." Usually it was an "interloper," a person who should not have been there in the first place, someone who did not fit the norms in the area, in the neighborhood, or on the job.

Differences

People seldom seem unwilling to hurt people like themselves intentionally, but they often inflict gratuitous harm on people who differ from them in obvious ways. One of the facts we collected was that people did not seem to be able to identify differences without making some qualitative judgment. People who dressed differently were classified with respect or contempt. People who ate differently were classified as "gourmets" or "pigs." Most of our respondents had a great many slang expressions to use on people who were different: nerds, slobs, jerks, bums, kooks, creeps, clods, whackos, and so on. The precise denotations of the words in this taxonomy were hard to pin down, but the connotations were obvious.

Differences were identified in an incredible number of ways.

Look at that *slob* eating mayonnaise on his corned-beef sandwich!
You've got to look out for those *bearded weirdos,* no telling what they'll do.
The *stupid bastards* can't even learn to speak English.
There ought to be a law about *fat slobs* like that sitting next to you in the theater.
Only a real *big shot* would drive a car like that.

That's *executive* style, I can tell.

Talk about *tacky?* Look at what she's wearing.

Only a *slut* would show that much leg.

She is really *classy* in that outfit.

They prance around like a bunch of goddamn *studs.*

Cut out that *egghead* crap and get to the point.

Stop stuttering, *stupid,* and tell me what you want to say.

You're assembling that like a friggin' *retard.*

Robert Ardrey (1967) pointed out that humans were territorial creatures just like many other animals and had to have a territory to own. We got the impression from our respondents they were territorial in "vertical" fashion; that is, they saw themselves owning niches in some kind of value hierarchy. Each person belonged to some group that was first on some hierarchy, and each new person, once identified, could be fitted into some position. Usually the new person's position was inferior but those on whom the individual wished to model were elevated to superior positions.

Once new people are classified, it is fairly easy to work out a way to treat them. People who are different in any apparent way must be treated accordingly. They must be either better or worse, to be ridiculed and rejected or imitated. Even such mundane differences as tall or short or what you put on your hamburger can elicit a classification comment that can make you friend or enemy without any expenditure of energy on your part.

We believe part of the source of this kind of distinction making is the psychoanalytic process called *transference.* Freud noticed that his patients tended to treat him like some important figure in their past: father or lover, for example. He ascribed complicated and deep motives to transference. It may really be quite simple. We need to have decision rules to guide our social behavior, and the simplest way to generate these rules is to classify people. When we meet someone, we try to find out who the someone "looks like," and initially, we treat the person as if he or she should behave exactly like the person they remind us of. Thus, if a young lady meets a young man who looks a bit like the punk who molested her, she is likely to be hostile toward him without ever giving him a chance. On the other hand, if a young man meets a young lady with breasts similar to those on the "playmates," he is likely to be spellbound without discovering that she is a very unpleasant human.

The effect of decisions based on transference is the creation of automatic enemies. When people remind us of others we hated in the past, our posture is usually one of suspicion. We respond coldly when we meet the new person. We begin our relationship with a distance between us; we are set for hostility. Little annoyances that we might tolerate in someone with whom we had a positive transference provoke us unreasonably and generate hostility.

EDWIN P.

I felt uneasy about Nicholas right from the start. I felt there was something suspicious, unlikable, about him, even though I couldn't put it into words. I had recommended against hiring him in the first place. I noticed he had a habit of staring off into space from time to time, like my old Latin teacher, Mr. Devers. Devers beat the crap out of me once when I did something when I thought he wasn't looking because he was staring into space, and I had the feeling that Nicholas was watching me all the time. I guess I began watching him a lot, too. He complained that I was giving him too much work and harassing him, and I thought he didn't have any right to complain. He was on a probationary period. I turned in a negative report to the supervisor, and—believe it or not—the supervisor accused me of being unfair. He told me everyone else thought Nicholas was doing well. When Nicholas finished his probationary period, he really went after me. It has been nearly two years and I haven't known any peace. He is on my case all of the time. It's as though he audits all my work, trying to catch me at something. I don't know what to do. I was honest in my evaluation of him, and he has no right to do this to me.

Edwin's reference to the Latin teacher provided a clue to his apparently irrational suspicion of the new employee. Whether Nicholas has a right to his hatred is not the issue. We presume no one has the right to hurt anyone else (without due process), but we are not concerned here with rights. The foregoing illustration typifies one pattern of the development of enemies. It explains some of the otherwise incomprehensible hostilities that occur from time to time. All of us have experienced a new person we disliked on sight. If love at first sight is irrational, we would assume hate at first sight is equally irrational. However, both do occur, and both usually bring trouble with them.

In an earlier chapter we discussed the special problems of friendship when there are major changes in the conditions of the relationship. Promotions often separate friends, as does changing residence. Differences in goals or in ways and means of achieving them also interfere with communication between friends, which in turn may generate actual hostility.

STEVEN P.

When Greg was transferred into New Product Development, he met some people who had a very different life-style. All of a sudden Greg was into their kind of life.

When we went to the game one Saturday, he got up and left during the sixth inning. He said baseball bored him lately. He called Sunday afternoon and asked me to go to a movie at the museum. I wanted to stay home and watch the game. We did very little together after that. I heard from some mutual friends that Greg was talking about me, and I told them that Greg was not very loyal and didn't know how to keep friendships.

GREG N.

The problem with Steve is that he forgot how to grow. There are only so many baseball games you can watch and only so many games you can rehash. Greg can't talk about anything interesting anymore. He doesn't like to meet new people or do new things. I have outgrown him.

The friendship ended, and hostilities developed. The two men gossiped about each other. Their wives retained their friendship, but it became impossible to socialize as couples anymore. Greg's wife reported that Greg talked aboout how Steven had changed, looked different, become ugly. Steven commented that Greg had acquired "some kind of strange expression on his face."

We had noticed this phenomenon before. We got the impression that people would literally change the way they perceived other people as they got more information about them. The young lady who rejected the man who looked like her molester reported that his appearance changed as she got to know him better. (Unfortunately, our questions reminded her of her original perception. The incident reminded us of the perils of this kind of research. It also explains why it is virtually impossible to get general support for this hypothesis. The kind of questioning required to get the information penetrates too far into personal space to be justifiable. We backed off very quickly.)

The same differentiation process goes on as we begin to note physical imperfections and personality flaws. Part of getting to know someone well is recognition of defects. Our judgments regarding the consequence of the defect vary from person to person. Our use of adjectives and adverbs offers a clue to our attitudes:

> He is talkative; he is effusive; he is eloquent; he is long-winded.
> She is sexy; she is sensual; she is lecherous; she is sluttish.
> She is shrewd; she is cunning; she is crafty; she is manipulative.
> He is impulsive; he is passionate; he is rash; he is foolhardy.

Personal attitudes thus shape expressed evaluations. Expressed evaluations guide behavior (within limits), and it is to our behavior that other people respond. Most of us cannot conceal our coolness for some people, our affection for others. People tend to respond to us as we respond to them; thus, hostility to a person may result in a self-fulfilling prophecy. We began to wonder how we could make use of this process. Could we get people to adjust attitudes by adjusting their language? Could we overcome prejudice, for example, by getting people to talk differently? There has been a concerted effort to get writers to remove "sexist" language from their books and to use women as examples of professions in which women are not commonly found. We questioned both the evidence and the conclusions. We found men, in particular, pay little attention to the language others use about women. They have their own. At the conclusion of this chapter we will discuss the impact of spoken language about women on the way they are regarded. Our tentative conclusion is that people suffer from first impressions (transference), from bigotry, and from myth. These three forces seem to generate the basic hostilities from which we gain our enemies. They are not easy forces to control.

MOTIVATIONS FOR ENEMIES

As yet, we have developed no systematic theory of enemies, nor even very systematic ways of discovering why people have enemies. However, we believe our data identify some common reasons about why people become enemies.

First, there are people who harm us in order to advance their own causes. For example, some books on how to "get ahead" advise that it is sometimes necessary to "clobber" people who get in your way. A great many managers and administrators do not consider how their decisions might affect individuals. They may not be able to. Their job is to produce particular results, and to consider the impact of decisions on human beings might impair the operation of the program designed to accomplish those results. Thus, individuals can do injury to others without even knowing them or being aware of the injury. The decision to close a branch office, for example, may throw several people out of work and have a frightful impact on their lives. The decision maker may only be aware of the color of the ink and the column in which it is posted. Competition and the urge to win often motivate frighteningly Eichmannlike decisions.

ANDREW P.
I had been with the company for nineteen years. I had turned down three opportunities to advance by relocating because I liked the town. I had sixteen years equity

in my home on a twenty-five-year mortgage. My wife was active in local politics. I had one kid in the local college and one each in the senior and junior high. We love this place. It is our home. So a new guy comes in at the home office and he has some rotation program that is supposed to improve productivity, and he tells me I am scheduled for El Paso. I asked him if I was doing anything wrong, and he said no, but if anyone got out of the track, it would ruin the whole system and the statistics wouldn't come out right or something. I said, "You can't treat me like this after all I've given to the company," but we don't have a union and we don't have that tenure business like you college professors, so he showed me he could do it to me. I am now out of work, the family is coming apart, and I swear, someday, as soon as possible, I will find a way to get that dirty little bastard.

Should Andrew get his chance to hurt the executive, chances are the executive won't be able to explain it. He may never make the connection between the hostility and his rotation policy. To him Andrew's hostility would appear completely irrational and clearly opposed to the good of the company.

Our narcissism induces us to make decisions in our own interest with little regard for the interests of others. One of the main arguments for *group* decision making in industry is that it provides an opportunity for people to express their personal concerns so the final decision can be as equitable as possible. Without our hearing from others, it is very hard for us to see how anything we do may hurt anyone else. It isn't that we are cold and rotten. It is just that it is very difficult to see things from another person's point of view. The noun *empathy* is the soothing syrup we take to explain ascription of our own motives to the other person. Thus we justify ourselves in moving ahead, demanding what satisfies us with little concern for others who might also be striving. All of us have, at one time or another, grabbed something from someone who at that moment was too weak to compete or protest. This kind of inadvertent and unthinking wrong can stir up considerable hostility.

NORTON P.

We had been considering three options for the 1978 campaign. I had a proposal in, and so did Tom and Frank. There was supposed to be a meeting, but I got called out of town. One of my kids had been in a car accident, and I was needed to help with the hospital arrangements and just be there with the kid. I told Tom I was going and to postpone the meeting. But Tom went right ahead and not only held the meeting, but he didn't even tell anyone why I wasn't there. By the time I got back, I was in hot water with the boss, and I had to explain my way out, and then he wanted to know why I hadn't notified him about my kid's accident—why did I tell Tom? I asked Tom why he hadn't told the boss, and Tom said that he just got "carried away." He thought his damned idea was so important that he pushed it through. Frank didn't have a chance and I got screwed. Well, his idea didn't work, and I got promoted over him, and I am slowly grinding him into the ground. It may sound like a little thing, but to take advantage of someone while his kid is in the hospital is too much. I will go a long way out of my way to hurt Tom. I won't talk to him, and eventually I will cream him.

Breaking relations with someone for personal convenience, not sharing a financial windfall with the family, or ignoring someone's personal request can lead to acts that injure others. In our urge to take care of ourselves, we often punish others who are trying to take care of themselves. We most often do this to people who are close to us. Our loved ones often learn to suppress their anger. But even they may feel so much resentment they learn to hate us. Others, such as the people with whom we work, owe us nothing. They have no necessary barriers to their resentment.

Second, there are people who hurt us because of a desire to "get even." Equity theorists Walster, Walster, and Berscheid (1978) have demonstrated that when a worker discovers an inequity—such as lower pay for the same work—she or he will calculate the difference and begin stealing, destroying tools, or wasting time on the job until equity is attained in his or her own mind.

The failure of "distributive justice" can result in hateful acts against the people who get the largest rewards. For example, workers are able to handle misery, provided it is equally shared. It is when one person receives a just reward while the others are denied reward that hostility begins. Jealousy leads to an urge to get even. Envy leads to acts designed to diminish the person's pleasure in what they have. Revenge is designed to equalize the score, and it is sweetest when you "get even" without having the object of your revenge know you even tried to.

TINA T.
I found out for sure that Carl had a thing going with his secretary. She was a pudgy little slob, but Carl was at the point where he needed someone to give him "unconditional positive regard," and I was frankly sick of his wimpy behavior. Still, if he was going to be unfaithful, he should have at least had enough taste to get someone with a little class instead of that pig. So, when I was absolutely sure, what I did was arrange a little time alone with Carl's boss. Now, Mr. D. is an old goat, but he is rich and he is important, and also impotent so I wasn't risking a lot, but I gave him strokes and cuddling and a lot of talk about what a bastard Carl was and how badly he was treating me, and I watched Carl lose his job and smiled and then I left him and sued for divorce.

Contrary to what we would like to believe, many people do seek revenge. It is customarily cold and calculated. The young assistant professor who has taken cheap shots at the senior professor discovers how powerful the revenge motive is at tenure time. The supervisor who credits himself with a subordinate's idea may discover later that the idea he took credit for failed because it was sabotaged by its originator.

BERT M.

The Japanese have a legend about a nobleman who seized the newlywed bride of a young villager and raped and killed her. The villager then entered the service of the nobleman and gradually worked his way up the hierarchy until he became the chief advisor and dear friend of the nobleman, the only person the nobleman trusted, and then he revealed who he was and he killed the nobleman. I've done that a time or two. The boss has worked me over, and I don't say anything, I keep being a good little "do-bee" until the crucial moment and then, with a smile, I just simply sell out. I tell a secret or two, or I screw up something important and then walk away so I don't have to hear the screams of agony.

The failure of equity is often inadvertent. Most people in power would like to believe they are fair-minded. Lovers would like to believe they look out for their mates. Friends would like to believe that they are true blue. People, generally, want to be trusted. Yet, in our interviews, with a bit of pulling and tugging, we could generally get a story of careful and calculated revenge even from the people who appeared kind and considerate. It appeared to justify Murphy's law "Just because you are paranoid doesn't mean they are not out to get you."

Third, there are people who hurt us because they do not recognize us as fully human. Members of ethnic and minority groups have long suffered the humiliation of second-class status, and no one should forget the Holocaust. When social scientists studied some of the Nazi death camp workers, they were astonished to learn that these people often believed that the Jews whom they sentenced to death felt no pain. We have already discussed the consequences of this kind of thinking as it affects minority groups or people who are different. Sometimes people can make you different in order to enjoy hurting you. Once they have found some name to call you or some hateful label to apply, they seem to be able to justify any kind of hostile act. Most of us are familiar with a person who has become a scapegoat, and perhaps we have even participated in name calling to soothe our guilt for not opposing the persecution.

MIKE V.

It started when Mr. C. blew up at Phil the day Phil pushed the wrong button on the machine and damn near burned the place down. I don't know how it happened. Phil must have had a drink or two at lunch. But Phil wasn't a drinker. When Mr. C. came in to yell at Phil, he must have smelled Phil's breath, because he said, "you f——n' lush, one more stunt like that and you'll be dragging your tail in the unemployment line." From then on, Phil became the "lush." Mr. C. was always on him. I don't think Phil ever drank anything since that day, but he was always catching it. It seemed like Mr. C. kept him around to be a punching bag. To this day, I'll never understand why Phil stayed around and took it, except fifty-year-old senior clerk types don't get new jobs easily. And I'll never understand why Mr. C. does it because in every other respect he is just a damn nice man. But the worst thing of all is that every so often I find myself doing something nasty to Phil or thinking about him as "stupid Phil, the lush."

Fourth, there are people who hurt us because of envy. In comic books people literally turn *green* with envy; you can recognize the emotion on their faces. In real life envy is less recognizable. The envious individual may wish you well, congratulate you for good work, and secretly harbor a strong desire to hurt you. It is understandable to be upset because of a failure of equity, to want your fair share. To feel like denying someone else his or her share seems irrational. Envy, in its extreme form, is one of our darkest emotions because it seeks to punish a person for something over which he or she may have had no control.

DR. WARREN S. (psychiatrist)
I had an attractive woman patient, dark-haired, large breasts, sensuous looking. She carried around a heavy load of guilt. Her story was very revealing. She said she hated slim blondes. She had a young blonde working for her. The girl really respected her, did her work well, and was an absolutely first-rate employee, but in her irrational envy of slim blondes, my patient did everything in her power to wipe the girl out. She was friendly to her, took her to lunch, complimented her, but she secretly sabotaged her work and tampered with her personnel records. Finally, she faked a small embezzlement of funds and got the girl fired. When she learned the girl had tried suicide, she came to me for help. It was almost impossible to repair the damage, but that's another story. For your purposes I tell you this story because I want to make it clear that people do harm to others because they do not want them to enjoy what they have. They hate them for the way they look or their brains or their friends or even their country of origin. There is a book, *Envy* by a man named Helmut Schoeck. You ought to read it. It is about how envy can explain a great deal of irrational behavior.

Like other powerful emotions, envy has received very little attention in the social sciences despite the fact we know it frequently affects people's daily lives. Envy is a form of subtle attack, an offensive tactic masquerading as goodwill. But where does it originate? What causes it?

We have described the competitiveness between friends or lovers.

We know we enter competitions in order to accomplish two interdependent tasks: (a) to participate in the game or interaction, and (b) to win or at least to improve over previous performances. For some, Vince Lombardi's credo "winning is not everything, it is the *only* thing" is a way of life. For others there is some truth in Grantland Rice's dictum: "when the one Great Scorer makes the mark against your name, it wasn't whether you won or lost, but how you played the game." There are a few who believe that "good guys finish last," some of whom consciously make sure they are not "good guys" and others who believe that being a good guy is compensation enough for finishing out of the money. The problem is, we seldom know who we are playing against until it is too late, and sometimes we do not even know our own motivations. Thus, we may feel that what we are doing is not terribly important because we do not believe we can lose, and when we lose, we must find a way to escape the blame. We can blame our mood, or we can blame our opponent for cheating or the referee for being unfair. In either of the latter two cases, we may need to feel they gained nothing by winning the prize. If you combine negation with the "mood" excuse, we may even claim diminished responsibility for the vengeful acts we committed out of envy.

Our respondents showed an interesting predilection to criticize and complain about the people closest to them, especially their spouses and friends. They griped about their parents, they told embarrassing stories about their friends, and they often burst out in irrational attacks against their lovers. The tensions that mount because of resentment and envy are often very hard to release. Some of the irrational hostility can be explained by the inability to "fight city hall." When you are aggrieved because of something done by a person too powerful to attack, then it is extremely hard to find relief. It is sometimes easiest just to lash out at the people closest to you. No one understands because we are generally unwilling or unable to admit we could even feel such dark passions as envy or a desire to get even.

Envy and jealousy seem to have a common form. The jealous person is dangerous and the jealous lover is malicious. Roland Barthes (1978) describes the jealous lover: "As a jealous man, I suffer four times over: because I am jealous, because I blame myself for being so, because I fear that my jealousy will wound the other, because I allow myself to be subject to a banality: I suffer from being excluded, from being aggressive, from being crazy, and from being common."

If jealousy can be described as outrage turned *inward,* then envy can be described as outrage turned *outward.* The jealous individual blames himself or herself for the emotion, recognizes its potential for motivating base and hostile acts, and suffers guilt because of inability to overcome the feeling. The envious person then shifts the blame to *the other person in the relationship* for causing the envy and seeks restitution for imagined harm. The envious person is an enemy disguised as a friend, lover, or co-worker. Because of the guise of friendship, the envious enemy can do a great deal of harm before the recipient even knows there is an enemy.

There is one more component of the jealousy-envy syndrome. People who are aggrieved or injured often injure back. When they obviously try to "get back" at someone, they may eventually offer restitution, either in the form of an apology or some small service or favor. The original aggressor usually feels that the restitution is not sufficient and rejects it. The person who tried to "get back" then rationalizes the act by deciding the original aggressor "had it coming." However, the original aggressor has now been twice injured, first by committing the act and second by the inadequate restitution. This can trigger a second round of malice. Thus, normal resentment at inequitable treatment can become pathological jealousy or envy.

It is difficult to detect envy simply because our culture teaches us not to ascribe evil to others. If we accept the principle of "dual perspective," we can ascribe to others only what we feel ourselves. If we deny that we can do evil, we must, at least consciously, deny that other people can do it. We would like to believe that the world is good and orderly. But, as Oscar Wilde once remarked, if you find yourself in a situation where the good are rewarded and the evil punished, you are probably in a novel. If you allow yourself the luxury of ascribing the possibility of evil to others, you run the risk of being regarded as paranoid. Thus, it is simply easier not to believe other people want to do you harm or that you can do harm to others. If you find that you have injured someone, you can retreat into Harry Stack Sullivan's famous copout and say "it was not me" as you claim diminished responsibility. If others do harm to you, you can claim not to understand what you could possibly have done to warrant the attack and then justify what you did to them in the first place.

Some of our older respondents were able to pinpoint the kinds of comments that might indicate jealousy or envy. "Gee, I wish I could be as good as you are" is a compliment laced with desire that may well be a clever disguise for envy. Aristotle, in his *Ethics*, pointed out that "men are good in but one way, but bad in many." Any excess of congratulations or praise should be examined closely, for in it may lie the roots of envy, jealousy, and malice.

We also need to listen for the conspicuous absence of truth in words spoken to flatter us. The woman who says to her attractive friend "You are the most beautiful person I have ever known" has a motive for the statement. There must be some desire behind flattery to gain a particular kind of response, or else the statement may indicate gratuitous, hidden envy.

It is important to be able to distinguish between a genuine compliment, such as "I like the way you do it, can you teach me how?" and the jealous-envious comments "How did you ever get that good?" or "I suppose your ability is a God-given talent." People have a tendency to give themselves away, if, and only if, we are attuned to their comments.

DR. JOHN B. (clinical psychologist)
Theodore Reick wrote this book called *Listening with the Third Ear.* It's a damn good book because it teaches us to see through some of the comments people make. I have a hard time with people who come to me depressed because other people seem to be hurting them. Sometimes they think they are unreasonably paranoid because they think others are out to get them. You are not supposed to think that in this society. It is very hard to have a completely honest, completely trusting relationship with anyone, your friend, your mother, your lover. There is always a little deceit, a little malice, and we tend to get bothered a lot by the people closest to us just because they are closest to us. So when something hurts, you have to deal with it, and you have to admit two possibilities at the same time: First, you have to believe that you may have done something rotten to motivate it. Second, you have to believe the other person can do it, whatever the reason. If you can get a grip on those two ideas, you might be able to understand and explain and maybe even talk about the behavior. Good Lord, in a marriage, you have to be able to do it. You have to understand that the real strength in a marriage lies in being able to get back together because being together is still fulfilling enough to overcome the hurts. You are going to hurt people and they are going to hurt you. There is no escape.

Finally, people will sometimes do us harm simply because it amuses them. People define pleasure in unique, and sometimes punishing, ways. Women have long recognized one special form of this behavior, which they call "cattiness." Being "catty" consists of dropping a word or statement designed to do harm in the midst of an otherwise friendly conversation. "Joan, we all know you have always been so *easy*" may bring a round of laughter, but underneath the laughter may be a malicious intent. The cat may not be an enemy, but the source of this rich form of one-upwomanship should be examined for its potential to hurt for the sake of amusement.

Men often play the same game with reminiscences. "Remember the

time you were drunk in the lobby of the Alamo Hotel and you pee'd into the potted palm" may sound affable and cute, but the person on whom the story is told may want to keep that kind of behavior to himself. Malice for the fun of it is not the property of only one sex. There is also the "practical joker," the person who takes real delight in making someone look small or foolish. The whole premise of the popular television program *Candid Camera* was the delight people took in seeing other people uncomfortable. The problem with practical joking is that it may be done with something approximating innocence, but the response to it may be far out of proportion. No one really knows how seriously a given person might take a personal embarrassment.

CONNIE U.
Alice promised me that she would arrange a date with that guy in the math class, the one with the curly black hair and the muscles. God, I wanted that guy to pay attention to me, and Alice said she knew him and would fix me up. She even had "him" call me, and he had a nice deep voice, and sounded really—I guess I'd have to say "groovy." Then on Saturday night it all turned out to be a gag. The guy that came for me was Al the joker. Al was a little fat guy who took real delight in grossing out girls, and I wouldn't be seen in public with him, and there I was in a restaurant sitting down at a table with him. I never forgave Alice. God, how I waited to get her! And then I had my chance. She asked for my notes to study for an exam, and I deliberately copied those notes and put in so many errors that she flunked the exam cold. She never found out what I did, but that flunk cost her an A and really worried her because she needed the A for grad school. I really enjoyed watching her cry about it and squeal, "I don't know what I did wrong." I wish I could have done worse to that bitch, but at least I did something.

172

Sometimes we organize our small societies around the capability to do injury to others. Some rituals rightfully fit into this category. "Hell night" at the fraternity is more amusing for the brothers than for the initiates. And every so often someone dies as a result of "brotherly" hazing, indicating that people are capable of doing things for their own enjoyment even at the expense of people they supposedly care for. It is hard to understand the principle of injury for the sake of pleasure, but the possibility cannot be ruled out in any relationship. There is, after all, a psychopathology called sadism, and people have to move toward it gradually.

More frightening is the sociopath, the individual who appears to be completely free of conscience and is therefore capable of inflicting considerable injury on others without ever feeling a twang of guilt. Sociopaths are skilled at social relations, and it is entirely possible to get trapped in a relationship with one and be forever the loser. The role played by the pimp to the prostitute is sociopathic, but it differs only in details from the following description:

ARLENE H.
After the mastectomy he divorced me. I guess I was flawed. Up to that time, I had been his toy. He would dress me in the best and bring me out and show me off. He had selected me, I guess from auditions. I was doing well as a dancer when we met, but he took me out of my career and he bought my services. I was not to talk in public, only to smile. I never prepared the company dinners; he hired a caterer and then bragged to his friends about what a cook I was. Occasionally he would tell me who to play up to, who to rub. I was his whore. He never made me go to bed with anyone, but I bet he would have tried if it suited his purposes.

A less brutal but equally demeaning behavior occurs when a "new employee" is initiated into the group. One friend of ours tells the story of his initiation into a group of electrical workers: He spent the whole day searching for a "left-handed" screwdriver and almost lost his job because of it. The bosses never even thought to blame the senior men who sent him on the search; instead, they blamed him for being stupid enough to fall for it.

We have examined the basis for enemies and the words of Nietzsche ring true: "It is not enough to love your enemies—you must also learn to hate your friends." Enemies are often made from among your friends or at least acquaintances who could be friends, which makes it hard even to discover who the enemies are. We will now look at some of the ways people report they deal with the unpleasantness of having an enemy and with some of the dangerous and unpleasant feelings enemies generate.

The ideal of Western religion is to "love your enemies." The life of Jesus illustrates, however, that you are likely to be betrayed by your friends, who will then stand by and watch your demise. People may live in the hope of heaven, said one wag, but they had better operate in fear of hell. And Brother Dave Gardner once commented, "Love your enemies, it drives 'em wild."

When it comes down to it, at least in the case of dealing with your enemies, you are probably your own best friend. Wishing, and hoping, and praying for salvation may pacify your soul and prepare you for immortality, but they won't make your problems, or your enemies, go away.

PETE M. (age ninety-one)
I heard this song on the local country-western station about this guy in the bar, and he was hungry, see, and thirsty, and this old guy comes up to him and they have some talk about guitar pickin', and anyway, the young guy gets the old guy to buy him a beer and sing him a song, and then the guy writes the song and sells it and becomes rich, and he says something like I won't say I actually beat the devil, but I drunk his beer for nothin' and then I stole his song. What I can say is that life is like that. The guy that's running against you, next to you—you've gone all around the track and then you see this guy, this hero, and he's moving at you like he's gonna' trip you, and you better make your move first. Now maybe you just think you saw him make that move, but the point is, he could make that move and so could you, so you better move first. I played baseball in the 1920s and I learned to slide with my spikes high. Hell, I can apologize for an accident and my insurance company can pay the claim, but I can't live with myself when I lose because I was playing fair and the other guy cheated. I've never taken welfare and I don't have social security. I have lots of friends because I can afford to pick up the bar tabs. I never got religion because the preachers are the worst hustlers of all. If there was really a God, He'd get an advertising firm to carry his message, not these pukes you have on Sunday morning television stealing money from old ladies. If you are going to fight, fight with the big boys, and if you are going to cheat, cheat the cheaters. You know what I do when I get a solicitation in one of those postage-paid return envelopes. I send it back empty. They have to pay the postage and open an empty envelope. It's something a man of my age can do to fight back.

We are biologically equipped for self-protection, despite the fact that we are culturally taught to avoid combat. However, some of our respondents had learned about enemies and had prepared themselves to handle interpersonal hostilities.

CAPTAIN ALAN G. (metropolitan police)
People are not normally murdered by strangers. It is the people closest to them who are most likely to do it. Most of the murders come from arguments: husband and wife, brother-in-laws, neighbors. There are very few cold-blooded, first-degree, premediated murders like in the Agatha Christie stories.

DR. KENNETH B.
When people recognize they have an enemy, it makes them very careful and very respectful. When two people understand, mutually, they are enemies, they often go to great lengths to avoid hurting each other. Sometimes you can count on your enemies being more reliable than your friends. They are less likely to hurt you with some silly error. When they get you, it is because they mean it, and you can prepare yourself to defend against that.

JANE B. (CEO, electronics firm)
I learned it from the Boy Scouts: *Be prepared.* The first thing you have to learn is that there are people who will hurt you if you give them the chance, and a lot of others that would do you harm if they thought they could get away with it. Your enemies are not far off. They are close by, and most of them don't even hate you. They are simply looking out for themselves.

CURTIS K. (accountant)
You don't have to fight fire with fire. If you play with fire, you are likely to get burned. You have to figure out what they can do and build a protection. If you think people will sell out your secrets, be careful who you tell your secrets to. For example, most executives dehumanize secretaries. They say and do all kinds of incriminating things in front of their secretaries. But secretaries feel, and hate, and talk. Same thing with your wife. I love my wife. Occasionally, on the road, I have had a roll in the hay. I make it a point to pay for my women and I make it a point never to confess. I think my wife knows that I am not made of wood but that I never do it for reasons other than biology. Nobody gets hurt because I pay for it. Understand? If you know how people can hurt you, you can be a humanitarian and help them keep peace in their souls by preventing them from hurting you.

WALT P. (chemical engineer)
I sometimes plant false rumors, and when I hear it come back, I know who has a big mouth. When I was a teacher, I used to leave fake answer keys lying around so I could find the people who were likely to steal answer sheets. I believe in security and protection. If you trap the people who try to hurt you, you can intimidate them into leaving you alone. People sometimes regard me as a little too hostile. I do it on purpose. I like to come on strong because it reminds people that I can hit back. That keeps some of the riffraff off my back. People also tend to pick on me because of my nationality. I let them know right from the start that is unacceptable, and if they make jokes about my nationality, I will strike back. I am a big guy, and I can get people to leave me alone.

ANNE W. (physician)
I want an honest and trusting agreement with my friends. I don't have many friends because I want to be sure I can count on them. I am prepared to go to the wall for my friends, but I want to be sure they will do the same for me. I try to see whether they give me credit for my ideas, whether they talk about me behind my back. I am over forty and I will probably never marry, so I have to be sure of my

friends. If you keep people at arm's length until you are sure of them, you can avoid getting hurt. I am very suspicious of people who are open and accepting of everyone. I think they get hurt a lot and I think they enjoy it.

CARL S. (radio station manager)

It's OK to learn how to fight back. Most people are so self-conscious about fighting at all that they fight spontaneously and badly. I like to plan my moves. I have a set of insults that I have memorized. I am prepared with information to support my controversial ideas. When I hear a rumor, I demand evidence or I go to the source and check it. If you are definitive enough, you can keep a lot of the hostiles away. Most people will only hurt folks they think are weaker anyway. One thing is for sure. If someone hurts you, it doesn't help to withdraw. In some way you have to stand up to it, even if you get punched, because if you withdraw and brood about it, you can get yourself sick, and even worse, you might find yourself hurting people you don't want to hurt. If this is a competitive society, then we'd better all learn to compete.

The law offers recourse to people who feel they have been injured. Our society is extraordinarily litigious, but people who can pay the price can take their case to court and either have arbitration enforced, or fight it out to a decision and get restitution and damages. The use of the court imposes a third party into the controversy and provides the added advantage (in most cases) of closure: The affair can be ended, legally. But the emotional legacy lasts on. There does not appear to be any reliable way to end interpersonal hostility, hatred, and the making of enemies. Each person must respond in her or his own unique way. We found some people who revised the way they saw the world in order to avoid hatred. They would, for example, simply reduce the affection they felt for a friend who had injured them.

RHONDA T.

When you are dating, there isn't much you can do to a guy who has hurt you or tried something you didn't like or talks too much. But you don't have to stay with them, you know. You can let logic overcome silly emotions and simply convince yourself that a person that acts that way is not worth knowing and when they call you, simply turn them down, or go with them and let them spend their money, but don't let them get you alone.

We found that some married women put up with injury by rationally concluding that the benefits of the relationship outweighed the insults.

CAROL D.

My husband "steps out" on me occasionally. I know when he does it because he doesn't respond to me in bed, and I am pretty good. I am also forty-one years old, and I do not have a great deal of value on the sex market. I am a little overweight and I do not care to be employed full time. My husband has an income of nearly a hundred thousand dollars a year. I go where I want to go. I see the shows, I am surrounded with comforts. I have a lot of friends and I get along with my children. Much of the time my husband is not a bad guy, and if I tried to hurt him, it would make me feel bad. So I do nothing at all, and it doesn't even bother me anymore.

We also found some people who have unique abilities to ward off possible enemy-like behavior by reversing the conditions by which harm may be perpetrated against them.

VINCE J.
If you don't accept the punishments as punishments, then you are OK. So, when it looked like some of us would have to teach freshman courses, I began talking about how much I liked to teach freshman courses, and so they didn't give me very many because the guy who assigned the courses hated my guts. And when I discovered they weren't going to nominate me for a teaching honor award, I give this humorous little riff about how silly those awards were. It's the old "sour grapes, sweet lemons" routine, but it keeps your enemies off guard, you know.

One of the most important things we found out is that there are powerful forces at work in all of us, and there are many negative emotions that interfere with our relationships. There is not much written about these emotions and not very many ways to help people understand them. We found very few constructive ways of dealing with them. But we feel it is very important to acknowledge some of the possibilities for dealing with these emotions. We have already discussed jealousy, envy, resentment, and revenge. Consider some of the following cases (this time described in our words):

Depression.
We found several individuals who seemed to use depression to intimidate other people into trying very hard to please them and get them interested. One psychologist explained to us that depression might be a chemical reaction in the brain or it might be a social strategy designed to attract compliments and control the behavior of other people.
Anxiety.
A great many people seemed to use their anxieties as excuses for avoiding responsibility to others or to perform in particular situations. We had the feeling that everyone is anxious when something is at stake or when the situation is unfamiliar. But there were some people who seemed to be all right who acted as if their anxiety was disabling. They made it clear to others that they were not going to do the job, and in so doing,

they were permanently excused from doing the task, almost as if they were physically disabled.

Anger.

Some people used anger as a bluff. We thought of the comedy routines where three people are holding a man who is yelling "Lemme at 'im." Releasing anger vigorously gets other people to back off and revise their demands. If it's done convincingly, it usually gets compliance, although sometimes it gets a punch in the jaw. We were convinced that some of our respondents had learned how to fake anger and used it as a "persuasive" technique. On the other hand, we found several people whose anger got them into more trouble than they could handle. Talking back at the wrong time to the wrong person can have serious consequences.

Pity.

Pity, we discovered, is a strategy that some people used to weaken a potential opponent. By pitying effectively, they displayed themselves as people of great humanitarian concern, and they persuaded others to regard the person they were pitying as something less than human, not to be taken seriously.

Embarrassment.

This is is a device people use to get off the hook. By confessing embarrassment and then indulging in self-abasement ("Ohh, I am such a klutz, I am always spilling") they are excused from providing equity (because I am a klutz I won't pay you for the thing I ruined).

Guilt and remorse.

Guilt and remorse are both techniques used to gain exemption from paying the price. By being sorry and acting remorseful, the person you injured is motivated to excuse you from responsibility. The psychiatrist Harry Stack Sullivan once pointed out that children who learn how to say "I'm sorry" convincingly can get off the hook, avoiding both punishment and the necessity to provide restitution. We look for signs of remorse in the courtroom and use it to justify reducing punishment for criminals. If the criminal is not remorseful, he or she gets the maximum sentence.

THE AUTHORS COP OUT

One of our more humorous respondents said, "Everyone ought to get just what they deserve—real hard!" This individual described to us the virtues of using humor as a form of attack. If we accept as a starting principle the idea that there is no idea that cannot, on one side, be dangerous and, on the other, be ridiculous, hostile and unpleasant responses can be managed by moving them to the ridiculous side of the scale. This is not easy to do, and more important, it is often dangerous, since people despise being laughed at. Still, this respondent seemed "together" with himself and the people around us. Among other things he said to us, "You enjoy looking through keyholes and seeing people in their psychic underwear." In a sense that is just what we have been doing. However, we have found, we think, some very important information concerning possibilities in human relations.

There is a danger, however, in prescribing remedies before sufficiently understanding the situation. We have attempted to avoid offering solutions. Several respondents asked us if we had attempted to fill out our own protocols. The answer is yes, and our discovery was that we were as amenable to evil and/or ridicule as anyone else we talked to. In fact, we found we could sometimes use our own comments as "typical" examples. The recognition that you are one of your own subjects is very sobering. It led us to ask other social scientists whether they ever considered themselves included in the conclusions they draw about the subjects they studied. We were dismayed, disheartened, and frightened to discover a great number of our scholarly and scientific colleagues regarded other humans as bugs or seeds, not as humans at all. We discovered one way to take away humanity from humans was to reduce them to numbers.

This, then, is our cop-out. Instead of telling what we have found out, we tell you what we *think* we have found out. We urge you to apply our ideas to yourselves, to think through our conclusions about people to see if you have observed similar phenomena in the people you know. We urge you to be very careful in reading the final section of this chapter.

SOME FRIGHTENING THINGS
WE THINK WE HAVE FOUND OUT
ABOUT WOMEN

When we were writing about how we dehumanize the people we are going to kill or injure, we began thinking about all the words men use about women. We call them chicks, dishes, cookies, cuties, playmates, pussies, dolls, floozies, tomatoes, babes, honeys, bunnies, bags, tootsies, pieces, skirts, dames, broads, cunts, and many more things related to their sexuality. There are far fewer pejorative words for men.

It occurred to us that when we refer to women by these words, we make them less than human. It is not that they are humans slightly different from men, it is that our language makes them appear not human at all. We conjectured that the ability to make women less than human may explain a great many of the aggressive acts men commit against women. It may explain why women are discriminated against in industry, why they are not often taken seriously when they offer advice or argument, why they are required to clothe themselves as sexual creatures most of the time, why they are required to groom themselves in order to meet male standards of appearance. It may also explain why some husbands justify beating their wives into bloody and battered pulps and why rapists justify violating a woman's most vital privacy. Consider this statement from an individual charged with rape and later acquitted.

MR. X.

It is not rape, it is a strategy designed to give them sexual gratification. Here's what I mean. When a woman goes on to graduate school to have a career and she does not get married, it means that she denies her mission in life. Women are to breed. They are to be at home and used for the gratification of their husbands, because they are designed to be gratified. They are insatiable sex machines, but our society has produced some renegades who do not admit it. What I do is get one of my students and I take her to my place in the country to show her the antiques. When I get her there, I do not fool around. I begin to take off her clothes. She may whimper and whine, but she knew what she was doing when she got into the car with me. I cannot believe there is a woman so innocent that she would not know what I was inviting her to do. I strip her and I lay her and then I take her back to town. Often I can repeat the performance on demand. They become, in a sense, mine, because I am permitting them to have sex without taking responsibility for it. You cannot call that rape. That is why they will not take me to court. The one case I had to defend, the jury found it perfectly reasonable when I said that no grown woman would go into a place alone with a man if she did not expect to have sex.

We found even more frightening the large number of women who seemed to believe they were obligated to behave as something less than human to meet the demands made of them by the men in their lives. We found highly competent career women who were turned to sex slaves when they entered the front door of their homes. We found that employed women were often unreliable colleagues, not because of their lack of competence, but because of the way they succumbed to a particular man who demanded they reduce their appearance of competency or betray their employers out of loyalty. We were reminded of Maurice Samuel's account of Queen Jezebel, excoriated in the Bible as the epitome of evil, who was loyal to her husband, courageous, innovative, strong, and wise in the service of her mate. It was interesting that she even took the punishment her husband earned.

During the course of our investigation we met a man who ran a pornographic book store. Our prurience led us to accept his guided tour of the pornography industry. He showed us the strange magazines, and we wondered what kind of woman might pose for the pictures. We asked if they were junkies. He said, "No, at least not in the high-quality magazines and films, since no one wanted to see needle marks." Some, he told us, did it purely for money. Others did it because their men demanded it of them. It is not unusual, he pointed out, if you consider the abuse the typical prostitute takes from her pimp.

As we investigated the dark side of human relationships, we came away wondering whether women in Western society were the punching bags of the male world, relegated to a position of use and abuse because the weakest of men needed to know there was someone more abject beneath them. But this position could not be defended. Racial and religious bigotry could be explained that way, but even the most confirmed bigots endow their enemies with the capacity to be fearful and dangerous. There is some identity to them, however malevolent it may be. For a great many men, however, women had no identity at all save that provided by their female organs.

The position of older women, we felt, was almost completely untenable. Older men acquire wisdom and dignity, but there are few older women who are major public figures. Once you have named Katharine Hepburn, there is very little left. Presidential wives are allowed controversies about food preparation. They are regarded as gallant when they confess their sins. But they really have no identity. The fact that we get so excited about the appointment of a female Supreme Court Justice indicates it is both rare and newsworthy.

Recently, some of the science magazines have been featuring articles on female scientists. We wondered why they were doing this so self-consciously until we recalled the journalist's adage "When dog bites man, it is not news, but when man bites dog . . ." The women with identity and impact is in the same category of the man biting the dog. It is rare enough to warrant self-conscious mention.

We apologize for bringing up this unpleasant topic. It means, of course, the men who dehumanize women and abuse them are flawed, and the women who permit this to be done to them are also flawed. Our respondents virtually all fell into this class, and we, the authors, wondered about our own orientations. Oddly enough, until that moment, we had not yet asked our wives what they thought.

chapter seven

Handling problem relationships and relationship problems

The First Law of Advice:
Don't ask the barber if you need a haircut.

Murphy's Collection

"Expert":
a man who knows thirty-nine positions
but doesn't have a girl friend.

Catskill resort one-liner

It is always a silly thing to give advice,
but to give good advice is absolutely fatal.

OSCAR WILDE

Advice is judged by results,
not by intentions.

CICERO

Sanity is not a norm;
it is an ideal!

GERALD M. PHILLIPS

RELATIONSHIP PROBLEMS

We wrote this chapter because we felt a great many people are locked into a world of fantasy and myth, in which things go badly because they lack orderly means to figure out what is going wrong and what to do about it. Our review of thousands of reports from our respondents convinced us there is a vast difference between a person with problems and a problem person. People with problems can usually solve them with personal effort. Problem people require the services of an expert. In this chapter we will describe some ways to criticize your own relationships and decide how much you can do by yourself to solve them. We will then propose alternatives for those who feel they need help in solving their problems.

THE ART OF SELF-CRITICISM

Criticism is the act of systematically applying standards to something and making a judgment about how closely it meets them. Rarely, however, do humans examine their relationships systematically to see how well they are doing. When we use the word *criticism* in this book, we mean *an orderly examination of a relationship, comparing what you seek with what you are getting. One result of relational criticism is trying to find out how you can get more of what you seek.*

Because we cannot read minds, the best way we can understand motives is to infer them from what people say and do. Therefore, we must learn how to observe our relationships systematically to draw sensible inferences about what is going on. People seem to agree on why they make relationships. The following statements sum up some of the possibilities suggested by our respondents:

I need someone to count on in emergencies, such as when I need a ride or to watch the kids when I am called away.

I need someone to spend the night with sometimes.

I need someone with experience, to give me advice about my job.

I need someone to tell me about the neighborhood and town and show me where to shop and about what doctors and dentists to go to.

I need someone to go out with.

I need someone to be with when I am feeling down, such as after a funeral.

I need someone to drink with without talking very much.

I need someone who can give me advice about women.

I need someone who can give me advice about men.

I need someone who can assure me that I am not crazy.

I need someone whom I can check with about the way I feel, about my bowel movements, and stomach, and my headaches.

I need someone to borrow money from when I need it.

I need someone to go camping with.

I need someone who will enjoy it with me when something good happens.

I need someone I can drop in on who will be glad to see me anytime.

I need someone to talk to.

We should be able to identify exchanges in our relationships. The value of the exchanges depends on both of us getting enough rewards to justify staying together. If we do not know what we want from others, we cannot persuade them to provide it. If we cannot identify why we are unsatisfied, we cannot negotiate for better terms. Relationship analysis depends on both parties knowing what they are after in a relationship. We can attain equitable exchange by getting people to do what we want them to do by doing what they want done.

Relationships can be analyzed as if they were contracts. People do not write these contracts formally, but over a period of time the process of relationship regularizes and the rules are apparent to a careful observer. The idea is to be able to see what outsiders see in order to describe the relational process accurately. Relationship contracts must be open-ended to accommodate changes. When one partner seeks a change and the other fails to respond, the stage is set for combat. Careful observation and prediction can help prevent or resolve conflict that might otherwise place stress on the relationship.

The main hazard in analyzing a relationship is that people tend to conceal important information from their partners. Part of the analysis must focus on obtaining this information.

Joseph Luft says there are ten types of information people conceal.

- People try to hide feelings of incompetence and inadequacy.
- People try not to talk about how hurt they are when they are rejected by others whose company they seek.
- People try to keep secret their feelings about needing to be punished or their urgency for revenge.
- People try to cover up their guilts and depressions. They learn to put on a "happy face" even when they feel terrible.

- People do not disclose their dependence on others and the weaknesses they feel in the presence of important people.
- People do not like to admit that they feel lonely or distant from people.
- People will not normally talk about their feelings of hostility to those they are supposed to love, such as children, spouses, and parents.
- People do not admit sociopathic feelings, such as their urge to have control over others or their desire to manipulate people.
- People do not call attention to the fact that they have qualities that they detest in others.
- People do not like to admit that they need strokes and cuddles, verbally and physically, from time to time.

Through the use of productive talk about the process of relationship, friends and mates can work through these hazards and work out effective exchanges. Experts agree that productive talk (1) seeks to change behavior of another person; (2) is adapted to that person; (3) is well organized and presented in intelligible language, and (4) is well spoken. These criteria can be used to analyze communication in intimate relationships in six categories: situation, participants, persuasions, constitutions, economics, and prognosis.

1. *Situation* refers both to the physical and psychological circumstances of a relationship and the reasons people are in it. Some situations are ritualistic: Everyone does the same thing, such as make small talk and sip drinks. Some situations are rule-governed, such as family gatherings, civic meetings, and committees, where the same people meet regularly to do the same thing. Participants in private situations are free to make their own rules so long as they do not try to enforce them in public. Partners need to consciously talk about what they seek in both public and private situations.

2. *Participants* refers to the people involved in a situation. Talk about participants seeks to discover what is required to make an effective relationship with each individual. The goals partners have must be discussed and assessed for compatibility.

3. *Persuasions* are the reasons people give others for doing what they want. People are constantly exchanging persuasions. Because persuasions are a natural form of talk, we may not be conscious of our attempts to persuade. The most effective persuasions are directed to the needs and preferences of the other person. Analysis of persuasions concentrates on the reasons partners give each other for sustaining the relationship. There are three sources of persuasion:

1. Persuasion can come from the amount of regard one person has for another or the degree of authority a person has over another.
2. Persuasion can be the good reasons people offer each other for creating, maintaining, or ending a relationship.
3. Persuasions can refer to the emotions and attractions people have for each other.

Conversation can be examined to discover the kinds of persuasions people exchange, and an assessment can be made of how effective their choices of persuasions are.

4. *Constitution* refers to the way a relationshp is managed. No matter how casual our relationship with another person may be, we will be able to find regularities in it. Constitutional analysis consists of describing each of the regularities of relationships: how decisions are made and carried out, how disputes are resolved, how outsiders are dealt with, how we behave in rituals and ceremonies, and so on. Partners ought to be able to identify how they accomplish these important goals.

5. *Economics* refers to what is exchanged between people. Exchanges do not necessarily take place in "kind." Services can be traded for emotions and sentiments; things can be traded for advice and counsel. Each partner must provide something of value. So long as the partners feel they are getting more out of the relationship than they are putting in, they will remain relatively content. Analysis of economics is carried out to identify the media of exchange and to assess degrees of satisfaction.

6. *Prognosis* refers to the future of the relationship. We must have an idea of where a relationship is headed. If we do not have something to look forward to, there is no real motivation to continue. Our acquaintances are all potential friends. When we develop new relationships, our goals will guide our social choices and provide a sense of the future. Prognosis is also precautionary. At the beginning of a romantic relationship the possibility of hurt must be considered. New people must be regarded as possible sociopaths as well as potential good friends.

To help guide your analysis, here are some important features of effective relationships that can be used to help focus your setting goals for improvement.

Relationships have long- and short-term goals defined at the outset. Partners should be able to define and plan a day's activity as well as consider how each activity contributes to future plans.

Partners usually develop some sort of method to test the strength of their bond. A successful relationship should be able to withstand the stress of partners depending on each other (and outsiders) for important services and sentiments.

A couple must have a way to display itself as a couple rather than as a pair of separate people. There ought to be an identifiable quality about the relationship so that the partners are seen as partners by others.

A clear medium of exchange must develop for the relationship to have a prognosis of permanence. The partners should be able to identify what they are giving and getting and be able to assess the value of the relationship to them.

Relationships must be capable of alteration. A good relationship should be amenable to change. The main reason for performing a relationship analysis is to discover whether or not the partners can work out ways to adapt to new situations.

There must be a way to handle conflict and irritants. The analysis should identify whether both partners are satisfied with the way decisions are made and carried out and with their opportunity to obtain equity in the relationship.

There must be reserved and private areas of space and mind available to both parties. The analysis should help discover how free partners are to be individuals and to assess whether there is sufficient commitment to the relationship to keep it together without jeopardizing each other's individuality.

It's probably not a good idea to compare your relationship with those of other people you know. Most relationships reveal to the world only their best or worst aspects. The ordinary day-to-day elements of a relationship are commonly concealed. So, the happily married couple you see across the street may be killing each other in private, and the couple that always bickers in public may have some really strong bonds keeping them together. We are really only an expert on our own relationships. To say "we should be more like the Joneses" is just a good way to get confused. The idea of relationship analysis is to focus on our own relationship to make the decisions *we* need to make to keep it mutually satisfying.

Many divorced couples we talked to pointed out they could have stayed together if they had only identified the strengths of their relationship while they were still together. Relationship analysis is most productive when people discover that *it is their behavior that may be at fault and that behavior may have to change.* After you consider what you have in a relationship, and your alternatives, you might feel like Jim.

JIM B.
Your questions really got me thinking about relationships I've had over the past sixty years. I tell you, you acquire a hell of a lot of people as you live. My wife is my deepest confidante and I tell her almost everything, but not everything. I will not tell how much it hurts me when she occasionally puts me off because of something I have done that she thinks is wrong. I can't confess that weakness, and anyway she needs some power over me, and if I tell her, she won't be able to keep me in line anymore. I can talk to my friend Rick about it, though. We talk about a lot of private stuff, and over thirty years neither of us has ever blabbed. Boy, if we did, could we kill each other! Rick and I never lent each other anything, and in fact, we have never even been together for a social evening with our wives. But he is my oldest friend and I can talk about my disappointments with the wife and kids, and he can tell me how he sometimes feels like a failure on the job. These are things we can't discuss with our mates.

RELATIONSHIP PROBLEMS THAT REQUIRE THERAPY

In this section we examine how various therapists deal with relationship problems. The idea of therapy is to help people with problems (or problem people) achieve effective socialization. Most symptoms associated with the so-called "neuroses" are relational. Therapists deal with "flat affect," "loss of affect," "sibling rivalry," various complexes, including inferiority, superiority, Oedipus, and Electra; extraversion and introversion; inauthenticity; alienation; inability to own and share feelings; and many more conditions with imaginative names and imprecise symptoms. Because symptoms of emotional problems are rarely if ever clear, it is hard for people to tell whether they have improved as a result of treatment.

People who are profoundly ill, such as manic-depressives or schizophrenics, often require hospitalization or pharmacological treatment. We are concerned with people who need no special treatment but who may bring their relationship problems to such professionals as psychiatrists, clinical psychologists, clergymen, social workers, marriage and family counselors, school counselors, and others who claim special competence in such matters.

There is no specific counseling for problems with friend making. There is considerable help for people whose friendly relationships might improve if they learned to communicate effectively. For those interested in improving their social communication, we recommend Phillips (1981). Interpersonal skills may also be improved by joining a local Toastmaster or Toastmistress Club or taking a Dale Carnegie Course. Colleges have performance courses in oral communication devoted to such skills as the ability to give and seek information, speak effectively in task groups, make public presentations, meet strangers, conduct ordinary business with professionals and tradespeople, and carry on conversations.

People often overcomplicate their lives by regarding their problems as more severe than they are. Our recommendation is to consider the possibility that your relationships might improve if you improved your communication skills. Try taking a course before you define yourself as emotionally ill. The training cannot hurt you, and it may help you communicate more effectively with a therapist if you have to see one.

MARRIAGE THERAPY
GENERALLY HAS A MORAL BASE

Most marriage therapists take the moral position that remaining married is better than divorcing. Divorce or separation is automatically recommended when either the wife or children are physically mistreated, although, even in these cases there is considerable concern about rehabilitating the husband.

The double standard has been an important component in marital therapy. Though it is not exactly all right for men to be unfaithful, it is considered natural and understandable. There is not much excitement about a wife upset by a philandering husband. Sometimes the wife is blamed and taught how to make herself more desirable to persuade the wandering boy to stay at home. Otherwise therapy is to learn how to "put up with it, if there are other benefits in the marriage." Liberated therapists may advise wives to "get a little for themselves." However, there is considerable concern about wives who do so. Such women are generally considered morally impure. Although we boast a veneer of civilization, the scarlet A of colonial times is still awarded to women, despite propaganda about "living free," "alternate life-styles" and "open marriage." Often marriage counseling is provided by such established institutions as church and welfare agencies, where traditional values prevail and therapy is as much moral training as revitalization or renovation of relationships.

The sexual implications of the double standard are very important. Most men distinguish between sexual contact for pleasure and a regular sexual association characterized by constancy and affection. There is a romantic notion that bittersweet attachments to third parties ought to be considered in therapy. Men assume they can have needs outside the marriage: someone to excite them, someone in whom to confide. The cliché runs like this:

Coming On at the Bar: A Sexual Vignette

Charlene, my wife is a wonderful woman, virtually a saint. She is a wonderful mother to my children and she manages a home that is the envy of everyone I know. But you make me a man. You make me strong and vital and passionate, for you are a woman for a man. That is why you mean so much to me that I will never let you go.

When will you divorce your wife, Harold? When the children are grown?

That's a long way off, Charlene. It will be at least five years before Gregory goes to college. Between now and then we will make music, we will be a symphony. Ohhh, God, Charlene, I have a belly full of stars for you. Your thighs, your breasts, the way you breathe when we are together on the bed. My God, Charlene, let's not dirty up this beautiful moment with talk of kids and divorces. Let's talk about your lusting eyes. Let's talk about you, the ultimate woman, let's talk about . . .

The foregoing scene was written with no apology to the many periodicals from which it could have come and with no sympathy for the life scripts in which it figures prominently. One basic axiom of marriage counseling is that the human male is very likely to be exploitive, dishonest, inconsiderate, greedy, and sometimes sociopathic in his dealings with his wife. There are very few exceptions.

An important component of the double standard is the woman's assigned role to support "her" man logistically, emotionally, and psychologically and be able to satisfy his sexual needs. This component guided roles in traditional marriages, where the man worked and the wife took care of house and children. However, in marriages of two working partners the norm is for the female partner to have similar logistical responsibilities and, in cases of conflict between two careers, to settle the dispute in favor of the husband. Cases where a husband sacrifices *his* career to advance that of the wife are so rare as to be newsworthy. The reason we sometimes read about them is because they are abnormal. Furthermore, while the idea that the wife must be at the husband's beck and call sexually is now being adjudicated in the courts, it appears it is not rape if the husband forces intercourse on an unwilling wife. Thus, working women have little advantage. In fact, many women have suffered from liberated divorce laws that regard men and women as economic equals.

Traditional marriage therapy has also advocated that husband and wife stay together and patch up the arrangement as much as possible—cosmetically, if necessary—in order for children to have two natural parents in the home. A corollary to this advice was the attitude that a discontented wife must be persuaded to stay in the marriage for the good of the children, whereas a discontented husband might be permitted to "follow his star" in order not to thwart his total growth.

These moral assumptions about marriage, romance and love, the role of sex, and the nature of the family provided therapists with a basis for advice. Because no one really knew what a "good" marriage was, it was hard to figure out how to attain it. Thus, though there have been some modifications in values and procedures, ostensibly to accommodate the contemporary needs of men and women, marriage counselors still seem to employ morally based therapy.

Another moral assumption is that marriage failure results from poor communication and that good communication can help a marriage. Counselors often assume if they can get a couple to talk, they can save the marriage, though little attention is paid either to the technique or to the content of the talk. This assumption engaged communication specialists in the process of marriage therapy. One proposition must be stated, based on the expertise of the communication specialist, for which we take sole responsibility:

Most couples who come for counseling have problems that are no worse than those affecting couples who work it out. It is possible to lip-synch the problems, since they are no different from those the authors have with their wives. Couples seeking counseling complain about their inability to meet the bills, problems agreeing on purchases or where to go on vacation, problems in child rearing, philandering, and finagling, nagging and pestering, and simple boredom. What characterized complaining couples was inarticulateness, an inability to speak coherently and specifically about their problems. They did not seem to understand the normal process of preparing, organizing, and adapting communication and delivering it competently to a listener. We assumed that if they were incompetent to speak to a therapist, they were probably incompetent to speak with each other. Our professional bias tells us that training in interpersonal communication skills might spare many people expensive hours of counseling and perhaps save a few marriages (and friendships).

We concede, of course, there are serious problems that require more than communication training: a few examples include major illnesses in the family, dealing with aged relatives, physical and psychological abuse. But we do believe communication skills would be helpful even in these cases.

SICKNESS

Perhaps the most insidious moral assumption is that marriages that are not going well are "sick." The notion of sickness pervades our society. Anyone experiencing difficulty with life is eligible to be classified as "sick." Disease theories are the basis of most psychotherapy. In order to understand this metaphor, we must examine the medical model to see how diseases are identified and what happens once a condition has been proclaimed as a disease.

In the first place a disease is assumed to be a physical pathology in which a given set of symptoms, similar in all cases, is presumed to arise from a single cause (the existence of such foreign organisms as bacteria, tumors, traumas, and so on). People who seek to treat the disease can do so by alleviating symptoms, by eliminating causes and by repairing damage.

The model is useful for organism-caused conditions such as measles and tuberculosis or for pathological conditions such as cancer and heart problems. Measles, for example, is characterized by fever, red rash, white spots inside the mouth, and the presence of identifiable organisms; "measles" is the diagnosis any time these symptoms are discovered. A pathologist has specific criteria for defining pathological states. There is very little guesswork. When interpretations are necessary, they are usually about how closely a particular observable condition compares with the criteria.

The technique is *not* useful for the problems people have relating to one another. In 1977 the President's Commission on Mental Health estimated about 10 percent of the population (about twenty to thirty-two million people) needed some form of mental health care. Problems included in this estimate ranged from such profound mental disorders as catatonic schizophrenia to such simple problems in living as loneliness.

Clearly, there are some mental problems that qualify as diseases and require medical treatment. There are other problems—depression, for example—that respond to various kinds of medication, although it has not yet been possible to isolate any consistent pathology. The extent to which depression is socially and physiologically induced is still not clear. Furthermore, even when treated successfully with medication, depressed patients need some kind of help readjusting to their physical and social environment.

It is the uniqueness of the individual case that casts doubt on whether emotional disorders are diseases in the common sense of the term. To paraphrase Tolstoy, adjusted people are all adjusted in the same way, whereas maladjusted people each have their own peculiar form of misery. People all have the same problems. They must work for money, buy goods and services, share space, obtain sex, and seek pleasure. For the most part, emotional and mental illnesses are identified by *evaluating* the quality of people's experiences and their responses to them. Short of hallucinations and compulsive phobias, most emotional illnesses are described in terms of affect, relationship, and attitude toward society. Emotional illnesses are not objective states. People can be ill when they evaluate themselves as such. There are no signs or symptoms that can be discovered and classified—only expressions of attitude to be interpreted. Thus, problems in relationships can be classified as emotional disorders because sufferers feel they have a problem. At the same time, emotional disorders can also be considered relationship problems.

If you think this reasoning is circular, you are correct. We do not know whether people develop emotional stress because they are not doing well in their relationships or the problems in their relationships arise because they feel emotional stress. Regardless, a "cure" depends on helping people get more satisfaction from their human contacts. The question is, if you get someone to feel better, will his or her relationships improve? Or is it necessary to improve relationships before the individual can feel better?

Basketball provides a good analogy. A basketball player is trained to shoot free throws. Sometimes a player clutches. He or she can no longer sink the free throws because of "tension." A form of therapy called systematic desensitization can be applied to relieve the tension, after which the players can customarily sink free throws again. Remember, however, the player *could* do it in the first place. When we deal with human relationships, the real question is *could the person having problems relate effectively before feeling the emotional tension?* If so, then we would assume that merely by removing the tension, the person could be restored to happiness. On the other hand, if the individual could not deal effectively with others before feeling miserable, reducing misery will not solve the problem.

There are serious problems in regarding emotional disorders as a disease. Therapists only agree on diagnoses one-third of the time. Physicians with that low a level of agreement in diagnosing measles would be drummed out of the medical society. Psychological diagnosis seems to be a process where experts try to agree on what nouns to assign to the behaviors they see. Once the condition is named, a "disease" has been diagnosed and may be treated. Once you are in treatment, it is clear that you have a disease, and so you can act as if you had a disease. There is no guarantee people whose problems have the same name have the same disease, and therefore, there is no way of knowing what chance the "treatment" has of being effective.

Furthermore, people who are diseased expect to be cured. Curing is often a passive process. A healer provides "medicine"—in the case of a marriage therapist, advice or a recommended activity. The sick person is spared from responsibility for deciding what changes to make or how to make them and thus need not take the blame for failure of the treatment.

There is also the issue of "diminished responsibility." It is a principle of the "common law" that persons cannot be held responsible if, in some way, they were unable to qualify as "sane." People who have a mental illness frequently excuse themselves from responsibility for their acts because of the illness. Thomas Szasz in *Myth of Mental Illness* argues that emotional sickness is often used as an excuse to avoid responsibility.

If therapy fails, the therapist can be blamed and a new therapist found. Treatment can prop up a marriage, because hope of success keeps the couple together even though nothing may happen. Furthermore, it is regarded as "dirty pool" for a partner to split while the couple is in therapy. Sometimes the couple works something out while in therapy. Our argument is that treating a failing marriage as a disease subverts the problem-solving process.

CLIFFORD O.

When Bernice and I started having trouble, we went to our minister. He told us that the family who prays together stays together and to ask God's guidance and to come to church regularly. We tried, but we didn't believe strongly enough apparently, and we fought after each church service. So we tried the local counseling center. The social worker told us to own and share our feelings and to release them, so we tried reflected listening and let it all hang out, and that seemed to make our fights worse. The kids were getting edgy, so we went to a family therapist, who tried to find out who was taking all the blame for family problems. We analyzed everything but our problems. Then we thought maybe if we could improve our sex life we could make it, so we went to a sex therapist. We learned a lot of positions, but I wasn't much of an athlete and Bernice couldn't get over her prejudice against sodomy, so that didn't work except we had some real sticky nights where we fought naked and loudly. Then I went to a shrink, and he tried to get me to recollect how I felt about my mother. Meanwhile, Bernice went to a woman's consciousness raising group, and then we split up. Bernice went back to work and got depressed and I started screwing around with some of the girls from the factory and I got herpes. It's been five years since the divorce, and I still think we could have worked it out. I'm single and miserable. Bernice is single and miserable and also broke. The kids aren't doing all that well, but I still can't figure out what I could have done. Maybe if I'd thought about what *I* could have done instead of what the therapists could do for me, I could have come up with something at the time.

It is clear that therapy doesn't always work. There is no way to predict what marriage therapy can help. In miserable relationships people have trouble making decisions and carrying them out. They can't resolve arguments. They are tempted by what they think other people can do for them, and they can't adapt to change. An essential problem of intimate relationships is learning how to change. Once we find a little "happiness" in a relationship, we want to hang onto it. So we try to keep everything the same, which is, of course, the best way to jeopardize it.

THE DYNAMICS
OF A SICK RELATIONSHIP

Let's examine how a pair of intimate partners discover their relationship is troubled. First, they analyze a special problem. Every couple has problems, but this couple decides their problem is not only unique but one that defies ordinary methods of solution. The problem can be almost anything from a dispute over what television program to watch to a kid on drugs. It could be a simple case of adultery, a complicated case of wife beating, a subtle case of middle-age burnout, an illness or loss of a job, or just malaise and discontent that won't go away.

So the couple seeks help. First, each partner looks for an individual remedy. She reads about people with similar problems in a woman's magazine, he talks about the problem with the boys at the athletic club. Each may get very excited about some "vital" new way or some "expert" who works little miracles. Each one tries to get the other to use the chosen remedy. They fight about it. During this period they may try tranquilizers, antidepressants, alcohol, and a little outside sex to soothe their aching psyches.

The first decision they make together may be to consult attorneys. The idea of divorce or separation may be their first agreement. Lawyers often suggest counseling (depending on how heavily their practice depends on divorce fees). If both attorneys suggest it, the result may be a *joint* decision to seek help. It is important that the decision to seek help be mutual. A marriage must be treated as a marriage and not as separate therapies. Few therapists will treat only one partner, and then will do so only when the other partner refuses to come. The worst happens when husband and wife try to make allies of friends or children. Involving others raises the stakes and intensifies the combat. If, however, the couple follows the advice of the lawyers, they may at least try one session. Another possibility is that the visit to the attorneys is very sobering. It leads many couples to rethink their decision. They have, after all, made the first mutual decision in a long while. Deciding to try therapy is a simple joint decision, but picking the therapist is another matter. There are so many different kinds with so many appeals. She may want a woman so she can feel she is being treated fairly. He may want a clergyman because of personal convictions. The fight over which therapist to choose may nullify the effectiveness of the first decision. The most effective therapy can be done when the spouses honestly decide they want to stay together and agree on therapy.

The therapist must first get information. The couple should agree on what happened. Some therapists try to get the couple to agree on a relational diagnosis, others work to get the couple to agree on details of relational events. The process may start with separate accounts being elicited from each partner, from which the therapist extracts perceptions of information. Sometimes the only agreement possible is that the partners are mutually and individually miserable. Often no objective consensus is possible. The therapist must often work with distorted perceptions of both events and feelings.

Counselors are often biased by their training. They seek the kind of information they have been taught is useful. Anything they emphasize means that something important is being left out. On the other hand, diagnosis of interpersonal difficulties is not like diagnosis of a physical condition. There is no objective data, and so it may not even matter what the therapist chooses to examine so long as he or she can get the couple thinking constructively. Because there is no common language or concrete book of symptoms, the language used can often bias the result. Consider the following terms that are commonly used in discussions of marriage problems; they are taken from *A Psychiatric Glossary* (prepared by a task force of the Committee on Public Information of the American Psychiatric Association. New York: Basic Books, 1975). Italics were in the original.

Idealization ... *a* mental mechanism, *operating* consciously *or* unconsciously, *in which the individual overestimates an admired aspect or attribute of another person.*

Conflict ... *A mental struggle that arises from the simultaneous operation of opposing* impulses, drives, *or external (environmental) or internal demands; termed* intrapsychic *when the conflict is between forces within the personality,* extrapsychic *when it is betwen the self and the environment.*

Emotion ... *A feeling such as fear, anger, grief, joy or love which may not always be* conscious. *See also* affect.

Affect ... *A person's emotional feeling tone and its outward manifestations. Affect and* emotion *are commonly used interchangeably.*

Depression ... *When used to describe mood, depression refers to feelings of sadness, despair and unhappiness. As such, depression is universally experienced and is a normal feeling state. The over manifestations of depression are highly variable and may be* culture specific. *Depression may also be a specific psychiatric diagnosis or component of illness. Slowed thinking and decreased purposeful physical activity accompany the mood change when the term is used diagnostically.*

Consider the possible meaning of the following note from a marriage counselor about a couple in counseling: "The emotional conflict arises from idealization by the husband of certain sex related aspects of personality the result of coping with depressive affect in the wife." Personality, incidentally, is defined in the *Psychiatric Glosary* as "the characteristic way in which a person behaves; the ingrained pattern of behavior that each person evolves, both *consciously* and *unconsciously* as his style of life or way of being in adapting to his environment."

We will not comment on the consistent use of sexist language, an inherent bias in counseling. But consider the meaning of such words as *ingrained, evolved, style of life, way of being,* or *adapting.* Diagnosis using this kind of language is evaluative, not objective like the diagnosis of measles or even the "flu." Even with a catchall diagnosis such as flu, there are still objective signs such as fever, aches and pains, loss of appetite, watery eyes, coughing and sneezing, and so forth.

What appears to happen when a couple selects a counselor is that their "symptoms" take on the colorations implied by the diagnostic and evaluative words used by the counselor. The counselor's first task is the development of a synthesis of language for the couple. The counselor induces the couple to develop a common therapeutic language that enables them to discriminate between therapeutic discussion and quarreling. Carrying the therapeutic language home may provide an opportunity for the partners to detach from their emotions in order to continue discussing their problem.

The first few visits to the counselor usually bring about some positive changes, at least in couples whose hope to stay together is sincere. However, a serious problem in marital combat is the lack of a referee. The therapist can only referee in the office. In order for the therapist to be effective, he or she must persuade the couple to be sick in precisely the way the therapist's rulebook defines it. Once this is accomplished, the therapist can associate symptoms (or signposts) and treatment and direct the couple about how to behave when they go home.

SAM T.

The therapist said me and Louise had a problem of apprehension about the sex act. We were not phobic, she said, but we had a diffused adrenalin reaction which kept us from concentrating on screwing. That was why I took so long to get it up and why Louise lay there like a stick. So, the therapist put us into systematic desensitization. We had to rank our fears, like coming too soon or pain when inserting and things like that. She [the therapist] wanted to know what would embarrass us the most, what we feared the most. She included oral sex to suggest that oral sex might actually be the least tense, since I could do it even though I was limp and I could play with Louise even after I came. Then we went through relaxation exercises, where we would think about the things that made us anxious and look at

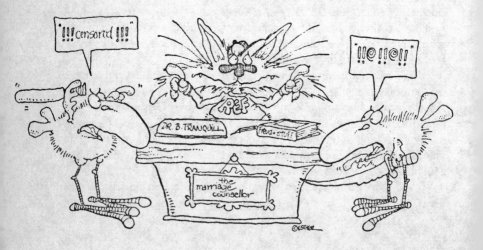

pretty pictures and listen to soft music while we relaxed. I would go to sleep, which was what Louise complained about anyway. So, the offshoot of it was we went home one night and we lost our heads and tried good old soixante-neuf and we had a better time that night than before we were married, when sex was sinful as hell. Louise said that maybe what we needed to make it exciting was to feel sinful, and I agreed that her idea was as smart as anything that therapist told us. The therapist helped us fight a holding action until we could work it out.

Sometimes the most effective aspect of the therapy is that by offering some hope, it encourages the couple to stay together long enough to work things out. The other side of the coin, however, is the *iatrogenic* possibilities. Again from the *Psychiatric Glossary,* "Iatrogenic illness . . . An illness unwittingly precipitated, aggravated or induced by the physician's attitude, examination, comments or treatment." A "drug kickback" is an iatrogenic disease. Couples in counseling can develop the disorders their therapist describes.

Medical diagnosis is essentially "empirical"; that is, it is based on events or circumstances that can usually be seen and measured consistently by others. One doctor can teach another doctor to diagnose an illness with a high probability of agreement between them. Medical diagnosis consists of observation, palpation (feeling around), measurement (temperature, blood pressure, EKG, and so on), testing (urine or blood samples), and comparing the findings with standardized tables. Some borderline conditions may be hard to specify, but the process concentrates on tangible identifications.

Consequently, a medical case history is different from the history taken by a marriage therapist. A physician may be interested in how the patient feels, but he or she must concentrate on getting specific answers to specific questions. The difference between "Doc, I can't stand these headaches" and "I get headaches about three times a week that are so severe I can't get out of bed" is a difference of objectivity. The physician can translate: "The patient *reports* headaches three times a week and claims they are so severe that he cannot get out of bed." The patient's statement is a matter of record, which guides the physician's search for objective facts. Physicians have been criticized for not being sufficiently concerned about "human" feelings. Indeed, many are edgy about emotional information because they do not know how to use it. Sensitive doctors recognize the importance of the patient's emotions and try to work with them, but they concentrate on alleviation of symptoms and remediation of causes.

Medical treatments are generally specific and applied by the physician. Recommendations are often made for "exercise" and "diet," with which the patient is expected to comply, and the specifications are quite precise—that is, you are dieting in order to eliminate salt from your diet because salt will aggravate your condition, which is ———. You are exercising to improve the strength of ——— because failure to do so will aggravate your condition, which is ———. The physician names a disease and is able to point to specific signs of it. A second opinion may be useful because both physicians will be looking at the same objective data.

The kind of history a psychologically oriented counselor takes may include the following from Benjamin Sadock and Harold Kaplan, *Comprehensive Textbook of Psychiatry*, 3rd ed., Baltimore: Williams and Wilkins, 1980, pp. 733–36: "in the patient's own words . . . about present states . . . normal activities, personal relations, changes in character, interests, moods, attitudes, dress, habits, level of tension and irritability." Of these possibilities, the only potentially objective component is "dress." The therapist does not actually observe any of this. Direct observation is impossible, because the therapist is interested in changes that took place over a long period of time, and what goes on in the therapist's office is not the same as what typically goes on in the patient's life. The physician can find the same symptoms in his office as at the patient's bedside at home.

The physician has another advantage. Hospitalization can be advised to allow more opportunity to gather data. Severe mental disorders often require hospitalization both to observe symptoms and monitor medication. Serious physical illness requires hospitalization until the symptoms are alleviated. Regular management is required for "chronic" conditions. The same is true of psychoses. Interpersonal problems must be dealt with by short visits to a therapist followed by return to the situation in which the difficulty developed. Marriage therapists sometimes try to increase their persuasive powers by using measurements of attitudes, values, and skills that induce the couple to believe their "symptoms" are being "treated."

MARY S.
The counselor told Peter and me that our problem was the way we used our language. We were too responsive, he told us—not reflective enough. He gave us this test to measure how reflective we were, and Peter and I both got very low scores. So he gave us instruction in how to listen reflectively and then gave us the test again. We got higher scores. "You see," he told us, "you can be more reflective." Then he dismissed us and we went home and fought reflectively. He never inquired about whether it helped us.

It is hard to interact naturally when a therapist is watching. Even therapists who make on-site visits have difficulty objectivizing their data, because they are seldom sure what effect they are having on the couple. Thus, psychologically trained marriage therapists may be able to spot both physical and severe mental illness (such as schizophrenia), but they have an inordinately difficult time pinning down the problems that are affecting the couple. According to a major psychotherapist, "the notion of disease is not a useful one . . . for the major difference between the medical and the behavioral disorders lies in the absence in the latter of a single 'cause' which is the invariant characteristic of the former."

SO WHAT IS THE NATURE OF THE SUFFERING?

With the exception of the obviously bizarre and dangerous problems (such as wife beating), the problems most couples suffer from are mundane. These maladies are characterized by an accentuation of their normal behavior to the point where they feel miserable. The following are some of the possibilities for relational disorders described by various therapists:

> They feel tense in the presence of each other. They often feel relieved when they leave each other.
>
> They feel that other people are watching them and paying too much attention to their hostility to each other.
>
> They believe that their partner is having excessive contact with another person or is too involved in other activities.
>
> They believe their partner is sexually unfaithful.
>
> They are angry about demands their partner imposes on them.
>
> They believe their partner is not doing a fair share in the relationship.
>
> They believe their partner is not paying sufficient attention to them.
>
> They think their partner is using more of the available resources (money) than they are.
>
> They do not think it is pleasant to be with their partner anymore.
>
> They feel their partner is consciously abusing them psychologically or physically.
>
> They feel the welfare of the children is being jeopardized by the behavior of the partner.

There is no couple that has not felt some of these symptoms some of the time. The distinguishing feature between a marriage and a marriage in counseling is that in the latter case there is the feeling there is something unusual about these feelings and there is a possibility that through therapy the unpleasant feeling can be alleviated. (We will not deal with actual physical abuse or other kinds of torment. In those cases, there is very little counseling can do except provide an avenue for relief for the injured party.)

Usually one partner is more eager for therapy than the other. Therapy is a weapon the weaker partner can use against the stronger partner. It capitalizes on guilt by making the partner who seeks to end the relationship feel that he or she must at least give lip service to trying to save it.

Couples in trouble want to be "normal," whatever their definition of normal may be. They don't want to think they endure excess misery or are denied an opportunity for happiness. They do not wish to be a gossip item. Thus, it is often useful for them to be able to label their misery. If they have a "communication problem," are "incompatible," or have some "sexual maladjustment," they can identify their problem in a magazine article or talk about it with friends without feeling strange.

PHILLIP Z.
Some couples come with elaborate stories about their sex lives. It used to be exciting for me to get into other people's bedrooms, but I've heard all the "he's too fast," "she lays there like a stick," "he always wants it," "she never wants it," "he wants to do kinky and immoral stuff," "she gets headaches," "he's getting it on the outside," "she's lusting for other men," and on and on and on that I want to hear. I feel that the real issue is that people in trouble thought originally that things ought to be rosy and they are disappointed when they have ordinary trouble. When people are disappointed, they look elsewhere for pleasure. Other people look good to them because it is easy to make something you don't know anything about valuable. Of course, I've seen a few bad ones—alcoholism, physical abuse, dangerous sexual aberrations. These kinds of things require immediate action. But the bulk of my clients are willing to pay me fifty dollars an hour to talk about their boredom, to bicker in front of me, and to confess that their lives are very, very ordinary.

The most frequent source of problems in relationships are economic. Individuals believe what they are getting out of the relationship is insufficient, not worth the effort, or possible to get with better quality and less effort elsewhere. One partner acting out of economic distress, does something to trigger a response so hostile that it leads to separation or divorce. Sometimes one or both partners, because of economic sanctity, wants to give it another try, and they seek help from professionals. There are a great many resources for troubled marriages and help takes a number of forms.

Religion.   Clergymen provide the most readily available form of marriage therapy. Traditional religion teaches that marriage is good and people ought to work at it. However dispassionate clergymen try to be, the thrust of their message is people ought to have something to cling to outside themselves. There is, of course, nothing wrong with this message. Presumably, if a couple chooses a clergyman as a counselor, it is because they have some commitment to religion to begin with, so to be reminded of goals and commitments beyond themselves encourages application of their beliefs to their problem. On the other hand, clergymen cannot be expected to be effective with marriages that must be dissolved. Some Protestant clergymen (Methodist, Episcopal, for example) and Reformed rabbis get excellent training in marriage counseling. Some of these denominations also have very advanced counseling about sex.

An advantage to counseling by a clergyman is that virtually every marital conflict has some component of guilt. Discussing the problem with a clergyman gives each partner an appropriate mechanism to discharge guilt by confession of responsibility. Confession in a religious setting is vastly different from the uncontrolled "dumping" characteristic of methods influenced by humanistic psychology. For one thing, the communication is privileged. It is not likely the clergyman will gossip or use the information against the people who divulged it. On the other hand, merely communicating information doesn't guarantee that anything will be done about it.

All in all, if it suits the denominational preferences of the couple, pastoral counseling may be effective. Even if it does nothing more than involve a mutually trusted third party to whom both husband and wife can speak freely, it has done some good. If it gets partners to deal with their guilt, it may encourage them to work on unpleasant habits. The couple may believe they are sinful (what's new?), but at least they don't have to believe they are sick. It is also the least expensive form of therapy.

Working it out.   There are enough books and articles on how-to-improve marriages that a couple can build its own do-it-yourself marriage. Much of the advice is nothing more than cliché: Talk it out; say what's on your mind; be orderly; don't seek revenge; don't involve third parties unnecessarily, and so on. A couple sincerely interested in working it out together can have fun selecting articles to read and share, and work out a procedure with which to rehabilitate their marriage. However, there must be a solid and mutual commitment made to the relationship before this method can be successfully invoked.

Sex therapy.   Many couples are upset because they are not satisfied with their sex life. It is hard to know when sex is satisfactory. No one has been able to establish norms. Thus, a useful operational definition is that sex is a problem when one or both partners think it is.

Sex problems may arise because of physical conditions. Competent sex therapists routinely require complete physical examinations before commencing their work. If the difficulty can be solved by prostate surgery or clearing up a yeast infection, the couple is ahead of the game. Sex problems also arise because of tension about pregnancy (in Catholics, for example, who are not on the pill) or about the ability to satisfy the partner. Sometimes individuals willing to blunder experimentally with sex get things worked out. However, once people get the idea that they have to satisfy their partner they can become apprehensive about possible failure and concentrate so hard on what they are doing that they are incapable of doing it. All of this may sound facetious. It is not meant to be. Sex is an easy topic to make overcomplicated. Many people have had problems with sex simply because they have read about problems with sex and are hypertonic enough in worrying about the sex act to acquire the problems.

There are some rare and complicated sexual conditions requiring the services of first-rate gynecologists and urologists as well as psychiatrists who specialize in sexual disorders. There are few couples who have these problems. Therapists are sometimes so desperate to work on one of these disorders they risk overcomplicating simpler problems.

Solving problems in mutual living.   This represents the largest proportion of marriage problems. People used to living alone have problems when they start to live with someone else. Even couples who have "played house" for awhile face some adjustments when they make their relationship official. The notion "I can get out any time I want to" makes a person a bit more tolerant. It is an escape clause that keeps partners from working too hard to change each other. Marriage is the beginning of serious "working it out." Sometimes the problems separating a couple are so simple they feel silly discussing them, and they are embarrassed when they find themselves scrapping about not putting the tops back on jars or squeezing the toothpaste from the middle. They may protect themselves by ascribing their difficulty to something more profound.

Marriage counselors who do not get overly psychological discover

some problems can be solved just by getting the couple to calm down and talk about ways and means. The third party spares them the necessity of saving face because the counselor can be a mediator.

Among the more abstract problems reported by couples are feelings of isolation, boredom, and ineffectiveness. These problems afflict individuals and have have nothing to do with marriage. Often, marriage problems do not reveal themselves until a couple has settled down. Then peculiarities glossed over during courtship become serious issues. Loneliness, boredom, and ineffectiveness are major problems of our times. They seem to exist in epidemic proportions. When they affect *individuals* who are married, they may also affect the marriage, but the marriage doesn't necessarily cause them or exacerbate them. They become problems only because they are now exposed on a regular basis to another person who expects something more than a sad or depressed partner. Thus, resolving unreasonable expectations becomes another important goal for effective marriage therapy.

Therapy itself has a distinctly utopian quality to it. It is presumed that therapy can make living and loving easier. Therapists sometimes find themselves trying to get people to "live with it," but they generally regard this as a less-than-satisfactory resolution. For many people, however, "living with it" may be the best that can be attained.

Cognitive modification. Revising attitudes toward the marriage is an important and often effective way of counseling when a couple displays serious misperceptions about what is possible in a marriage and how to get it. People often try very hard to be regarded as sick in order to avoid the pain of learning and revising. Cognitive restructuring can help a couple get a realistic view of what is possible in their marriage and help them set sensible goals for mutual and individual accomplishment. Unfortunately, sometimes attaining goals requires skills the couple does not have. If, for example, the couple aspires to goals that require a lot of money, which they are not capable of earning, they must either set new goals or split up. Cognitive modification used in conjunction with skills training can bring about successful change. Couples can be trained to manage money; they can learn more valuable job skills to get more money. First, however, the problem must be clear to them.

Skills training programs' net effect is to keep a volatile or hostile couple apart evenings for a period of time while they each learn useful skills. Training also gives them something interesting to talk about with each other. Most important, it creates a "scarcity economy," that is, it keeps them constructively apart so they often learn to value each other's company. Learning to be more effective will work only if both partners want to maintain the marriage. If one partner seeks bliss in the arms of a seductive someone and is irreconcilable about escaping, a training program will only be an irritation. Training programs work best when inexperience causes the difficulty.

DR. LINDA B. *(marriage counselor)*
I have the feeling that narcissism is such a powerful force in our society that most of the people who marry or live together do so out of selfish motives. Most do not understand how to give and get. They think they are so desirable that merely being with them is enough to keep their partner loyal and caring for their every need. When they find they have to work things out together some fall back on their narcissism and demand their rights. If the other one is an altruist or masochist, things might work out as a convenient master-slave relationship. But altruists and masochists are hard to come by these days, and so two narcissists have to learn how to think about other people. They have to get that dual perspective you spoke about and learn that other people also have feel-

ings. If you can teach them some of this, something about giving and getting, you can get some positive movement. I am convinced that the only deep relationships that work are the ones that are cynical enough to involve two people who understand that no one can be happy alone.

CAVEAT EMPTOR: YOU PAYS YOUR MONEY AND YOU TAKES YOUR CHOICE

Our data convince us that in the vast array of possible therapies, the most effective can be found in pastoral counseling, problem solving, unapologetic sex therapy, and cognitive modification accompanied by skills training. None of these remedies is essentially psychological. There are a vast number of psychotherapeutic types of counseling available. They must be approached with caution because they commence with the premise that one or both of the partners is ill and must be cured. The following review of therapeutic types is oversimplified, filled with editorial opinion, and based largely on experience with our sample. We provide references you can examine to get your own idea of what is involved. We could not find victory records for very many of them.

Behavior modification. Behavior modification is based on Skinnerian principles of conditioning. It is highly effective in changing annoying personal habits and eliminating irrational fears and phobias. It can also be used to teach relaxation. It does not seek to understand your insides, and pays little or no attention to your personal feelings. If the problem in the marriage is a bothersome behavior of fears, behavior modification can be a very rapid and permanently effective form of therapy. Most pure form behavior modifiers are quite straight about what they can and cannot do. (Read A. E. Kazdin and L. A. Wilcoxon, "Systematic De-sensitization and Non-Specific Treatment Effects: A Methodological Evaluation," *Psychology Bulletin,* 1976; Perry London, *Behavior Control* [New York: Harper, 1969].)

Psychoanalysis. Psychoanalysis is rarely proposed for marriage therapy. However, in looking for help for real and imagined emotional and mental illnesses, you are bound to encounter the concept. It is often useful for people who want to understand the developmental dynamics of some of their behavior they cannot rationally explain. For a quick review of principles see D. Stafford-Clark, *What Freud Really Said* (New York: Schocken Books, 1974) or E. A. Bennet, *What Jung Really Said* (New York: Schocken Books, 1975). The individual psychology of Alfred Adler is somewhat more useful. It is based on a notion that people tend to develop strengths to compensate for real or imagined weaknesses. You can read about it in detail in H. L. and R. R. Ansbacher, *The Individual Psychology of Alfred Adler* (New York: Harper Colophon Books, 1964).

Interpersonal psychiatry.   Interpersonal psychiatry is largely the invention of Harry Stack Sullivan, although a great many neo-Freudians and systems people eventually got into the act. It operates from a basis that personality depends on social contact, and deficient social contact generates a defective personality which in turn generates deficient social contact. While it makes no specific comment about marriage therapy, there are a number of contributors worth examining because much of what they had to say about relationship has now passed over into the mainstream of interpersonal behavior theory. Of particular importance is Karen Horney, *The Neurotic Personality of Our time* (New York: W. W. Norton, 1937). Although this is a very old book, it contains a message of importance to and about women. Horney believed that women often get sex and affection confused and as a result make some neurotic substitutions. Horney offers a wise method of examining your life in her books. Reading Sullivan is very hard indeed. There are two basic works that detail his theories in readable form. See A. H. Chapman, *Harry Stack Sullivan: The Man and His Work* (New York: G. P. Putnam's Sons, 1976) and Patrick Mullahy, *Psychoanalysis and Interpersonal Psychiatry: The Contributions of Harry Stack Sullivan* (New York: Science House, 1970).

Humanistic psychology.   There are a variety of contributors to collect under this heading. The main names to look for are Abraham Maslow, Carl Rogers, and Fritz Perls. The premise of humanistic psychology is we all have the ability to relate honestly and effectively with each other, but we need to learn more about ourselves and our feelings and how to share them openly with others. In order to make authentic relationships, we learn to release both good and bad feelings toward the other person and to accept with unconditional positive regard what the other person says. The therapeutic method most commonly used is the encounter or sensitivity training group.

This orientation to therapy has been widely used in marriage therapy. Unfortunately, the record of results is not very good. See Bruce Maliver, *The Encounter Game* (New York: Stein and Day, 1973) for a very hostile review. For a more scholarly examination of effects see Morton Lieberman, Irvin Yalom, and Matthew Miles, *Encounter Groups: First Facts* (New York: Basic Books, 1973). Maslow's most important books are *Motivation and Personality* (New York: Harper & Row, 1954); *The Further Reaches of Human Nature* (New York: Viking, 1971). Carl Rogers's major work is *On Becoming a Person* (Boston: Houghton, Mifflin, 1961).

Transactional analysis. Eric Berne took the world by storm with his little book *Games People Play* (New York: Grove Press, 1964). This book was the basis for the transactional analysis movement. Transactional analysis assumes that all of us can operate in one of three ego states—child, parent, and adult—and effective relationships demand proper matching of these states. The conceptualization, while sensible and useful in the hands of a trained psychotherapist, was easily corrupted and became the basis of a pop psychology cult that employs relatively untrained practitioners. TA should be approached with caution.

Systems theory. The psychotherapy based on general systems theory is generally highly effective in the hands of trained practitioners. Such contributors as Jay Haley (*Strategies of Psychotherapy* [New York: Grune and Stratton, 1963] and *Problem Solving Therapy* [New York: Harper & Row, 1976]) have worked systems theory into rational and productive methods of treating entire families. Other contributors, such as Jurgen Ruesch (*Therapeutic Communication* [New York: W. W. Norton, 1972]), provide a theoretical basis in communication, while others, such as Paul Watzlawick and Milton Erickson, devote a good deal of attention to personal control of behavior attained through resolving paradoxes. The vocabularies of these therapies is highly convincing, but care must be taken to obtain a well-trained and experienced practitioner, because in the hands of a novice this kind of therapy can be dangerous.

General communication training. Because so many marriage counselors and therapists claim that communication is the basis of a satisfying marriage, couples experiencing difficulty will find it useful to obtain interpersonal communication training. There are a number of good books that can guide you toward effective interpersonal skills:

Ron Adler, *Confidence in Communication*. New York: Holt, Rinehart and Winston, 1979.

H. Lloyd Goodall, Jr. *Human Communication: Creating Reality*. Dubuque: William C. Brown, 1983.

Mark Knapp. *Social Intercourse: From Greeting to Goodbye*. Boston: Allyn and Bacon, 1979.

Elaine Langer and Carol Dweck. *Personal Politics*. Englewood Cliffs, N.J.: Prentice-Hall, 1973.

Gerald Phillips. *Help for Shy People and Anyone Else Who Ever Felt Ill at Ease on Entering a Room Full of Strangers*. Englewood Cliffs, N.J.: Prentice-Hall, 1981.

Gerald Phillips and Nancy Metzger. *Intimate Communication*. Boston: Allyn and Bacon, 1976.

Gerald Phillips and Julia T. Wood. *Communication and Human Relationships*. New York: Macmillan Co., 1982.

Philip Zimbardo. *Shyness*. Reading, Mass.: Addison-Wesley, 1979.

There seems to be no end to the books about relationships. Our conclusion is that anything that productively alters the way you talk and behave toward your partner may be useful. Anything that turns inside to discover hidden ideas and feelings often disrupts. This is only a rule of thumb, but when you have to make decisions about relationships, it is important to recall that people respond to behavior, not attitudes.

Our respondents who were doing well were singularly characterized by the ability to speak well. They were considerate of their partners, understood and served their needs and sensitivities, and consciously avoided hurting them. One respondent offered advice that seemed to be an excellent conclusion for this book.

WESLEY T.

I celebrated my Golden Wedding Anniversary yesterday. I remembered something I learned long ago playing football at Yale when football required the sixty-minute services of a young gladiator. I learned the way to learn was to find someone who was doing what you wanted to do well and watch him carefully to figure out what he was doing that made it come out so well, and then figure out which of those things you could do and which you could learn.

I learned to sell by watching good salesmen and I learned to be an executive by studying the behaviors of successful executives. I watched some damn good husbands, my father for example, and how they treated their wives, and I figured out how to behave. I learned how to listen and I learned how to talk to show I cared, and I learned how to bring some surprises and smiles into her life and I learned how to take it easy on her and remember that she had feelings, too. I also learned to trust her strength and count on her when she was the only person in the world that I could count on. That was mighty advanced for 1930, when I got married. It may even be mighty advanced today, but I bet if you tell your readers about it, it might do them some good.

Bibliography

CHAPTER ONE

David Barash. *The Whisperings Within.* New York: Harper & Row, 1979.

Ernest Becker. *The Deniai of Death.* New York: The Free Press, 1975.

Leon Cooper. "Source and Limits of Human Intellect." *Daedalus,* Spring 1980, pp. 1–18.

Charles Derber. *The Pursuit of Attention.* New York: Schenkman, 1979.

Collette Downing. *The Cinderella Complex.* New York: Summit Books, 1981.

George Gilder. *Sexual Suicide.* New York: Quadrangle, 1973.

George Homans. *Social Behavior: Its Elementary Forms* (rev. ed.). New York: Harcourt, Brace, Jovanovich, 1974.

Christopher Lasch. *The Culture of Narcissism.* New York: W. W. Norton, 1978.

William H. Masters and Virginia Johnson. *Human Sexual Response.* Boston: Little, Brown, 1966.

George Herbert Mead. *Mind, Self, and Society.* Chicago: University of Chicago Press, 1934.

Wilder Penfield. *The Mystery of the Mind.* Princeton, N.J.: Princeton University Press, 1975.

Gerald M. Phillips and Nancy J. Metzger. *Intimate Communication.* Boston: Allyn and Bacon, 1976.

Carl Rogers. *On Becoming a Person.* Boston: Houghton, Mifflin, 1961.

Jordan Scher, ed. *Theories of the Mind.* New York: The Free Press, 1962.

John Silber. "Masks and Fig Leaves" (audio tape). Santa Barbara, Calif.: Center for the Study of Democratic Institutions, 1972.

Thomas Sowell and Andrew Greeley. Letter to the Editor in *Psychology Today,* December 1981, p. 9.

Harry Stack Sullivan. *Interpersonal Theory of Psychiatry.* New York: W. W. Norton, 1953.

Edward O. Wilson. *On Human Nature.* Cambridge, Mass.: Harvard University Press, 1979.

CHAPTER TWO

Ernest Becker. *The Birth and Death of Meaning.* New York: Free Press, 1962.

Murray Davis. *Intimate Relations.* New York: The Free Press, 1973.

Mark Knapp. *Social ˟˟ˣˣcourse.* Boston: Allyn and Bacon, 1979.

Lawrence Kohlberg. ˟˟ge and Sequence: The Cognitive Developmental Approach to ˟˟ialization," in *Handbook of Socialization Theory and Research,* eˋ ˟˟ Goslin. Chicago: Rand-McNally, 1969.

Gerald M. Phillips and Julia T. Wooa, ˟˟nication in Human Relationships. New York: Macmillan, 1982.

CHAPTER THREE

Grace deLaguna. *Speech: Its Function and Development.* Bloomington, Ind.: Indiana University Press, 1963.

Dennis Fry. *Homo Loquens: Man, the Talking Animal.* Cambridge, Eng.: Cambridge University Press, 1977.

George Homans. *Social Behavior: Its Elementary Forms.* New York: Harcourt, Brace, Jovanovich, 1974.

Karen Horney. *Our Inner Conflicts.* New York: W. W. Norton, 1945.

Lane Jennings. "Brave New Words." *The Futurist,* June 1981, pp. 7–15.

Abraham Maslow. *Motivation and Personality.* New York: Harper & Row, 1954.

Rollo May. *Power and Innocence.* New York: W. W. Norton, 1972.

George Herbert Mead, *Mind, Self, and Society.* Chicago: University of Chicago Press, 1934.

Gerald M. Phillips. *Help for Shy People or Anyone Else Who Ever Felt Ill at Ease on Entering a Room Full of Strangers. Englewood Cliffs, N.J.: Prentice-Hall, 1981.*

David Riesman, Nathan Glazer, and Reuel Denney. *The Lonely Crowd.* Garden City, N.Y.: Doubleday and Co., 1950.

Philip Slater. *The Pursuit of Loneliness.* Boston: Beacon Press, 1970.

Harry Stack Sullivan, *The Interpersonal Theory of Psychiatry.* New York: W. W. Norton, 1953.

Daniel Yankelovich, *The New Rules: Searching for Self-fulfillment in a World Turned Upside Down.* New York: Random House, 1981.

CHAPTER FOUR

Christine R. Arrington. "The Paupered Princesses." *Savvy,* July 1981, pp. 32–37.

Jules Henry. *Pathways to Madness.* New York: Random House, 1971.

Richard Rabkin. *Inner and Outer Space.* New York: W. W. Norton, 1970.

Scott Spencer. *Endless Love.* New York: Alfred Knopf, 1978.

Lionel Tiger. *Men in Groups.* New York: Vintage Books, 1970.

CHAPTER FIVE

Christopher Lasch. *The Culture of Narcissism.* New York: W. W. Norton, 1978.

Richard Sennett. *The Fall of Public Man.* New York: Vintage Books, 1978.

CHAPTER SIX

Robert Ardrey. *The Territorial Imperative.* New York: Atheneum, 1967.

Roland Barthes. *Lover's Discourse: Fragments.* Trans. Richard Howard. New York: Hill and Wang, 1978.

Saul Bellow. *Mr. Sammler's Planet.* New York: Viking, 1970.

J. I. Rodale, ed. *The Synonym Finder.* Emmaus, Pa.: Rodale Books, 1961.

Elaine Walster *et. al. Equity Theory.* Boston: Allyn and Bacon, 1978.

William White. *The Organization Man.* New York: Doubleday, 1951.